BHC

Essential Reflexology

First published 1999.

Published by Essential Training Solutions Ltd.
PO Box 5116
Badby
Daventry
Northants
NN11 3ZB

www.essential-training.co.uk

D1437923

IMPORTANT

Throughout this book much emphasis is placed on practicing reflexology in a safe and professional manner and every effort has been made to provide as much relevant safety information as possible. Whilst the advice and information in this book is believed to be true and accurate at the time of going to press, neither the author nor the publisher can accept any legal responsibility or liability for any errors or omissions that may be made.

This package has been designed to support conventional reflexology courses, not replace them. Whilst it provides a vast amount of information and allows you to test your understanding, it does not replace the important 'hands-on' practical element.

Any practical use of reflexology is entirely at your own risk. Therefore, unless caused by the proven negligence of Essential Training Solutions Ltd., Essential Training Solutions Ltd. accepts no liability whatsoever for any injury, discomfort or disorder, howsoever caused, to any person or property, as a result of the practical application of reflexology.

ISBN 0-9553425-1-1
ISBN 978-0-9553425-1-6

2

Contents

➢ Introduction to Reflexology .... Page 5

➢ History .... Page 17

➢ The Principle .... Page 31

➢ The Treatment .... Page 67

➢ Safety .... Page 91

➢ Conditions .... Page 103

➢ Hand Reflexology .... Page 189

➢ Developing Professional .... Page 199

➢ Anatomy and Physiology .... Page 221

➢ Case Studies .... Page 327

➢ Revision and Exam Tips .... Page 353

➢ Answers .... Page 359

➢ Foot and Hand Charts .... Page 395

➢ Glossary .... Page 409

➢ Product List .... Page 423

➢ Index .... Page 425

This page has intentionally been left blank.

Introduction to Reflexology

This page has intentionally been left blank.

Reflexology is a **pressure therapy** primarily involving the **feet**. It revolves around the understanding that there are **reflex points** on the feet (and hands) that relate to the structure and function of **all** parts of the body. **Applying pressure** to these reflexes using a gentle **on-off** pressure may **influence** the state of the body in many ways. For example, reflexology has been found to reduce stress and tension, relieve pain, improve bodily functions and generally restore the body to a better state, so improving physical well being.

The way in which a reflexology treatment achieves its sometimes startling results has **not** yet been **scientifically established**, although there are a number of **theories** (see 'The Treatment'). Irrespective of how it is actually achieved, reflexology is thought, in many cases, to **influence** the **functioning** of the body. It has been shown to:

> ➢ induce a state of deep relaxation
> ➢ reduce stress and tension
> ➢ improve the blood supply
> ➢ promote the flow of nerve impulses
> ➢ reduce inflammation
> ➢ encourage the release of toxins
> ➢ reduce congestion
> ➢ assist the body to regain its natural equilibrium

The fact that reflexology is capable of inducing a state of deep mental and physical **relaxation** may, in itself, provide a favourable **environment** in which **healing** can take place. Also, the **psychological** benefits of being involved in a one-to-one treatment involving physical contact should not be overlooked.

As well as being used to help relieve specific disorders, reflexology may also be used to **maintain** the efficiency of the body. We have mentioned that reflexology may assist the body to regain its natural equilibrium, but it may also be used to **maintain** harmony in the body. Irrespective of the state of the body, it is highly unlikely that a reflexology treatment will do any harm. Reflexology is a **very safe** treatment with very **few contra-indications** or **precautions** to consider (see 'Safety'). There is **no limit** to the number of treatments that could be carried out - even daily is acceptable. **All ages** can benefit, from very young babies to the elderly.

The **origins** of reflexology can be traced back many **thousands** of years (see 'History'). Many civilizations and cultures have used this **ancient** form of healing throughout history. The main principle of reflexology that has evolved with time and research is that **the feet mirror the body**.

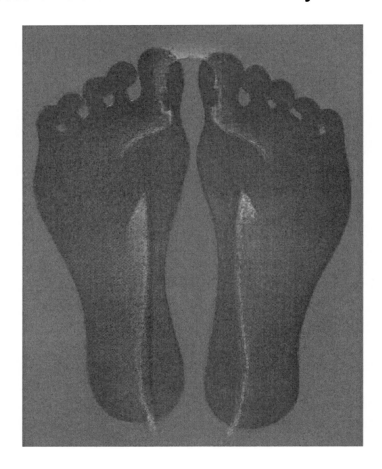

You can see how the **left** foot reflects the **left** side of the body and the **right** foot reflects the **right** side, **both feet** combining to create the **whole**.

Notice how the **shoulders** (the widest part of the body's skeleton) relate to the **widest** span of the foot, at the base of the main toe joints. The natural **waist** (the narrowest part of the body) relates to the **narrowest** span of the foot. The foot then **widens** to image the **hips**. This principle leads to the positioning of the **guidelines**.

Guidelines are the lines that divide the feet into the **main sections**. These guidelines assist in the location of the specific reflex areas. There are four main guidelines and one secondary guideline:

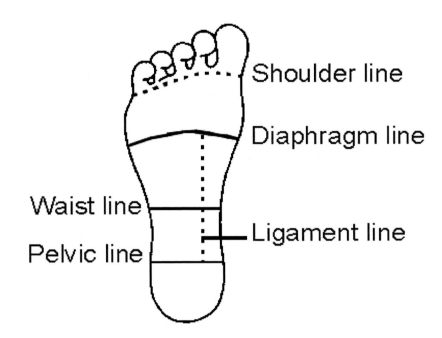

The **diaphragm line** is located just beneath the joints of the **phalanges** and the **metatarsals**. This line is easy to determine because the skin colour is darker above this line than it is below it. As the feet mirror the body, the heart and lung reflex areas are located above the diaphragm.

The **waist line** runs across the **middle** of the foot. Its exact position can be determined by locating a small bony protuberance called the **metatarsal notch**. The metatarsal notch is present on the lateral edge of the foot, at the end of the 5th metatarsal. Drawing a line across the foot from the metatarsal notch shows the position of the waist line. Areas relating to the main digestive organs, including the stomach, pancreas and liver, lie between the waist line and the diaphragm line.

The **pelvic line** can be derived by drawing a line across the plantar aspect of the foot from one side of the **ankle bone** to the other. There is often a change of skin colour from lighter above the line to darker below it.

The fourth main guideline is the **ligament line**. The ligament line runs down the foot between the first and second toes. It follows the line of the ligament that can be felt just below the surface of the skin when the toes are pulled back. The ligament should **not** be pulled tight in this way when treating reflex areas on this line, as this would cause pain. The ligament line is useful for locating reflex areas such as the kidney and adrenal.

The final line is the **shoulder line**. This line is not so important as the others and is referred to as a **secondary** line. The shoulder line is situated just **below** the line of the **toes**. As you would expect, the head and neck reflex areas lie above the shoulder line.

These guidelines are literally **guides**. Based on the feet mirroring the body, they help you to locate the reflex areas.

Three of the five guidelines that we have looked at on the foot can also be found on the **hand**. The hand is not as sensitive as the foot and does not mirror the body so closely. However, parallels are there and hand reflexology has shown to be particularly useful for self-treatments. The hand guidelines are covered in the 'Hand Reflexology' section.

So, the guidelines show the basic layout of the body as mirrored on the feet. In 'The Principle' we look at and discuss **detailed foot charts**, showing the specific locations of the various reflex areas. If you wish to look at these charts now, they can be found on page 397.

The story so far…

We now know that reflexology is a **pressure therapy**, based on the understanding that there are **reflex points** on the feet (and hands) that relate to the structure and function of **all** parts of the body. Applying pressure to these reflex points has been shown to **influence** the **body** in many positive ways. The principle behind reflexology is that the **feet mirror the body** and, based on this, **guidelines** can be drawn to assist in the **location** of the various reflex areas.

We'll now look very basically at the **treatment** itself. More information can be found in 'The Treatment'.

Each foot has **7,000 - 7,200 nerve endings**, each of these being a reflex point. These reflex points are **tiny** – just the size of a pinhead – so any treatment has to be carefully conducted to ensure that as many as possible are contacted. A reflex area associated with a particular part of the body may **overlap** another reflex area (in the same way that organs overlap in the body) so it really is important that the treatment is comprehensive.

To achieve both the **pressure** required to stimulate the reflex points and to gain maximum **coverage**, most of the treatment is carried out using the **thumb** in a 'creeping' motion. The thumb is used to creep **forward**, little by little, creating **on-off pressure** across all areas of the foot, including the toes. To assist with this, powder (preferably low aluminium or aluminium free) tends to be used as it helps to prevent the thumb from sticking.

The pressure applied should be **firm**, **consistent** and **acceptable** to the patient. It should not be so hard as to cause the patient stress or the withdrawing of the foot. Always remember that the primary objective, required to obtain the maximum benefit from the treatment, is **relaxation**.

A **sensitive** reflex area on the foot may indicate **congestion**, **inflammation**, **stress** or **imbalance** in the associated part of the body. Working this reflex area may well improve its functioning. However, it is not the role of the reflexologist to make assumptions as to the condition of the patient, nor should the reflexologist offer a diagnosis or profess to cure.

Reflexology is a **holistic** treatment. Each treatment should therefore be **thorough**, encompassing **all** parts of the body. This is not to say that an identified sensitive area could not be revisited for further attention, indeed this is good practice. However, a treatment should not be carried out just on a specific area as it is very important that the **whole** body receives the benefit of this balancing therapy to help to regain or maintain physical well being.

Summary

> Reflexology is a **simple**, **safe**, **pressure therapy** that can be traced back to **ancient** times.

> It deals with the principle that there are **reflexes** on the feet (and hands) that relate to **all** parts of the body.

> **Applying pressure** to the reflex points has been shown to **influence** the **body** in many positive ways.

> The **feet mirror the body.**

> **Guidelines** can be drawn to assist in the **location** of the various **reflex areas**.

> Each treatment should treat **all** the reflex areas to influence the **whole** body.

> The 'creeping' thumb movement provides the necessary **on-off pressure**.

> A **sensitive** reflex area on the foot may indicate **congestion, inflammation, stress** or **imbalance** in the associated part of the body.

Questions (Answers on Page 361)

1. Which of the following statements best describes reflexology?

    a. Reflexology involves massaging the feet.
    b. Reflexology is a pressure therapy.

2. True or False?

    The only benefit derived from reflexology is a state of deep mental and physical relaxation.

3. Anatomically, the heart is located mainly to the left side of the chest. On which foot do you think the main reflex area relating to the heart is located?

    a. left
    b. right

4. Fill in the missing word.

    The _____ notch is used to locate the waist line.

Questions 5 – 9 refer to this graphic:

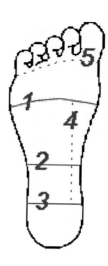

5.   Which is the waist line?

6.   Which guideline are the heart and lung reflex areas situated just above?

7.   Which secondary guideline is represented here by line number 5?

8.   Which guideline is shown here as line 3?

9.   Which is the only guideline that runs down the foot, shown here as line number 4?

10. The skin on the foot changes colour at the pelvic line. Which other guideline, shown here as line 1, can be located by identifying where the skin on the foot changes colour?

This page has intentionally been left blank.

History

This page has intentionally been left blank.

The origin of reflexology **cannot** be traced to any **one civilization**. Evidence suggests that primitive forms of reflexology existed in ancient Egypt, India and China some 5,000 years ago.

In **Egypt**, at **Saqqara**, a painting found in tomb of **Ankhmahor** appears to show a reflexology treatment being performed:

This dates back to the early 6th Dynasty, about **2330 B.C.**. Ankhmahor was a **physician** and an official of great importance, second only to the King. The hieroglyphic is thought to translate to the patient requesting "Don't hurt me," and the practitioner replying "I shall act so you praise me." The symbols shown in the painting are thought to be symbols of **healing** techniques:

The **owl** represents **wisdom**, education and learning.

The **pyramids** symbolize **energy**. It was believed that the apex of the pyramid has the maximum accumulation of energy.

The **birds** are symbols of **peace** and **paradise**. They are omens of good health, peace and prosperity.

The **eyes** represent the **windows of the soul** and indicate the ability to read the body through the eyes.

The **zig-zag** symbol represents **power**. In this painting it is indicative of the **power** of **reflexology** and the ability to read the body through the feet. The zig-zag is the Egyptian character for the letter 'N'. This connects with the River **N**ile and symbolizes flowing water. In Egypt, the River Nile is the "bringer of life and death" and symbolizes energy and power. This character is always drawn in blue in hieroglyphics.

The remaining symbols are **surgical instruments** used in ancient Egypt.

An ancient form of reflexology can be traced back to ancient **India**, some **5,000** years ago.

Hinduism, a major religion of India, is one of oldest religions in the world. One of the three most important Hindu Gods is **Vishnu**, preserver of the universe. The painting 'Vishnu-padas' shows the feet symbolically representing the unity of the universe. The **meaning** of many of the symbols has been lost over the course of time and there is no evidence to suggest that they represent the human anatomy. However, coincidentally or otherwise, the **locations** of the symbols closely **correspond** to the positions of many reflex areas used today.

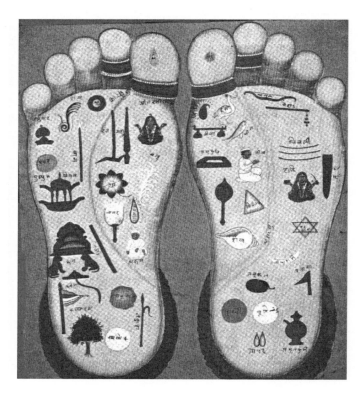

There is also a picture, dated around **1760**, of **Vishnu reclining** having his feet treated. An excerpt from this painting is shown below. It can be difficult to identify, but to the left of the picture there is a lady sitting, treating the feet of Vishnu, who is lying down. His head is to the right of the picture.

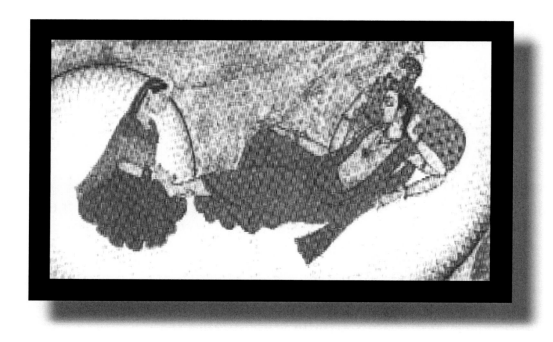

Evidence of reflexology can also be found in ancient **China**.

A form of reflexology is said to have developed in China under **Emperor Hwang** in conjunction with **acupuncture**, about **4,000** years ago.

A form of reflexology is also referred to in the Chinese medical book "**Hwang Tee International Text**", where it is referred to as "**Examining Foot Method**".

In **Kusinara**, **China**, a footprint representing that of **Buddha** can be seen carved in the rock. The carving, shown below, shows many symbols on the feet.

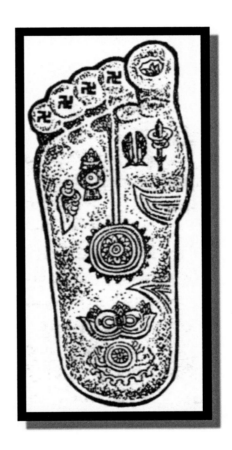

Despite basic foot charts being available in ancient times, it took the **rediscovery** of a different **ancient belief** to bring what we now know to be reflexology into the 20th century. **Doctor William H. Fitzgerald** (1872-1942), an American physician and ear, nose and throat surgeon, is credited with rediscovering '**zone therapy**', a treatment used in **India** and **China** about **5,000** years ago.

Zone therapy hinges on the belief that the body is divided into **10 longitudinal zones** of **energy** that extend from the **feet** and **hands** to the **brain**.

Five zones originate on each foot, with the **big toe** representing **zone 1** and the **little toe** representing **zone 5**. Notice that the zones originating in the **left** foot run up the **left** side of the body. Zones originating in the **right** foot run up the **right** side of the body.

These zones also originate on the hands, with the **thumb** as **zone 1** and the **little finger** as **zone 5**.

Zone 1 is considered to be the **most powerful**.

Zone 1 includes the spine, brain, pituitary gland, nose, mouth, thymus, beginning of the liver, lungs and solar plexus, and the bladder, uterus and prostate. It is usually the most sensitive.

Remember that each zone of energy incorporates a **longitudinal segment** of the body. In each of these zones it is believed that nothing occurs in isolation. Any abnormality, sensitivity or congestion in any part of a zone causes an imbalance throughout

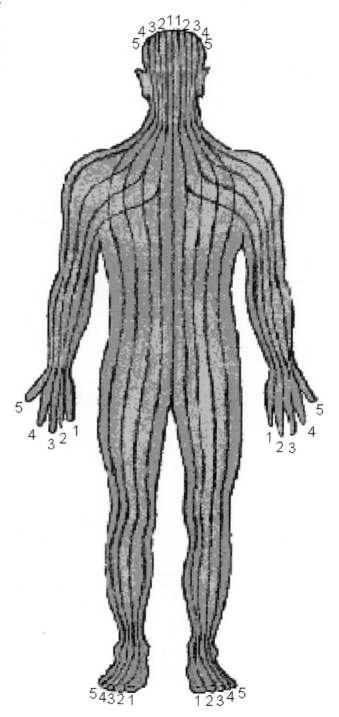

that **whole zone**. Likewise, any treatment performed on any area within a zone will have a healing effect on the **whole zone**.

From a reflexology perspective, when pressure is applied to an area on the foot, **all** parts of that originating zone are affected. Therefore, based on zone therapy, a **full** reflexology treatment, covering **all** zones, can influence the **whole body**.

Dr. Fitzgerald did much of his research using the **hands**. He found that applying pressure by attaching clamp-like devices and bands to the fingers could be used to relieve pain, as it caused a local anaesthetic effect to the hand, arm and shoulder, continuing up through the jaw, face, ear and nose.

He carried out minor surgical procedures using this technique to create the anaesthesia. Allegedly, he also improved a concert singer's vocal ability by applying pressure to a callous on her right big toe!

Although an American, Dr. Fitzgerald also worked in **Europe**, including Vienna, Paris and London.

In 1917 he wrote, in association with **Dr. Edwin Bowers**, "Zone Therapy, or Relieving Pain at Home". Two years later they published "Zone Therapy or Curing Pain and Disease".

Fitzgerald's work caught the attention of American physician **Dr. Joe Shelby Riley** (below).

He wrote four books, devoting much attention to zone therapy. His first book was published in 1919 and was entitled "Zone Therapy Simplified".

As well as extensively using zone therapy, Dr. Riley made the first detailed drawings of the **reflexes** on the foot. He also added **8 horizontal** lines to the 5 longitudinal lines originating from zone therapy.

In the early 30's, Dr. Riley had a physiotherapist in his office called **Eunice Ingham** (1889-1974).

Eunice Ingham (left) became engrossed in zone therapy. With the aid of visiting Chinese doctors, who gave her documentation illustrating how the Chinese perceive the feet to mirror the body, she started equating areas on the feet with the anatomy of the body and drew up detailed foot charts.

Eunice Ingham's work became more and more **reflex** based but, confusingly, she continued to use the term 'zone therapy' for some time. She found that not only did 'zone therapy' relieve pain but it also **promoted healing**.

In 1938 she published a book entitled "**Stories the Feet Can Tell**" and then "**Stories the Feet Have Told**". Over the course of her work she changed the term from 'zone therapy' to 'compression massage' and finally settled with '**reflexology**'.

Hanne Marquardt trained with Eunice Ingham. Hanne then became the first practitioner in **Germany** to work using pressure on the feet only. She was also credited with introducing the concept of **transverse lines** across the feet. These lines are now commonly used as the main **guidelines** (see 'Introduction to Reflexology'). Hanne went on to **train** a large number of **medically qualified** professionals to be reflexologists.

Eunice Ingham's nephew, **Dwight C. Byers**, assisted her with her work and carried it on after her death in 1974.

The **National Institute of Reflexology** and the **International Institute of Reflexology** were formed, dedicated to the teaching of the **Original Ingham Method**.

In the 1970's **Ann Gillanders** (below) began to study reflexology with Dwight Byers and she qualified in 1976.

Ann worked with Byers for 16 years, teaching and setting the future of reflexology in motion. Ultimately she was a Director of the **International Institute of Reflexology**. During her time with this Institute, she established schools in Hong Kong, France, Switzerland and Israel. Ann founded the **British School of Reflexology** in 1987. She also has a school in Japan. Ann travels and lectures throughout the world promoting reflexology and other aspects of natural healing. Her many books have sold worldwide and she is now considered to be one of the leading authorities and teachers of modern day reflexology.

Summary

➤ The history of reflexology **cannot** be traced back to any one civilization.

➤ In **Egypt** a wall painting in the tomb of **Ankhmahor**, dating back to **2330 B.C.**, shows a reflexology treatment being performed.

➤ The **Indian** painting 'Vishnu-padas' shows the feet of a Hindu God marked with symbols to represent the unity of the universe.

➤ In **China**, about 4,000 years ago, reflexology was used to enhance the effectiveness of **acupuncture**. A rock carving in China representing **Buddha's footprint** shows many symbols positioned on the sole of the foot.

➤ In the early 20th century, **Dr. William Fitzgerald** rediscovered '**zone therapy**'. Zone therapy is based on the theory that the body is divided into **10 longitudinal zones** of energy that extend from the feet and the hands to the brain. Fitzgerald found that applying pressure to a finger caused an anaesthetic effect through the corresponding zone.

➤ **Dr. Riley** took Fitzgerald's work further, **added** to the zones identified on the feet, and made the first detailed **drawings** of the **reflex areas**.

➤ Dr. Riley's colleague, **Eunice Ingham**, began to extensively equate areas on the feet with the **anatomy** of the body. She found that treatments of the feet could **promote healing** and is credited with coining the phrase 'reflexology'.

➤ **Hanne Marquardt** trained with Eunice Ingham and became the first practitioner in **Germany** to work using pressure on the **feet only**.

➤ Eunice Ingham's nephew, **Dwight Byers**, **continued** her work and **influenced** many of today's leading reflexologists, including the Founder of the British School of Reflexology, **Ann Gillanders**.

Questions (Answers: Page 363)

1. In which physician's tomb can a painting be found, dating back to 2330 B.C., that appears to show an early form of reflexology being performed?

    a. Emperor Hwang
    b. The King of the 6th Dynasty
    c. Ankhmahor
    d. Vishnu

2. Where in Egypt is this tomb?

    a. Kusinara
    b. Saqqara

3. All of these symbols appear in this Egyptian painting. Which is thought to represent power and, in this context, the power of reflexology?

    a.

    b.

    c.

    d.

    e. ᨆᨆᨆᨆᨆ

4. Which ancient Hindu God, known as the preserver of the universe, is pictured having his feet treated?

5. Fill in the missing word:

    The painting Vishnu- _____ shows the feet of Vishnu symbolically representing the unity of the universe.

6. Which therapy, used in conjunction with a developing form of reflexology, was used in ancient China about 4,000 years ago?

7. Where in China can this footprint of Buddha be found carved in rock?

    a. Kusinara
    b. Saqqara

8. Who, in the early 20th century, rediscovered zone therapy, a treatment used in India and China about 5,000 years ago?

9. According to zone therapy, how many longitudinal zones of energy are there?

10. Which zone originates from the big toe on the foot and the thumb on the hand?

11. True of False?

    Zone therapy supports the fact that stimulating the feet can affect the whole body.

12. Who, influenced by Dr. William H. Fitzgerald's work, devoted much attention to zone therapy and published his first book entitled "Zone Therapy Simplified" in 1919?

    a. Dr. Joe Shirley Rily
    b. Dr. Jo Stanley Riley
    c. Dr. Jo Shelby Rily
    d. Dr. Joe Shelby Riley

13. Who worked as a physiotherapist with Dr. Joe Shelby Riley and is credited with coining the term 'reflexology'?

14. Who was trained by Eunice Ingham and became the first practitioner in Germany to work with pressure on the feet only?

15. Name Eunice Ingham's nephew, who assisted Eunice with her work and continued it after her death in 1974.

16. Who trained with Dwight C. Byers and later founded the British School of Reflexology?

The Principle

31

This page has intentionally been left blank.

The fundamental principle of reflexology is that the **feet mirror the body**. The right foot mirrors the right side of the body and the left foot mirrors the left side. In treating **both** feet you are treating the **whole** body.

A foot has 7,000 - 7,200 nerve endings, or **reflex points**. These nerves can be traced to every structure and function of the body. Therefore, by applying pressure to these reflex points the corresponding structure and function may be influenced. Based on this principle, the locations of the various reflex points on the feet have been **charted**.

There are a number of commonly used reflex charts. They are **fundamentally** the **same** but may contain just very subtle differences. Throughout this package we will be using the foot and hand charts created by Ann Gillanders, Founder of the **British School of Reflexology**.

Take a look at the plantar foot charts on page 397 now. The **guidelines** that we explained in 'Introduction to Reflexology' are shown and the **reflex areas** are labelled. As you can see, there is a lot to remember!

The key to remembering the locations of these areas is to **visualize** how the feet mirror the body. To help you do this, we will look at the **anatomy** of the body systems and **compare** the position of the major structures with the **location** of the corresponding **reflex areas**. We'll start with the skeletal system.

Please note that it is not the purpose of this section to teach anatomy. The anatomy and physiology of the main body systems is covered in the Anatomy and Physiology section.

Skeletal System

The skeleton is **symmetrical**, with the **spine** running down the **centre** line of the body.

As you would expect, based on the feet mirroring the body, the corresponding reflex areas are located symmetrically on the feet, with the spine running down the medial edge of both.

Let's take a look at the location of the skeletal reflex areas.

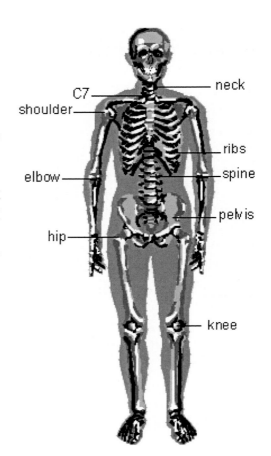

Skeletal structures reflected on the plantar aspect of the right foot.

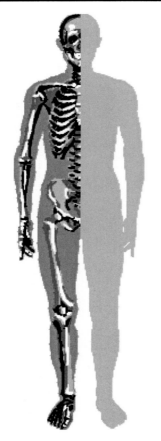
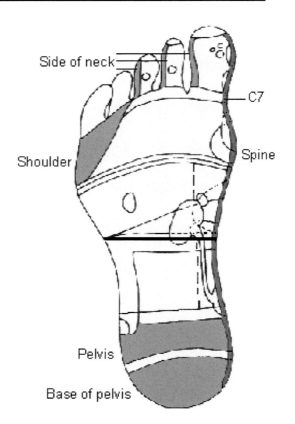

Skeletal structures reflected on the plantar aspect of the left foot.

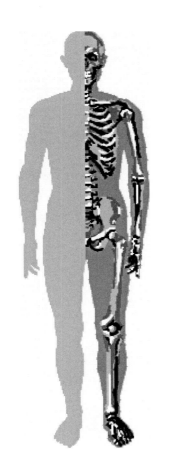
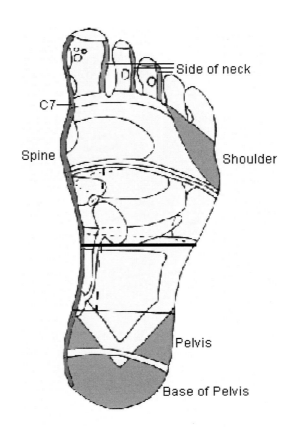

The medial view of the feet clearly shows how closely the shape of the feet **mirror** the shape of the spine. From here you can also identify the location of the various vertebrae.

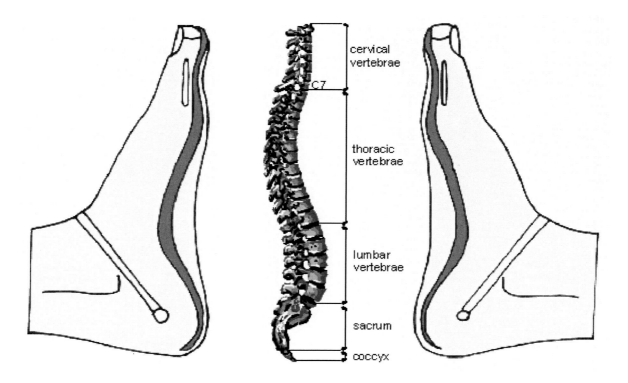

Below, you can see how the **knee/elbow** and **hip/pelvis** areas are reflected on the **lateral** view of the feet.

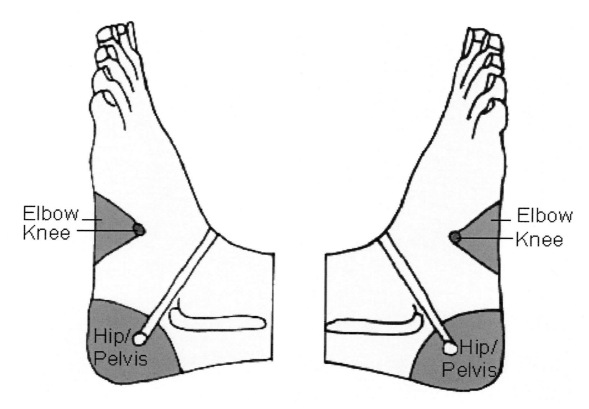

A large area on the **dorsal** aspect of each foot represents the **ribs**.

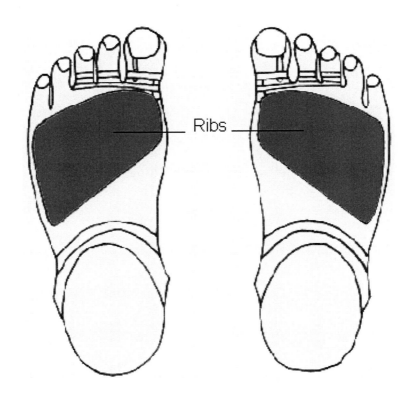

Ribs

Nervous System

The **brain** sits **centrally** in the skull.

There are 12 pairs of **cranial nerves** that leave the brain. One of these is called the **trigeminal nerve**, which extends to the facial muscles.

The spinal cord runs down the vertebral column, extending as far as the top of the second lumbar vertebra.

There are 31 pairs of spinal nerves, including the **sciatic nerve**, which runs down each **leg**.

The **solar plexus** (a network of nerves arising from the spinal cord) is positioned on the **left** side of the body, behind the stomach.

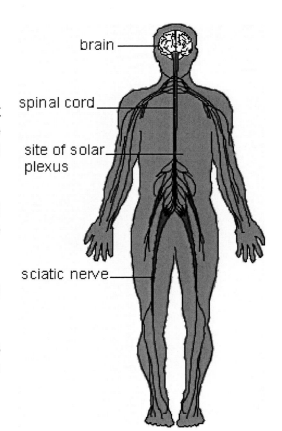

Nervous system structures reflected on the plantar aspect of the right foot.

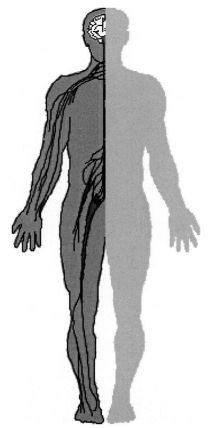

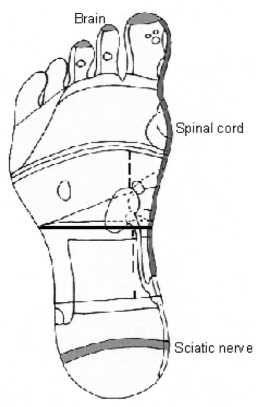

<u>Nervous system structures reflected on the plantar aspect of the left foot.</u>

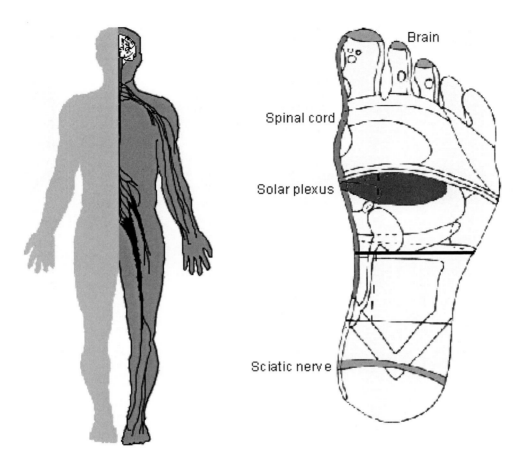

The **sciatic nerve** also has a reflex area on the **lateral** part of the feet.

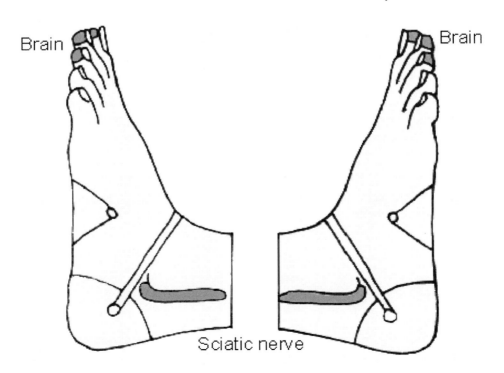

The **trigeminal cranial nerve** reflex is located on the **dorsal** aspect of the **big toes**.

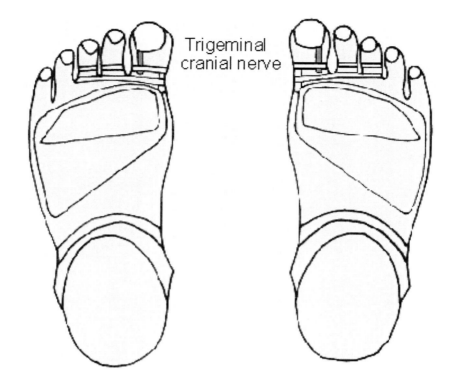

Trigeminal cranial nerve

Cardiovascular System

The **heart**, the principal organ of the cardiovascular system, is positioned **mostly** to the **left** of the thorax.

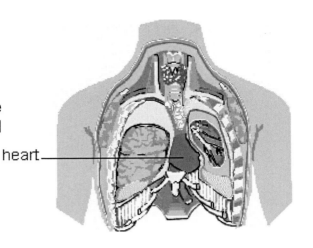

heart

Cardiovascular system structures reflected on the plantar aspect of the right foot.

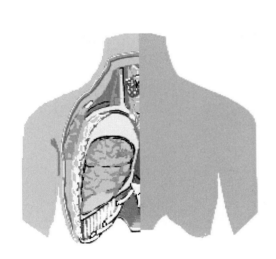

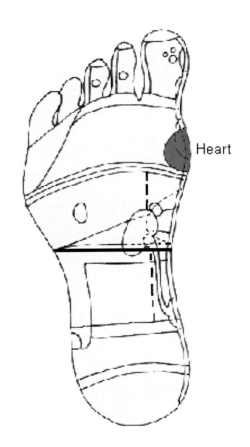

Heart

41

Cardiovascular system structures reflected on the plantar aspect of the left foot.

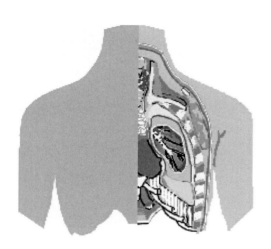

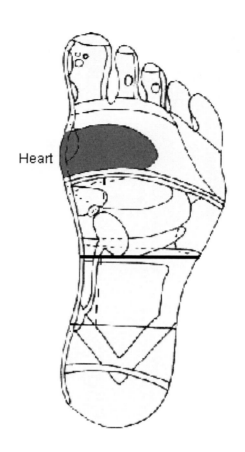

Heart

Respiratory System

The organs of respiration lie fairly **symmetrically** in the body. The reflex areas are therefore fairly symmetrical too.

The **diaphragm** is a major **guideline** and can clearly be found on the feet as the line below which the skin lightens.

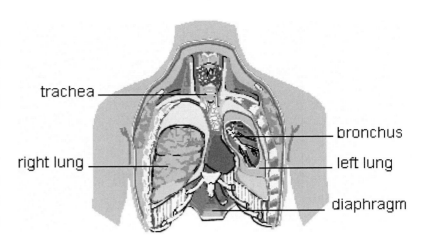

Respiratory system structures reflected on the plantar aspect of the right foot.

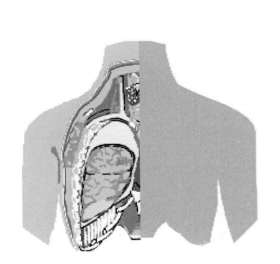
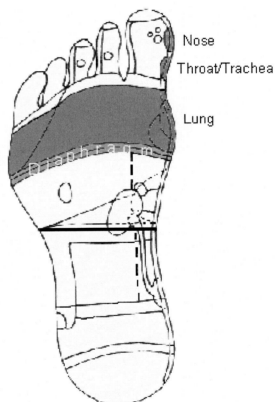

Respiratory system structures reflected on the plantar aspect of the left foot.

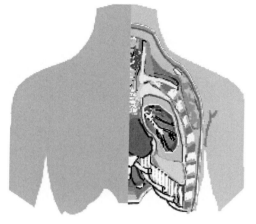
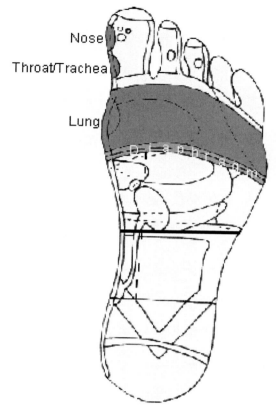

There is also a reflex area for the **lung** on the **dorsal** aspect of the foot. You may recall that there is an area on the top of each foot that represents the ribs. The lung area is located within this. The **trachea/bronchi** reflex area is located on the **big toe**.

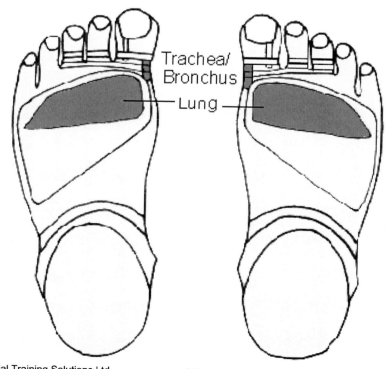

44

The **trachea/bronchi** are also represented on the **medial** view of the feet.

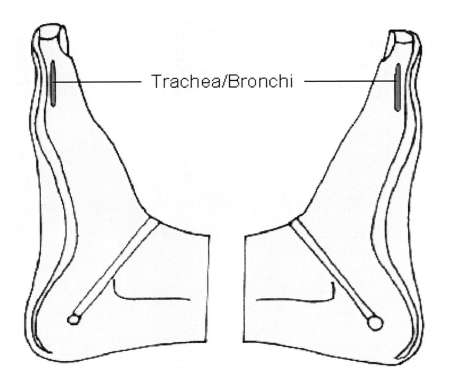

Trachea/Bronchi

Digestive System

The structures that make up the digestive system are not located symmetrically.

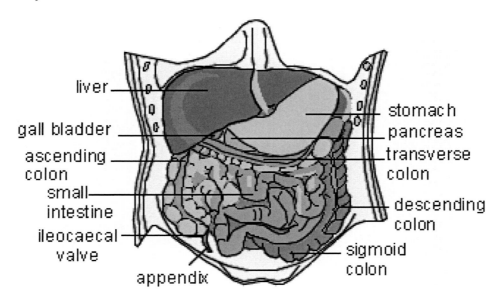

The **gall bladder**, **ileocaecal valve** and **appendix** are completely on the **right**, and only the right side has the **ascending colon**.

The **transverse colon** runs **across** the body. The small intestine lies centrally.

Only the **left** side has the **descending colon** and the **sigmoid colon**. The **stomach** is located primarily on the **left**, but with a small portion crossing the mid-line. The pancreas is located below and behind the stomach, mostly on the left. As it is situated behind the stomach, it can not be seen extending to the left on this graphic.

The **liver** is **mainly** on the **right** with a small portion crossing the mid-line of the body. Therefore the digestive reflex areas on the left and right feet differ considerably.

<u>Digestive system structures reflected on the plantar aspect of the right foot.</u>

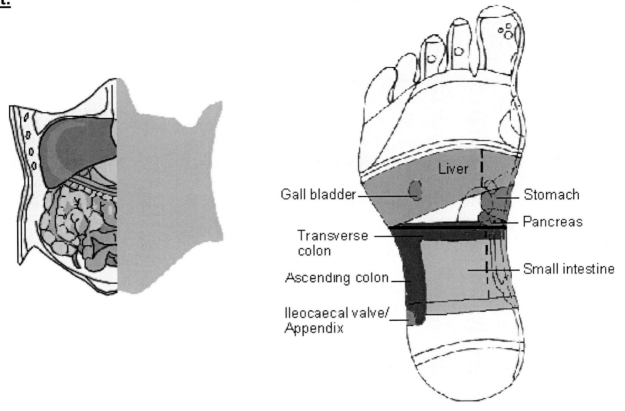

<u>Digestive system structures reflected on the plantar aspect of the left foot.</u>

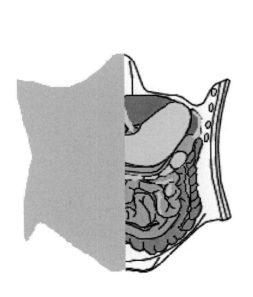
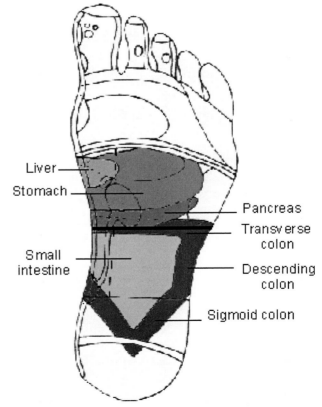

Copyright © 2006 Essential Training Solutions Ltd.   47

Urinary System

The urinary system is fairly **symmetrical**, although the right kidney is slightly lower.

The associated reflex areas are located only on the plantar aspect of the feet.

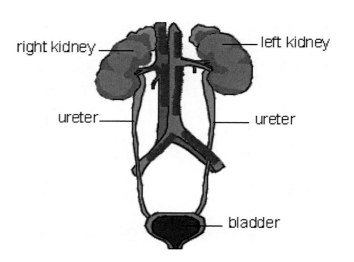

Urinary system structures reflected on the plantar aspect of the right foot.

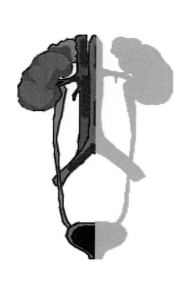

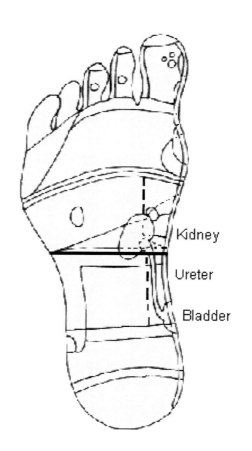

Urinary system structures reflected on the plantar aspect of the left foot.

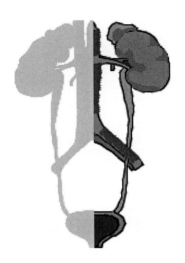
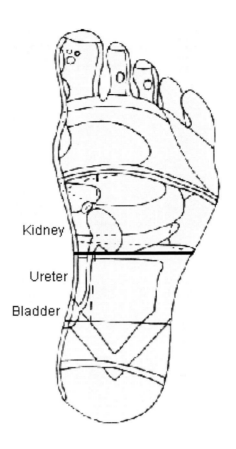

Kidney

Ureter

Bladder

Reproductive System

Both the **male** and **female** reproductive systems are **symmetrical**, however **none** of the associated reflex areas are on the **plantar** aspect of the foot.

The **testis** reflex area is located in the **same** position in the male as the **ovary** reflex area in the female. This area is on the **lateral** aspect of the foot.

The **prostate** in the male and **uterus** in the female also share the **same** reflex area location. The prostate/uterus reflex area is on the **medial** aspect of the foot.

Similarly, the **vas deferens** reflex area on the male is in the same location as the **fallopian tube** reflex area in the female. This area runs over the **dorsal** aspect of the foot…

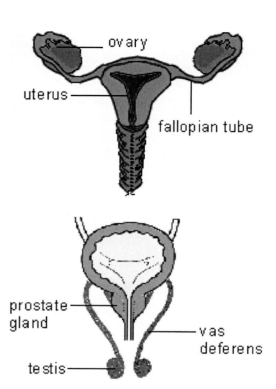

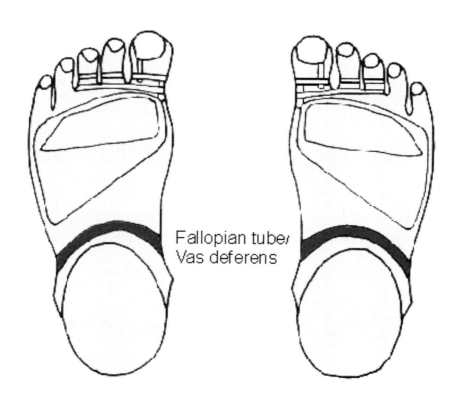

Fallopian tube/
Vas deferens

Reproductive system structures reflected on the lateral aspect of the feet.

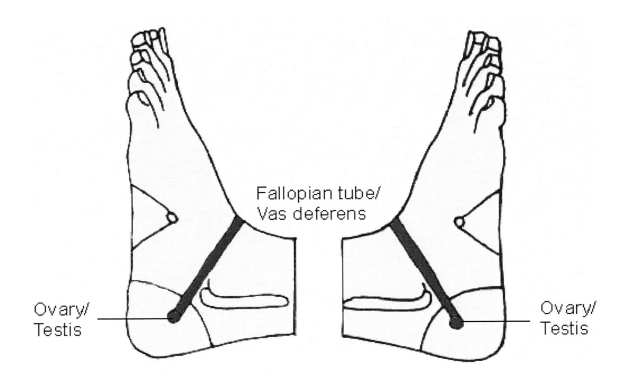

Fallopian tube/ Vas deferens

Ovary/ Testis

Ovary/ Testis

Reproductive system structures reflected on the medial aspect of the feet.

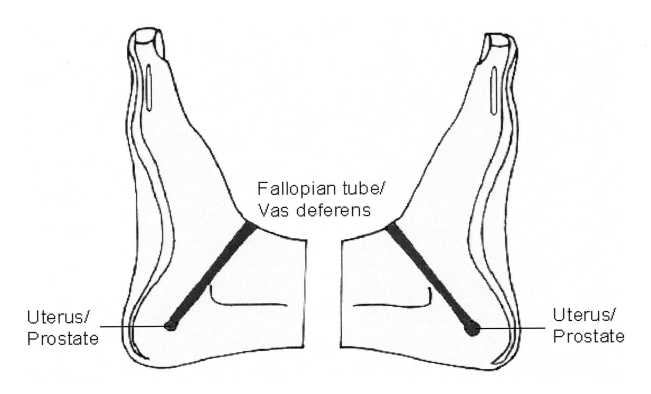

Fallopian tube/ Vas deferens

Uterus/ Prostate

Uterus/ Prostate

Endocrine System

The positions of the main endocrine glands are shown.

With the **exception** of the **pancreas**, these glands are located fairly **symmetrically** and are therefore represented on both feet.

Notice the ovaries and testes. As well as playing an obvious role in reproduction, they secrete hormones and so they are also included in the endocrine system.

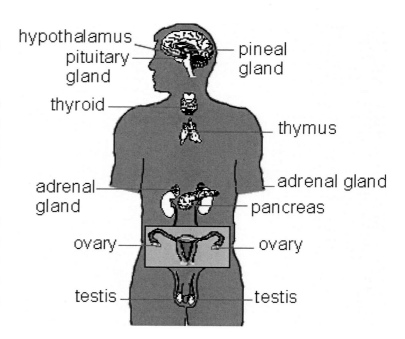

Endocrine system structures reflected on the plantar aspect of the right foot.

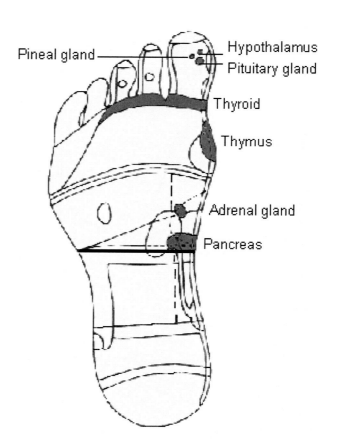

Endocrine system structures reflected on the plantar aspect of the left foot.

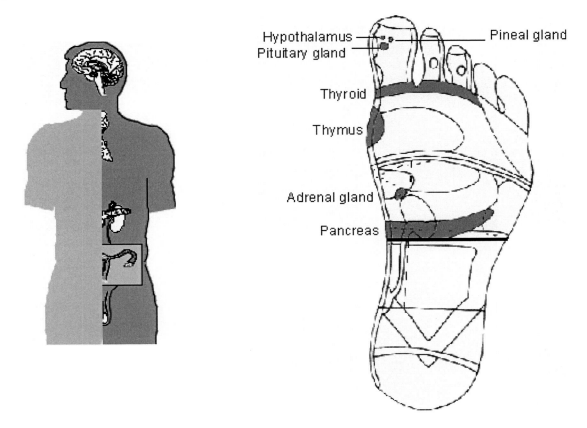

Hypothalamus — Pineal gland
Pituitary gland
Thyroid
Thymus
Adrenal gland
Pancreas

There is another **thyroid** reflex area located along the base of the **first three toes**.

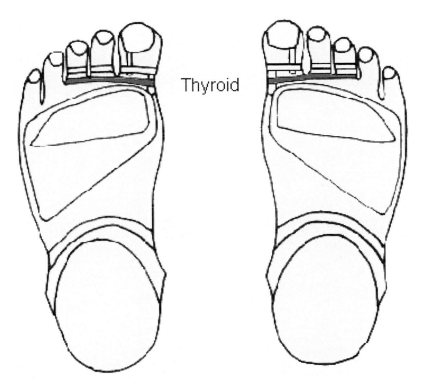

Thyroid

53

The **ovary/testis** reflex area is on the lateral aspect.

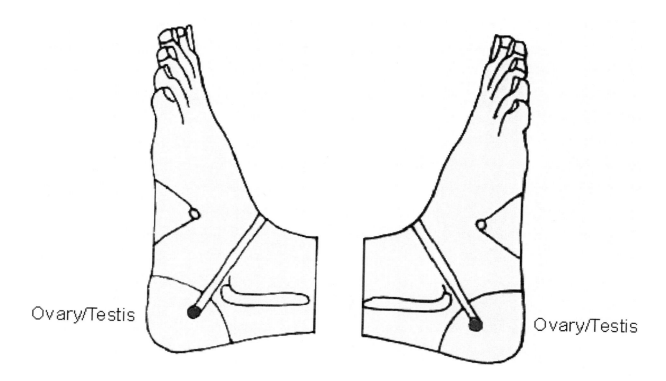

Ovary/Testis   Ovary/Testis

54

Lymphatic System

The lymphatic system runs **throughout** the body.

Its main vessel, the **thoracic duct**, is in the **chest** area. There is an accumulation of **lymph nodes** in the **axillas** (arm pits), **neck** and **groin**.

The **spleen** is located to the **left**.

The **thymus** is a centrally located lymphatic structure, as well as being an endocrine gland.

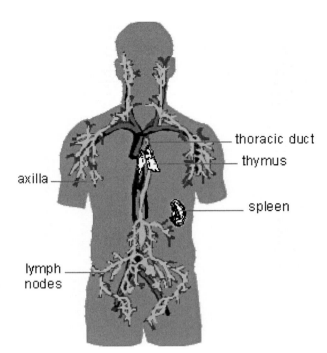

Lymphatic system structures reflected on the plantar aspect of the right foot.

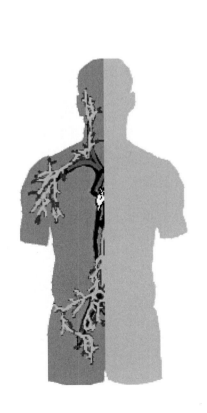
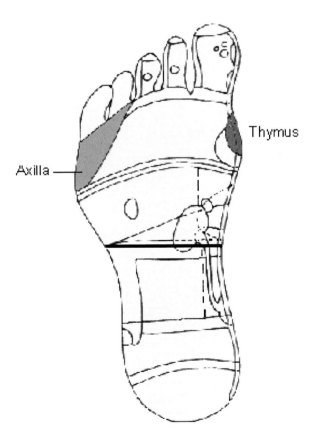

Lymphatic system structures reflected on the plantar aspect of the left foot.

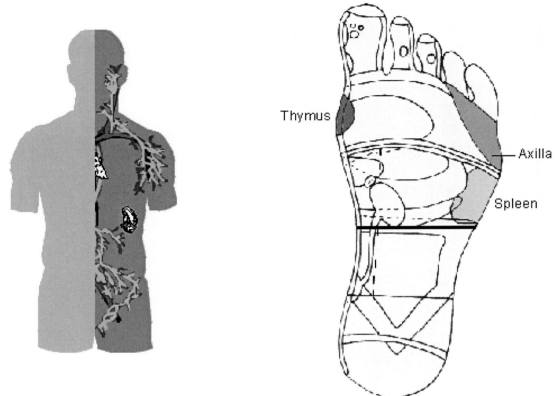

On the dorsal aspect of the feet, the **lung/breast** area corresponds to the **lymph nodes** and **thoracic duct** in the **chest**. The **lymph nodes** in the **groin** area are reflected in the **vas deferens/fallopian tube** reflex area.

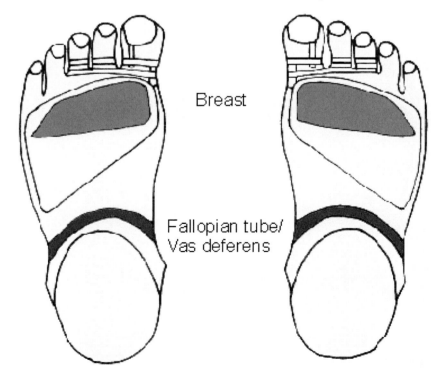

Senses/Facial area

The only areas remaining are the senses and facial area reflexes.

These have **symmetrical** location in the body and so, as usual, this is mirrored in the feet.

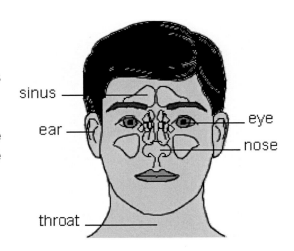

Senses/facial structures reflected on the plantar aspect of the right foot.

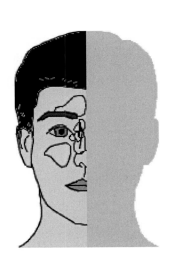
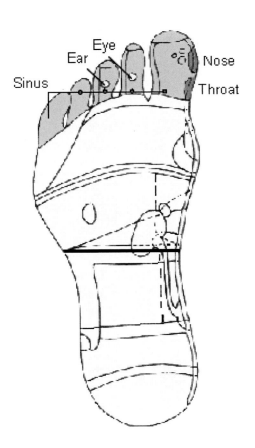

Senses/facial structures reflected on the plantar aspect of the left foot.

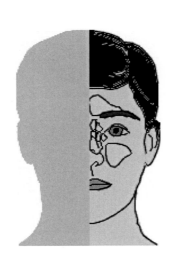

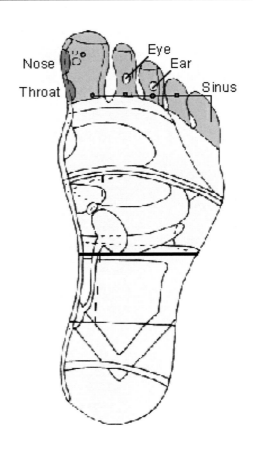

The **teeth** and **face** reflex areas are on the **dorsal** aspect of the **first three toes**.

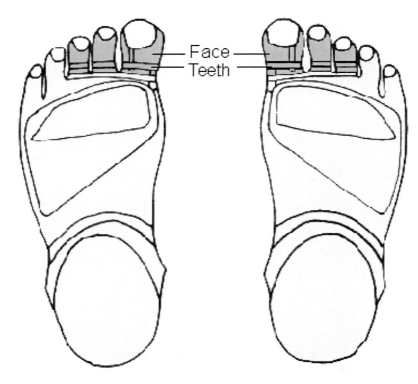

So, the principle of reflexology is that the **feet mirror the body**. As we have seen, by comparing the location of anatomical structures with the location of the corresponding reflex areas, the foot charts that have developed are based on this principle.

However, also remember that the development of reflexology has been heavily influenced by **zone therapy** (see 'History').

Zone therapy promotes the idea that there are **10 zones** of **energy** running longitudinally through the body, originating in the feet. Applying pressure to a zone on a foot may influence all the anatomical structures within that zone. If you consider the anatomical structures located in each zone and visualize them reflected on the foot, zone therapy generally supports the basic principle of the feet mirroring the body.

Zone therapy can also help to explain how an abnormality in one part of the body can cause a detrimental effect on another part, providing of course that both occur in the **same** zone.

Additionally, zone therapy helps to explain how, when **treating** a reflex area that is **neurologically** connected to a specific part of the body, **another**, seemingly physically **disassociated**, structure can be **affected**. However, do bear in mind that **any** nervous stimulation will be registered by the **central nervous system**, which is connected to **every** part of the body. Therefore it could be argued that the central nervous system itself might have a part to play in this phenomenon.

Due to the complexities of the body's anatomy and physiology, and the possible presence of zonal energy fields, the reflexologist must be aware that it is sometimes necessary to treat **additional** areas of the body, away from the area in difficulty, to assist a particular condition.

These additional areas are called **Areas of Assistance**. For example, there is an area of assistance associated with shoulder conditions. Although the shoulder is the primary target area for these treatments, it has been shown that working on the hip reflex area may ease the problem. In this case the hip is the area of assistance.

A number of areas of assistance have been found. Sometimes the area of assistance seems totally disassociated with the primary target area and, at first, it may seem difficult to comprehend the connection between them. However, areas of assistance can generally be **explained** by one, or a combination of, the following:

Zonal Link

The area of assistance may be in the **same zone** as the primary target area. Based on zone therapy, treating one area in a zone can influence all of the structures within that zone. As we have mentioned, the hip is an area of assistance for the shoulder. The shoulder is also an area of assistance for the hip. The hip and the shoulder are in the same zone. These examples of areas of assistance could therefore be explained by the presence of a zonal link.

Organic Link

The **condition** itself may be **influenced** by a **secondary body** part. In some cases, this secondary body part may be the actual originating source of the condition. An example of a condition with an organic link is asthma. For this condition the digestive system is an area of assistance. Asthma is a predominantly respiratory complaint, but superfluous secretions of mucus from the digestive system can worsen this condition. Therefore, treating the reflex areas associated with the digestive system may benefit the asthma.

Structural Link

There may be a **physical structural connection** between the primary target area and the area of assistance. For example, an ankle problem may be caused or exacerbated by a knee, hip or pelvic problem that is disrupting the weight distribution. Therefore, treating the structurally connected reflex areas (in this case the knee, hip or pelvis) may assist the ankle problem.

Neural Link

The condition may be caused or worsened by the impairment of the **nerves**, originating in the spine, that serve a particular part of the body. This may lead to the malfunction or altered sensation in the affected part. For example, tingling in the hands may originate from the compression of the related nerves in the cervical vertebrae. In this case, the cervical spinal reflex area would be treated as the area of assistance.

In this section we have looked at how the feet mirror the body. We have also drawn your attention to the influence of zone therapy and the presence of areas of assistance. Here's a summary…

Summary

➤ The **feet mirror** the **body**.

➤ Anatomical structures on the **left** side of the **body** have corresponding reflex areas on the **left foot**.

➤ Anatomical structures on the **right** side of the **body** have corresponding reflex areas on the **right foot**.

➤ **Foot charts** show the location of the reflex areas.

➤ **Zone therapy** has strongly influenced reflexology. The theory helps to explain how treating one reflex area can influence other structures located in that particular zone.

➤ Some conditions have an associated **area of assistance**. Treating this additional, sometimes remote, reflex area may benefit the condition.

➤ An area of assistance generally has a **zonal**, **organic**, **structural** or **neural** link to the primary target area.

Question (Answers: Page 365)

1. True or False?

   The reflex area corresponding to the spine runs down the medial edge of both feet.

2. Where is the pelvic reflex area located?

   a. on the toes
   b. centrally on the feet
   c. below the pelvic line on the plantar and lateral aspects of the left foot only
   d. below the pelvic line on the plantar and lateral aspects of both feet

3. Anatomically, the solar plexus is located on the left of the body. Based on the principle of the feet mirroring the body, on which foot do you think the solar plexus reflex area is located?

4. How many reflex areas representing the brain are there on each foot?

5. True or False?

   The heart reflex area is on the left foot only.

6. True or False?

   The lungs are represented on both the plantar and dorsal aspects of the feet. The trachea/bronchi reflex areas are located on the top of the big toes and on the medial edge of the big toes.

7. On which foot are the gall bladder, ileocaecal valve and appendix reflex areas situated?

8. Which foot has the largest liver reflex area?

9. On which foot are the descending colon and sigmoid colon reflex areas?

10. True or False?

    Only the left foot has a reflex area for the transverse colon.

11. The prostate reflex area in the male and the uterus reflex area in the female share the same location. Which aspect of the feet shows this reflex area?

    a. lateral
    b. medial
    c. plantar
    d. dorsal

12. The ovaries and testes are a part of the reproductive and endocrine systems. On which aspect of the foot is the associated reflex area located?

    a. lateral
    b. medial
    c. plantar
    d. dorsal

13. It has been found that, for some conditions, treating another specific reflex area may be beneficial. What name is given to these additional areas?

14. The pressure of the stomach on the heart can cause palpitations. The stomach is therefore an area of assistance for palpitations. What link exists for this reason between the heart and the stomach?

    a. zonal
    b. organic
    c. structural
    d. neural

15. Many knee conditions are caused by the compression of nerves in the lumbar spine. The lumbar spine area is therefore an area of assistance. What link exists here?

    a. zonal
    b. organic
    c. structural
    d. neural

16. What link exists between the hip and the shoulder?

17. The ankle is an area of assistance for knee conditions and vice versa. There is a zonal link. What other link exists to help to explain these areas of assistance?

65

This page has intentionally been left blank.

The Treatment

This page has intentionally been left blank.

As a holistic therapy, a reflexology treatment should, whenever possible, cover **all** the body systems. This means treating **all** the reflex areas and this complete treatment usually takes about **1 hour**. However, always bear in mind that every treatment is **unique** with its own **individual** circumstances that may affect the structure of the treatment.

Before the treatment is started, a full **case history** should be taken (see 'Developing Professional'). This will ensure that any **contra-indications** or **precautions** that may influence the treatment are identified (see 'Safety'). Finding out what **conditions**, if any, the patient has, allows the treatment to be **tailored** appropriately.

Having taken the case history and found out as much relevant information as possible about the patient, you may decide:

> - to **reduce** the **duration** of the treatment
> - to **reduce** the **pressure** applied
> - to **avoid** a particular **reflex area**
> - to **avoid** the **feet** but treat the hands
> - to **refer** the patient to their **General Practitioner**
> - **not** to **treat** at all

The case history may also highlight a condition that may benefit from **extra attention** to a particular **reflex area.** For example, you may decide to spend more time on the respiratory reflex areas for an asthmatic patient.

The identified condition may have an associated **area of assistance** (see 'The Principle') which also needs attention. In the case of asthma, the digestive system is an area of assistance. Therefore, you may decide to further treat the digestive reflex areas.

During the treatment itself, sensitivity may be discovered in a specific reflex area suggesting **congestion, inflammation, stress** or **imbalance** in the corresponding part of the body. As a result of this, you may decide that extra attention is required to the sensitive area.

In cases when extra attention to a particular area is required, the reflex area should be **re-visited** at the **end** of the standard treatment. It is not recommended practice to treat an individual reflex area in isolation.

The case history should establish if the patient is taking any **medication**. Taking medication may impact on the treatment due to the **side effects** of many commonly used drugs. Unfortunately, many modern drugs cause an **imbalance** in various parts of the body. Often the parts of the body affected are disassociated with the original condition. The imbalances caused by the drugs may cause **sensitivity** in the associated reflex areas. These sensitive areas may therefore need extra attention.

You should be aware of the effects of the most **commonly** used drugs, so we'll take a look at them next.

Anti-histamines

Anti-histamines counteract the effects of **histamine**, a chemical in all body tissues that can cause **allergic reactions**. They are classified according to their **sedative** effect. Anti-histamines are used to treat allergic reactions such as skin rashes, hay fever, nettle-rash, certain forms of eczema and some irritant coughs. From a reflexology perspective, anti-histamines may cause sensitivity in the **kidney** reflex area.

Steroids

Steroid is the group name for compounds derived from **cholesterol**. Some **hormones** are included in this group. Steroids are often used as **anti-inflammatories** for conditions such as arthritis, heart conditions, asthma and severe allergic reactions. Steroids, often seen as a last resort drug, may cause **kidney** problems if used over a long term. They may also reduce vitality. From a reflexology perspective, the use of steroids can cause **insensitivity** in the feet. This may reduce the reaction to the treatment but does not negate its beneficial effects.

Aspirin

Aspirin (acetylsalicylic acid) **relieves pain** and **reduces fever** in infectious diseases. It also may help to **promote sleep**. It is commonly used for headaches, colds, flu and minor cases of insomnia. Vast quantities of aspirin are used every year, but it does have associated side effects. Aspirin can have a detrimental effect on the **stomach**, from minor irritations and inflammation to ulceration and bleeding in some sensitive individuals. The **stomach** reflex area may therefore be sensitive if the recipient is taking aspirin. Aspirin may also cause the skin to bruise easily. Look out for signs of this and reduce the pressure applied accordingly.

Painkillers

Medicines that **relieve pain** can affect the **intestines** and may cause **constipation**. These side effects may therefore cause sensitivity in the **intestine** and **large bowel** reflex areas.

Antibiotics

Antibiotics are **antibacterial** agents derived from micro-organisms. They are capable of destroying or injuring living organisms. Antibiotics, such as penicillin, are commonly used to control infections in the body. Antibiotics can destroy the natural bacteria in the gut that aid digestion, causing

constipation or **diarrhoea**. The **liver** can also be affected. The associated reflex areas may therefore be sensitive in individuals taking a course of antibiotics.

Anti-depressants
Anti-depressants are used to **relieve depression**. Anti-depressants can cause great sensitivity in the **brain** reflex areas.

Sleeping Tablets
Drugs given to **induce sleep** can cause great sensitivity in the **brain** reflex areas.

Beta-blockers
Beta-blockers **inhibit** the **parasympathetic** and **sympathetic** nervous systems. They have a **depressant** effect on the **adrenal glands** and the **heart** and so they are commonly used to control heart conditions and hypertension. The **liver** may be adversely affected by taking beta-blockers. This may cause the associated reflex area to be sensitive.

Amphetamines
Amphetamines are a group of drugs closely related to **adrenaline**. They **stimulate** the sympathetic nervous system. When taken orally, amphetamines have a profound stimulating effect on the **brain** producing, in the short term, a sense of well being and confidence. The capacity for mental work is also temporarily increased. Amphetamines inhibit **appetite** and so can be used for slimming purposes. They should be used only under strict medical control as they can cause adverse effects and can be addictive. From a reflexology perspective, the use of amphetamines causes sensitivity in the **brain** and **adrenal gland** reflex areas.

Antacids
Antacids correct excessive **acidity**, usually in the stomach. They tend to be **peppermint** flavoured and **chalk** based. The chalk content of antacids can cause **kidney stones** if large quantities are taken over a long period of time. The **kidney** reflex areas may therefore be sensitive.

As we have mentioned, sensitivity in a reflex area may be indicative of congestion, inflammation, stress or imbalance in the associated part of the body. However, it is of vital importance that you do not make assumptions as to the cause or reason for this.

Remember that it is **not** the role of the reflexologist to diagnose. Neither should a reflexologist profess to cure.

Now that we've looked at how treatments must be tailored to meet the needs of each individual, let's take a look at some of the **general features** of the treatment.

The **right foot** is always treated **first**.

The right foot is first because the treatment follows the direction of the **large intestine**. Following the flow of the large intestine helps the body to gently eliminate the toxins released as a result of the treatment. Anatomically, the large intestine originates on the right of the body and therefore the right foot is treated first.

Once the treatment has been completed on the right foot, it is started on the **left**.

The main movement of a reflexology treatment is the **creeping thumb**. The thumb always creeps **forwards** – never backwards. The creeping movement must take **slow**, **small steps** to contact as many reflex points as possible. The rest of the hand and fingers should be in a **natural** position to avoid unnecessary strain or contortion.

The pressure applied should be **firm**, **consistent** and **acceptable** to the patient.

To facilitate the smooth, creeping thumb movement, the feet can be dusted with a light coating of powder. These powders absorb any natural dampness on the feet and reduce stickiness. This allows the thumb to travel easily over the skin but without making the feet slippery. There are a growing number of powders available which contain little or no aluminium. You may choose to use cornflower or a similar product.

Take care if you choose to use creams, lotions or oils because they lubricate the feet too much if used generously. The thumb therefore slips on the surface of the foot, reducing the number of reflex points that are contacted. There is also a danger that the patient could slip as they step onto the floor after the treatment, or the feet may slip within the shoes as the feet warm – especially if wearing tights or stockings.

The thumb creeps over the foot following **imaginary lines**. These show the direction in which the area should be worked.

Individual reflex areas have their own associated direction of working using the creeping thumb technique. The suggested direction of working for each reflex area **varies from school to school**. Make yourself aware of the directions used by your school **now**.

For many of the reflex areas, particularly those on the plantar aspect relating to the major organs, the movement used is often **bi-directional**.

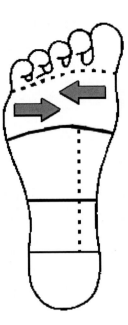

The thumb first creeps over the foot following the imaginary lines in one direction. The other thumb is then used to creep back along these lines in the opposite direction.

For a bi-directional reflex area that requires the thumb to creep across the foot, the thumb first creeps forward from the **medial** edge to the **lateral** edge of the foot.

Once the reflex area has been covered, the direction is reversed to work from the **lateral** edge to the **medial** edge. As the thumb always creeps forwards, **changing direction** involves **changing hands**.

The foot must always be **supported** correctly.

The holds and supports used are as important as the creeping thumb technique. If the foot is not well supported it will get pushed away and much of the pressure applied by the thumb will be lost. As we have mentioned, hand changes have to be made frequently during the treatment and so you need to be comfortable with your grips.

The way in which the foot is supported largely depends on the area of the foot that is being worked.

When working **above** the **waist line** on the plantar aspect of the foot, the foot is supported at the **toes**. For reflex areas on the plantar aspect **below** the **waist line**, the foot is supported at the **heel**. Let's take a look at the grips used on the right foot.

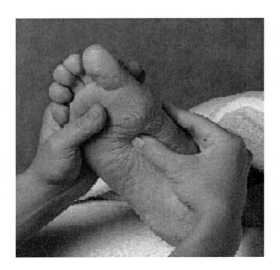

Here, the right foot is being treated **above** the **waist line**. It is therefore supported at the **toes**.

Initially the right foot is supported by the **left hand**. This allows the right thumb to work from the **medial** to the **lateral** edge of the foot.

The easy way to remember this is to keep in mind that the **initial working hand** always **matches** the **foot being worked**. So, initially, the right foot is worked by the right hand. The left hand must therefore support the foot.

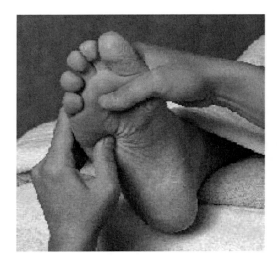

To **reverse** the direction, the **supporting hand changes**.

The **right hand** now supports the foot so that the left thumb can work from the **lateral** to the **medial** edge of the foot.

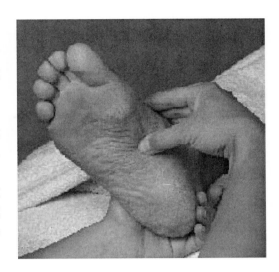

Here, the right foot is being treated **below** the **waist line**. It is therefore supported at the **heel**.

Initially, the right foot is supported by the **left hand**. Remember that the initial working hand matches the foot being worked. So, initially, the right foot is worked by the right hand. This allows the right thumb to work from the **medial** to the **lateral** edge of the foot.

To **reverse** the direction, the **supporting hand changes**.

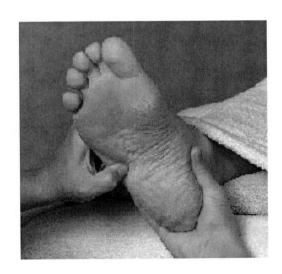

The **right hand** now supports the foot so that the left thumb can work from the **lateral** to the **medial** edge of the foot.

The grips on the left foot work on the same basis...

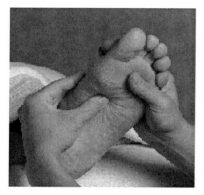

Above the waist line,
medial to lateral.

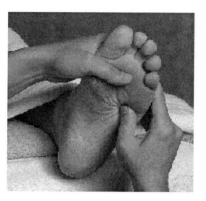

Above the waist line,
lateral to medial.

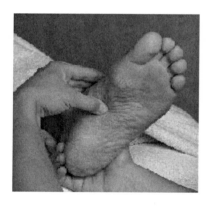

Below the waist line,
medial to lateral.

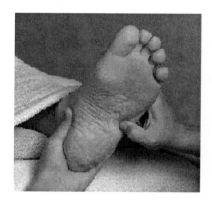

Below the waist line,
lateral to medial.

Let's now look at how the foot is supported to treat the reflex areas on the **medial** and **lateral** edges of the foot.

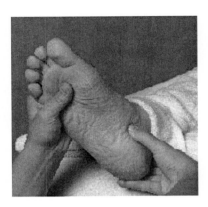
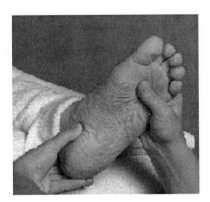

These are the holds for working the **medial** edge of the feet. To work the medial edge, the foot is held at the **base of the toes**. The foot is gently pushed towards the patient and angled out slightly to give good access to the area. Notice that the working hand matches the foot being worked.

These are the holds for working the **lateral** edge of the feet. To work the lateral edge, the foot is again held at the **base of the toes**. The foot is gently angled inwards which pushes the lateral edge forwards making it easier to access. The opposite hand to the working foot is used to work the lateral edge.

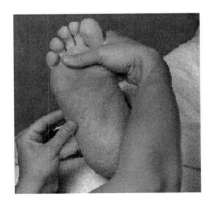
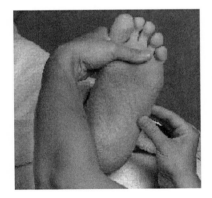

Summary

Here is a summary of the points covered in this section so far:

➢ Treat **all** reflex areas whenever possible.

➢ Take a full **case history** to identify any factors that may affect the treatment.

➢ Tailor the treatment to meet the **individual's** needs.

➢ Start with the **right** foot.

➢ Support the foot at the **toes** if working on the plantar aspect **above** the **waist line**.

➢ Support the foot at the **heel** if working on the plantar aspect **below** the **waist line**.

➢ Support the foot at the **base of the toes** and **angle** the foot to work the **medial** and **lateral** edges.

➢ Use a slow, **forward-creeping thumb** movement to apply firm and consistent pressure to contact as many reflex points as possible.

➢ Many reflex areas are worked **bi-directionally**.

➢ Work from the **medial** edge to the **lateral** edge first.

➢ Initially, the **working hand** matches the **foot being worked**.

➢ **Revisit** reflex areas identified as needing extra attention at the **end** of the treatment.

The actual **treatment sequence varies** from **school to school**. Find out now which treatment sequence you use, and then apply the rules that we have covered in this section.

All reflexology treatments incorporate **relaxation techniques**.

There are many relaxation techniques that can be used during a treatment and their importance should not be understated. Remember that the ultimate aim is to **relax** the patient to **encourage** a more **receptive environment** for the treatment. We'll look at the **uses** of relaxation techniques **before**, **during** and **after** the treatment.

Relaxation techniques can be used **before a treatment** to:

> ➢ introduce the patient to the practitioner's touch
> ➢ warm and relax the foot
> ➢ put the patient at ease
> ➢ signal the start of the treatment
> ➢ assess the level of flexibility of the foot which may reflect the patient's stress level

During a treatment, relaxation techniques can be used to:

> ➢ keep the foot relaxed
> ➢ keep the patient relaxed
> ➢ provide a link when moving from one area of the foot to another during the treatment sequence
> ➢ provide a respite for the reflexologist's thumb, so that constant pressure can be applied throughout the treatment

At the **end of a treatment**, relaxation techniques can be used to:

> ➢ signify that the treatment has come to an end
> ➢ relax the foot
> ➢ relax the practitioner's hands
> ➢ provide a comforting and reassuring end to a professional treatment

There are many relaxation techniques that can be incorporated into the treatment sequence. It is up to you which you use.

Details of 20 relaxation techniques follow. For each, we advise where it is most suited to fit into the treatment sequence, its function, and how to perform the technique.

Side to Side Relaxation

This can be used to start a treatment. It initiates the treatment, introduces the patient to the practitioner's hands and relaxes the patient. It also loosens and relaxes the upper foot.

To perform this relaxation technique:
- Loosely cup the hands on either side of the upper half of the foot.
- Gently rock the foot back and forth, using alternate hand movements.

Achilles Pinch and Slide

This technique can be performed at the beginning of the treatment. It relaxes and gently stretches the Achilles tendon making it more supple and sends a feeling of relaxation up the leg.

To perform this relaxation technique:
- Support the foot at the toes.
- Place the thumb and fingers comfortably on either side of the Achilles tendon.
- Gently apply pressure as you glide up the Achilles tendon for about 10cm.
- Repeat several times.

Double Hand Effleurage

This technique can be used after the spinal and other skeletal areas have been treated. It relaxes the foot and the practitioner's hands. It is generally very soothing and can link with the next area to be worked.

To perform this relaxation technique:
- Using a small, circular movement, with both hands working in a mirror image, move down the dorsal area from the base of the toes to the ankle.
- Loop around the outside of the ankle bones with the fingers. This leaves your thumbs naturally placed on the plantar area.
- Work up the plantar area, using alternating deep, slow thumb circles until you reach the toes.
- Repeat for 5 circuits of the foot.

Crescent Moon

This relaxation technique can be used after the respiratory system has been treated but prior to working the spine. It stretches the metatarsals, relaxes the whole foot and improves the blood supply to the muscles between the metatarsals. It is similar to the rib cage relaxation technique but in reverse.

To perform this relaxation technique:
- Brace both thumbs firmly over the lung reflex area.
- Starting at the centre of the dorsal area, using a moderate pressure, gently draw the fingers back across the dorsal aspect causing the foot to form a crescent shape.

Diaphragm Relaxation

This technique can be performed at the beginning of the treatment. It relaxes the patient by helping to slow down the breathing. It also allows the practitioner to gauge the patient's level of relaxation and flexibility of the foot.

To perform this relaxation technique:
- Place the working thumb on the medial edge of the diaphragm line.
- With the other hand, gently but firmly pull the foot over the thumb, using the thumb as a pivot.
- Continue this across the foot, from the medial edge to the lateral edge, change hands and then return.

Dorsal Channels

This technique can be performed at the beginning of the treatment. It gently encourages venous flow and therefore can assist with swollen feet and ankles. It is very relaxing for the whole foot.

To perform this relaxation technique:
- Place the thumbs on the plantar aspect to act as a base.
- Using sliding movements with alternating index fingers, slide gently down the channels (grooves) between each toe on the dorsal aspect of the foot.

Spinal Twist

The spinal twist can be used at the beginning of the treatment. It gently stretches the longitudinal arch of the foot in preparation for later work on the spinal reflex area.

To perform this relaxation technique:
- Hold the medial edge of the foot at the toes with one hand and position the second hand at the heel.
- Gently twist the foot as though wringing a cloth. The main emphasis of the twist comes from the upper hand.

Metatarsal See-Saw

The metatarsal see-saw can be used prior to treating the digestive system. It exercises the joints of the foot, massages the muscles between the metatarsals, eases stiffness and increases flexibility.

To perform this relaxation technique:
- Using the fingers on the dorsal aspect and the thumbs on the plantar aspect, take hold of the metatarsals below toes 1 and 2 using one hand for each.
- Using a firm but gentle pressure, move the hands alternately up and down, similar to a see-saw. Repeat five times and then release.
- Repeat for metatarsals 2 and 3.
- Repeat for metatarsals 3 and 4.
- Repeat for metatarsals 4 and 5.

Dorsal Stroking

This technique can be used after all the systems have been treated. It is very soothing and a good linking technique to use between movements. It also helps to drain excess fluid.

To perform this relaxation technique:
- Using all four fingers of each hand, gently make short, circular strokes.
- Alternate the hands and work from the base of the toes to the ankle, and then return.
- Repeat several times.

Ankle Circles

Ankle circles can follow the dorsal stroking relaxation technique. It is soothing and eases puffiness and tension around the ankle bone. The ankles are often neglected so they appreciate the attention!

To perform this relaxation technique:
- When the ankle is reached using the dorsal stroking technique, concentrate on circling the ankle bones using just two fingers.
- Give extra emphasis to the underside of the ankle bone as this is often a very tight area.

Plantar Petrissage

Plantar petrissage follows the ankle circles relaxation technique. It relaxes yet tones the foot muscles and keeps the foot joints supple. Plantar petrissage also feels wonderful!

To perform this relaxation technique:
- From the ankle, transfer your thumbs onto the plantar aspect at the heel.
- Using slow, deep, circular movements, work the thumbs up the sole of the foot.
- Repeat this several times to thoroughly cover the whole area.

Medial Petrissage

This technique can follow on from the plantar petrissage. It stimulates the spinal reflexes and is soothing and comfortable.

To perform this relaxation technique:
- Start on the medial edge at the base of the big toe.
- Use both thumbs in a slow, deep, circular movement and work your way down to the heel.
- Work your way back up the medial edge to the big toe.
- Repeat several times.

Knuckling

This technique can be used following the spinal area but prior to treating the digestive system. Knuckling stimulates all nerve endings in the feet and is both relaxing and beneficial to the foot.

To perform this relaxation technique:
- Hold the foot firmly at the top of the lateral edge.
- Make a loose fist with the hand that matches the foot being worked.
- Rotate the fingers so that the knuckles make small circles over the skin, whilst moving the fist up over the plantar surface and down over the dorsal surface of the foot.

Ankle Freeing

This technique can be used prior to treating the reproductive and urinary systems. It relaxes and loosens the ankle joint, increases circulation and prepares the ankle for the reflex work.

To perform this relaxation technique:
- Place the padded heel of each thumb in the natural grooves either side of the ankle bone.
- Gently apply an inward pressure using an alternating back and forth movement.
- Doing this correctly encourages the foot to wag from side to side like a dog's tail!

Under-grip and Over-grip

These grips can be used prior to treating the reproductive and urinary systems. The upper-grip relaxes and gently stretches the calf muscles and Achilles tendon. It also relaxes the ankle in preparation for the reflex work. The over-grip concentrates on relaxing different muscles in the shin. It too relaxes the ankle in preparation for reflex work.

To perform these relaxation techniques:
- For the under-grip, hold the foot at the heel using the opposite hand to the foot being worked.
- Grasp the foot at the top of the medial edge.
- Slowly, using the upper hand to guide the movement, rotate the foot in circles of approximately 15cm in circumference, inwards towards the other foot.
- Pause, and change to the over-grip position.

- To do this, release the grip of the lower hand and pivot the thumb to allow the hand to 'saddle' over the top of the ankle.
- Keeping the upper hand in place, continue to rotate the foot in circles as for the under-grip.

Metatarsal Kneading

This technique can be used prior to commencing the lung/respiratory reflex areas. It spreads the metatarsal bones. This allows the muscles to stretch so that they can receive fresh blood and eliminate old blood. It relaxes the whole foot and the lower leg.

To perform this relaxation technique:
- Make a fist with the hand that matches the foot to be worked.
- Place the fist at the top of the plantar area at the base of the toes.
- Cup the other hand around the dorsal aspect at the base of the toes, with the main contact on the outside edges.
- Using slow, alternate movements, push with the fist causing the foot to spread slightly to fill the cupped hand.
- Then, as you relax the pressure from the fist, gently squeeze the foot on the outside edges with the cupped hand.
- This makes a gentle two stage rocking movement.
- Repeat several times.

Foot Moulding

This technique can follow on from medial petrissage. It massages and loosens the toe joints, increases the flexibility of the feet and improves the blood supply to the toes. It is calming and very relaxing.

To perform this relaxation technique:
- Place one hand on the plantar side and one hand on the dorsal side of the foot, to sandwich the foot between the heels of your hands.
- Apply gentle pressure.
- Rotate each hand alternately, keeping the pressure on so that the hands resemble bicycle pedals turning.

Rib Cage Relaxation

The rib cage relaxation technique can be used prior to treating the respiratory system. It helps to stimulate the reflexes in the chest and lungs in preparation for the treatment.

To perform this relaxation technique:
- Place both thumbs firmly over the lung reflex area to act as a brace.
- Starting at the outside edges and using all 4 fingers, gently creep forward over the dorsal aspect until you meet in the middle.
- Repeat several times.
- Be careful not to make contact with your nails and take care not to apply too much pressure in this delicate area.

Gliding Off

This technique can be used as the last movement of the treatment. It is a very gentle way of signalling to your patient that you have finished.

To perform this relaxation technique:
- Link with the previous technique using a gentle, gliding stroke to ultimately position one hand on the plantar aspect and one hand on the dorsal aspect of the foot at the ankle.
- Slowly and gently, glide your hands up the length of the foot, drifting off at the toes.

Revitalizing Point

This can be used after the gliding off technique to help to revitalize and re-awaken the client.

To perform this 'relaxation' technique:
- Locate the revitalization point. It is at the start of the kidney meridian, which is located below the diaphragm line, in line with toe 2.
- Using a thumb on each foot, press firmly into this point on the plantar aspect and then release.
- Repeat, asking the patient to breathe in as the pressure is applied, and out as the pressure is released.

A reflexology treatment has been seen to induce many positive changes in the body. For example, it has been found to reduce stress and tension, relieve pain, improve bodily functions and generally restore the body to a better state of well being.

Despite much research, the way in which a reflexology treatment achieves its somewhat startling results has **not** yet been **scientifically established**. There are, however, a number of theories or explanations. We'll take a quick look at some of them now, but do remember that these are only **suggested** explanations as to how reflexology may work.

One suggested explanation is the **Physiological Response Hypothesis**. This is based on the widely acknowledged belief that reflexology creates a state of **deep relaxation**.

According to the Physiological Response Hypothesis, when this state of deep relaxation is achieved, a series of physiological responses occur. **Muscles** begin to **loosen**. **Organs** and body **systems** begin to lose their **tension**. This allows the **blood** to circulate more **freely**, taking oxygen and nutrients to previously inaccessible areas. The stagnant blood and accumulated **toxins** are **flushed out** of these areas, rejoin the cardiovascular system, and are subsequently **removed** by the liver and kidneys. Thus the deep state of relaxation, induced by reflexology, encourages natural healing processes to take place.

Dobbs, B.Z. (1985) considers that reflexology is based on **several hypotheses**. The main ones are listed here. Remember, they are only hypotheses.

The Energy Hypothesis
Inside a living organism, energy circulates in a rhythmical way due to an electromagnetic field. The energy touches all cells and maintains communication between all organs. Sometimes 'blocks' occur on the energy pathways. Reflexology helps to clear the blocks and re-circulate the energy.

The Lactic Acid Hypothesis
Lactic acid is sometimes transformed into microcrystals and deposited in the hands and feet. These deposits stop or disturb the flow of life energy. Reflexology crushes and recycles these microcrystals, so allowing the energy to circulate again.

Proprioceptive Nervous Receptors Hypothesis
There is a direct connection between certain parts of the feet and hands and the body's organs. Therefore a reflexology treatment can affect these organs.

Relaxing Effect Hypothesis

Persistent stress and tension can induce many physical problems. Reflexology is a relaxing therapy. This property of the therapy can induce its beneficial effects.

Psychological Hypothesis

Reflexology is a contact therapy. This physical demonstration of care and concern has psychological benefits which, in turn, are reflected in the physical body.

Although how reflexology works hasn't yet been scientifically established, it can be said that the treatment has been seen to improve the state of the body in many ways.

To maximize the effectiveness of the treatment, **obtain** as much **information** as possible about the patient. Take a full **case history**. **Listen** to the patient and to your **intuition**. Be **perceptive**. **Open** your mind. Take the various **theories** as to how it may work, combine these theories with **your** own **experiences** and **thoughts**. Your opinion is as valid as anyone else's until the scientists can determine the underlying physiology behind the therapy.

Irrespective of the lack of scientific proof, reflexology is a **powerful** holistic treatment. A professional reflexologist has the potential to do an amazing amount of good, safe in the knowledge that it is highly unlikely that they will do any harm.

Questions (Answers: Page 367)

1. True or False?

   A full case history is taken to ensure that only the reflex areas relating to the identified conditions are treated.

2. Which commonly used drug can cause stomach irritations and, in extreme cases, stomach ulceration?

3. Fill in the missing word:

   Anti-histamines may cause sensitivity in the _____ reflex areas.

4. Which large organ can be affected by the use of antibiotics and beta-blockers?

5. Three of the four drugs listed below may cause sensitivity in the brain reflex areas. Which drug doesn't?

   a. anti-depressants
   b. sleeping tablets
   c. steroids
   d. amphetamines

6. Which foot is always treated first?

7. Most schools consider that the reflex area associated with the small intestine is bi-directional. The direction of working is across the foot. What would be the correct technique?

   a. Creep from the medial edge to the lateral edge and then move on to the next reflex area.
   b. Creep from the lateral edge to the medial edge and then move on to the next reflex area.
   c. Creep from the medial edge to the lateral edge, change hands and then creep from the lateral edge to the medial edge.
   d. Creep from the lateral edge to the medial edge, change hands and then creep from the medial edge to the lateral edge.

8. Where is the foot supported when treating reflex areas on the plantar aspect that are below the waist line?

9. True or False?

   When treating the plantar aspect of the feet, the initial working hand always matches the foot being worked.

10. True or False?

   To work either the medial or lateral edge of a foot, the foot is supported at the base of the toes and turned gently either outwards or inwards to make the edge comfortably accessible.

11. When working which edge does the working hand NOT match the foot being worked?

Safety

This page has intentionally been left blank.

Reflexology is generally a **very safe** therapy with no associated dangers. There is **no limit** on the **frequency** of treatments – even daily is safe.

Age is not an issue. Reflexology can be beneficial to all age groups, from very young **babies** through to the **elderly**. The amount of **pressure** applied and the **duration** of the treatment is adapted according to the recipient.

For tiny **babies**, a **feather-light touch** is used and the treatment only lasts a **few minutes**. The movement always starts at the **heel** and works **towards** the **toes**.

Children under the age of **16** should only be treated if a **responsible adult** accompanies them. The **pressure** used should be **lighter** and the **duration** of the treatment **reduced** from the standard hour. The treatment should be clearly explained to the adult - without ignoring the child. Depending on the age of the child, toys or books should be available to keep their attention. Take care if using a massage couch – use lower equipment if possible to ensure the safety of the child.

When treating the **frail** and the **elderly**, always be aware of the possibility of **osteoporosis**. Use **light pressure** and ensure that the treatment is always comfortable. Never attempt to bend a stiff foot or straighten bent toes. **Reduce** the **duration** of the treatment and use gentle massage to relax the feet and legs. For safety reasons, assist the patient on and off the massage couch and never leave them on it unattended.

The **pressure** applied and the **duration** of the **first** treatment should also be **adapted** if the recipient is in **poor health**. In these circumstances, a pressure lighter than normal should be applied and the session reduced to about 30 minutes. It is always best to 'dilute' the treatment in this way and see how the recipient feels afterwards. The next treatment can then be adapted accordingly.

During the treatment, adverse reactions are **not** usually encountered. However, a **hypersensitive** individual may display some of the following symptoms:

> ➢ dramatic feeling of coldness
> ➢ nausea
> ➢ faintness
> ➢ trembling
> ➢ excessive sweating
> ➢ change in pallor
> ➢ hyperventilation
> ➢ uncharacteristic restlessness and agitation

Should any of these symptoms be displayed, **stop** the treatment **immediately** and attend to the patient's needs.

Generally there are **no significant side effects** to reflexology. Indeed, it often leaves the recipient with an increased feeling of well being and some enjoy better sleep.

However, due to its balancing effect on the body, some existing symptoms may be **exacerbated** in the short term. This may cause the recipient to feel a little worse immediately after the treatment or the following day. These effects are usually short lived, leaving the recipient feeling the true benefit of the treatment.

Various **minor** reactions may be experienced **after** a treatment. Remember that each recipient is an **individual** and will react as such to a treatment. Symptoms sometimes encountered after a treatment include:

> ➢ sleepiness and constant yawning
> ➢ weeping or easily upset and emotional
> ➢ shivering
> ➢ flu-like symptoms/runny nose/headache
> ➢ frequent urination and defaecation and/or diarrhoea
> ➢ increased thirst
> ➢ nausea/dizziness
> ➢ mild skin rash
> ➢ feeling blue or depressed
> ➢ irritability
> ➢ aches and pains in a specific reflex area on the foot or in the associated body part
> ➢ restless sleep

Why a reflexology treatment should cause some recipients to display the symptoms listed on the previous pages is uncertain, but it is thought that it may be due to one (or a combination) of the following reasons:

> ➤ the elimination of toxins
> ➤ the body trying to re-balance
> ➤ a shift or re-balancing of subtle energies within the body
> ➤ a sudden deep relaxation which initiates an emotional release

After a reflexology treatment, the recipient should be encouraged to drink plenty of **water**. This aids the removal of the toxins from the body and may help to prevent some of the symptoms mentioned earlier from occurring.

Before a patient is treated, a full **case history** must be taken (see 'Developing Professional'). Taking a case history highlights aspects of the patient's condition that may affect how you carry out the treatment.

If the patient uses **medication** for conditions that can suddenly onset, e.g. angina and asthma, make sure that you find out if the patient carries the medication and, if so, where it is kept. Medical Alert jewellery can be a valuable source of information in an emergency, so remember to ask if any is worn.

You should also find out when the patient last had a **meal**. Ideally, a treatment should not be performed on a recipient who has just eaten a heavy meal, as the body will be working to digest the food, making it impossible to fully relax. The reflexologist should avoid heavy meals before a treatment too! Performing a treatment on a full stomach can cause drowsiness.

It is also best to avoid treating someone who has **not eaten** for a significant period of time. An empty stomach may increase the possibility of dizziness and nausea.

Having taken the case history and found out as much relevant information as possible about the patient, you may decide:

> ➤ to **reduce** the **duration** of the treatment
> ➤ to **reduce** the **pressure** applied
> ➤ to **avoid** a particular **reflex area**
> ➤ to **avoid** the **feet** but treat the hands
> ➤ to **refer** the patient to their **General Practitioner**
> ➤ **not** to **treat** at all

There is a strong consensus of opinion that there are very few circumstances that actually **prevent** a reflexology treatment from taking place. Aspects of the patient's condition that **prevent** the treatment are called **contra-indications**.

There are various schools of thought on what circumstances constitute a contra-indication. However, a view shared by all is "**if in doubt – don't!**"

Common sense should always prevail and the reflexologist must always take into account their own **experience**, **knowledge** and **limitations**.

We'll take a look at the conditions that are generally considered to be contra-indications next.

Pregnancy

Reflexology is considered to be of benefit to **pregnant** women. It has been shown to be useful in reducing fluid retention, lowering blood pressure and reducing stress. However, it is generally considered wise to **avoid** treating women during the first **three months** of pregnancy. Although there is no evidence to suggest that a reflexology treatment increases the likelihood of a miscarriage, declining to treat women in the early stages of pregnancy eliminates the risk of blame should a miscarriage occur.

When there is a **history** of **miscarriage**, **avoid** performing a treatment for the first **three months** and then take **extreme care** for the **rest** of the pregnancy. There are no hard rules here and much is left to common sense. It is down to the individual reflexologist to decide whether it is best to get a letter of **approval** from the General Practitioner, give a **light relaxation** treatment or **decline** to treat.

Infectious or Contagious Illness

Generally, it is considered best to avoid treating a patient with an infectious or contagious illness. Quite apart from the obvious risk of **cross-infection**, reflexology **stimulates** the **detoxification** processes. This causes the effects of toxins, at a high level due to the infection, to become more apparent. If these toxins cannot be successfully removed from the body, a more toxic environment may be created in which the disease will manifest.

Cancer

There is much debate as to whether or not cancer is classified as a contra-indication. There is no evidence to suggest that reflexology encourages cancer to spread and most feel that this is unlikely. It is generally thought that treatments can be valuable at all stages of the illness to help reduce pain, counteract the side effects of drug and radiation therapies, reduce stress and increase the body's general resilience. It is, however, widely considered that a **novice** practitioner should treat cancer as a **contra-indication** and therefore decline to treat. An **experienced** practitioner may choose to treat based on his or her own **opinion** and **experience**. In either event, the site of the tumour should be avoided. A letter of consent may be wise.

Thrombosis, Phlebitis, Venous or Lymphatic Inflammations

Many reflexologists decline to treat sufferers of these conditions, due to the dangers of **blood clots** being displaced and circulated. Others do treat them but with great care. Medical liaison is vital.

Psychosis

Only **experienced** reflexologists with specialist training should treat patients suffering from severe psychological disorders. The treatments should only be carried out under **medical supervision**. It is also wise for the patient to be accompanied during the treatment.

Continued Extreme Negative Reaction

Should the recipient continuously display a negative reaction to reflexology, the treatments should be **stopped**.

Internal Bleeding

Patients suffering from any form of internal bleeding should not be treated. Internal bleeding constitutes an emergency situation. Refer them to their General Practitioner immediately.

As well as the contra-indications that prevent the treatment, there are also circumstances under which **care must be taken**. These are called **precautions**. The precautions include:

Terminal Illness
It has been found that reflexology may help to relieve the pain associated with terminal illnesses. The duration of the treatment should be reduced, but the frequency of the treatments increased. The comfort of the patient is of great importance and more time than usual should be spent on the relaxation techniques. Be prepared to listen to the patient's concerns and offer reassurance, but be careful not to give false hope. Pay extra attention to the liver and elimination systems to help with the metabolism of the drugs.

Fever
The **cause** of the fever should be established. If it is due to an infectious disease then the treatment should be declined. Some believe that working on the pituitary reflex area could help to bring the temperature down.

Asthma and Epilepsy
Only practitioners trained to deal with asthmatic attacks and epileptic fits should treat asthmatics and epileptics. **First Aid Training** is therefore highly recommended.

Foot Conditions
Minor foot conditions such as verrucae and small cuts should be covered with a plaster and direct touch avoided. Areas of broken skin should also be excluded. Athlete's foot does not in itself limit the treatment - infected areas can be avoided or covered with a plaster, but do ensure that your hands are washed well before and after the treatment. Wearing gloves is an option, but few therapists show enthusiasm for them. Major foot conditions, such as open sores, and bad varicose veins may limit the reflexology treatment to the hands. In cases of gangrene of the feet or legs, the feet should not be treated, treat the hands only.

Heart Conditions
Reflexology can be beneficial to sufferers of heart conditions, but obtain consent from the Doctor before commencing any treatment.

Menstruation
When the recipient is menstruating, it is advisable to work over the **uterus** and **ovary** reflex areas only **briefly** and **lightly**. This avoids the possibility of causing an excessive menstrual flow.

Osteoporosis

The treatment given to sufferers of osteoporosis should be very **light** and carefully conducted. If the bones in the feet are brittle, reflexology is prevented as the treatment may cause the bones in the feet to break.

Pre and Post Surgery

Reflexology, used pre-surgery, has been shown to help increase resilience during the operation. The Doctor's consent is required. Any post-operative treatment should be very **gentle** at first, but it has been shown to reduce stress and shock, promote healing and boost the immune system.

Hypertension

Should the recipient suffer from hypertension (high blood pressure) the reflex areas associated with the **adrenal glands** must be **avoided**. Working these reflex areas may cause an increase in the metabolic rate, which could cause a further increase in the blood pressure.

Diabetes

Some reflexologists believe that it is best to **avoid** the **pancreas** reflex area should the recipient be diabetic. Also, diabetes frequently **impairs** the **circulation** to the extremities and therefore the feet are often cold, clammy and less mobile than usual. The skin may be 'thin' and tear easily. The utmost care must be taken to ensure that the skin isn't damaged during a treatment. The amount of **pressure** applied should be **reduced** and the practitioner's fingernails must be kept short and smooth to prevent aggravating the skin in any way.

Drugs and Alcohol

Drugs and alcohol inhibit the therapy as they affect the nervous system. Only a very light treatment should be given so as not to significantly increase the toxin level. The treatment should be declined if the client is obviously under the influence of drugs or alcohol when they arrive for a treatment.

As you have seen, there are a number of contra-indications and precautions to keep in the back of your mind. As there are very few rules, and most advice you will find is based on personal experience and opinion, much comes down to your own common sense. When deciding what course of action to take, look at the picture as a whole.

Take into account **everything** you know about the **condition** and accumulate as much knowledge as possible about the **patient**. You will then be well placed to decide what treatment, if any, is appropriate.

If in doubt, don't do it, but remain realistic. Reflexology is a very safe treatment and it is highly unlikely that it will do any harm.

Summary

➢ Reflexology is generally a **very safe** treatment with **no major side effects**.

➢ There is **no limit** on the **frequency** of treatments.

➢ There are **no age restrictions**.

➢ The treatment should be **adapted** to the patient's needs.

➢ There are only a **few contra-indications** to prevent the treatment.

➢ Contra-indications that may **prevent** a reflexology treatment from taking place include **pregnancy, cancer, infectious and contagious illnesses, thrombosis, phlebitis, venous or lymphatic inflammations, psychosis, internal bleeding** and a continued **extreme negative reaction** to the treatment.

➢ Conditions that require **caution** include **terminal illnesses, fevers, foot conditions, heart conditions, menstruation, osteoporosis, hypertension, asthma, epilepsy** and **diabetes**. Caution should also be taken with treatments performed **pre- and post surgery** and with patients under the influence of **drugs** or **alcohol**.

Questions (Answers : Page 369)

1. True or False?

    Reflexology is generally a very safe treatment with no associated dangers or major side effects. It is suitable for all ages.

2. A reflexology treatment can be adapted to make it suitable for the recipient. The length of the session can be reduced. What other major factor can be altered?

3. During a reflexology treatment, your patient starts to shiver and feels nauseous. What do you do?

    a. cover the patient with an extra towel for warmth
    b. ask if they would like a drink of water before you continue
    c. stop the treatment immediately

4. Which of the following is a contra-indication?

    a. infectious illness
    b. verruca
    c. menstruation

5. True or False?

    There is no evidence to suggest that reflexology induces miscarriage, however it is wise not to treat women in the first three months of pregnancy.

6. Which is a precaution that restricts the treatment from the adrenal reflex areas?

    a. psychosis
    b. thrombosis
    c. phlebitis
    d. hypertension

Conditions

This page has intentionally been left blank.

This section contains information on the 72 conditions listed below:

Amenorrhoea	Indigestion
Anxiety	Insomnia
Arthritis – osteo	Irregular ovulation
Arthritis – rheumatoid	Irritable bowel syndrome
Asthma	Kidney stones
Back pain	Laryngitis
Bell's palsy	Lumbago
Blurred vision	Mastitis
Bronchitis	Menopause
Cancer	Menorrhagia
Catarrh	Migraine
Chilblains	Multiple sclerosis
Colds and flu	Muscular fatigue
Compression of spinal nerves	Myalgic encephalomyelitis
Constipation	Nausea
Cramp	Oedema
Cystitis	Ovarian cysts
Depression	Palpitations
Diabetes	Panic attacks
Diarrhoea	Parkinson's disease
Dysmenorrhoea	Pregnancy
Eczema	Pre-menstrual tension
Endometriosis	Prostatitis
Facial neuralgia	Raynaud's disease
Female infertility	Sciatica
Fever	Seasonal affective disorder
Frozen shoulder	Sinusitis
Glue ear	Stress
Headache	Stroke
Heart attack	Tennis elbow
Heartburn	Tension
Hiatus hernia	Thrush
Hypertension	Tinnitus
Hyperthyroidism	Ulcer
Hypotension	Varicose vein
Hypothyroidism	Vertigo

To provide you with a concise revision and reference tool, we have summarized the information for each condition to display it in a chart. For each condition a definition is given, along with a list of possible causes, general signs and symptoms, primary target areas, areas of assistance and holistic advice. There is a vast amount of information here but, for the developing reflexologist, this is just the beginning!

Many research papers are available, giving detailed information about specific conditions. The Association of Reflexologists and the Danish Reflexologists Association both offer a research paper service. Please note that there is usually a fee involved. Here are the appropriate contact details:

Chairman
Association of Reflexologists
27 Old Gloucester Street
London
WC1N 3XX
Tel: 0870 5673320

Forenede Danske Zoneterapeuter
Tollosevej 7
DK-4330 Hvalsoc
Denmark
Tel: +45 7550 1250
E-mail: fdz@fdz.dk
Web site: www.fdz.dk

AMENORRHOEA

Definition: Absence of menstruation.

Possible Causes: Pregnancy, slow development of the ovaries or womb, anaemia, anxiety, tuberculosis, malaria and anorexia nervosa. A sudden fright, stress or intense grief may cause menstrual stoppage for several months.

General Signs and Symptoms: Absence of menstrual flow.

Primary Target Areas:
Reproductive system

Areas of Assistance:
Endocrine system (organic)

Holistic Advice: First, before any treatment commences, establish whether the condition is caused by pregnancy. If it is, it is recommended that reflexology treatments are avoided during the first three months (see 'Safety'). Establishing the cause of this condition is a priority, for then the subsequent and correct treatment can follow.

ANXIETY

Definition: A reaction to a stimulus that results in the body pumping adrenaline, which helps the body to cope with difficult situations.

Possible Causes: Stress, fear, worry and apprehension.

General Signs and Symptoms: Anxiety, under normal circumstances, is healthy. Anxiety becomes a problem when it is permanently present or when it occurs at extreme levels. It may then produce insomnia, dizziness, tension, palpitations, sweating, weakness, lethargy, raised blood pressure, raised pulse rate and even vomiting and diarrhoea.

Primary Target Areas:	Areas of Assistance:
Solar plexus Give a thorough treatment and use plenty of relaxation techniques.	

Holistic Advice: Try to keep stress levels low. Try to adopt a positive attitude. Take regular exercise and practice relaxation exercises. Chamomile tea can be calming. Take time out to relax. Inhaling the aroma of one drop of lavender essential oil from a tissue can be calming. The Bach Rescue Remedy can also be helpful as a first aid treatment. Consult a doctor if symptoms persist. Counselling can help to get to the root cause of the anxiety.

ARTHRITIS - OSTEO

Definition: A degenerative inflammatory disease of one or more joints.

Possible Causes: Excessive joint usage, congenital bone deformity or simply wear and tear. Can follow injury (e.g. fracture), other inflammatory diseases and diabetes.

General Signs and Symptoms: Localized inflammation due to the bones rubbing together. The joints (often the knees, hips, spine and finger joints) may be swollen, stiff and deformed causing a lack of mobility. The pain is generally worse in the evening.

Primary Target Areas: Affected joint area	**Areas of Assistance:** All systems of elimination (organic) e.g. digestive system, urinary system and the liver

Holistic Advice: Avoid red meats, pork products, tea, coffee and alcohol. Suggested supplements: vitamins A, B complex and E, cod liver oil, calcium and aloe vera juice. Take gentle exercise. Consider acupuncture and homeopathy. Always treat the whole person. Look at the cause of any stress, any obesity and diet. Arthritis often affects people who are bottling up rage or grief and those who are unable to express a specific talent.

ARTHRITIS - RHEUMATOID

Definition: Inflammation of the connective tissue, tendons and ligaments. Characterized by progressive joint destruction, especially of the feet, fingers, wrists, knees, shoulders, ankles and elbows.

Possible Causes: Auto-immune disease affecting the synovial membrane around a specific joint or joints (mostly small joints). Auto-immune enzymes eat into the synovial membranes first and then into the cartilage. Could be triggered by a virus or an allergy.

General Signs and Symptoms: Deformity of the thumbs and fingers. Stiffness, weight loss, fatigue, anaemia, fever, tendon rupture, muscle wastage and restricted movement. Blood test shows rheumatoid factors. Pain and swelling is generally worse in the early morning.

Primary Target Areas:
Affected joint area

Areas of Assistance:
All systems of elimination (organic) e.g. digestive system, urinary system and the liver

Holistic Advice: Avoid red meats, pork products, tea, coffee and alcohol. Suggested supplements: vitamins A, B complex and E, cod liver oil, calcium and aloe vera juice. Take gentle exercise. Consider acupuncture and homeopathy. Always treat the whole person. Look also at the cause of any stress, any obesity and diet. Arthritis often affects people who are bottling up rage or grief and those who are unable to express a specific talent.

ASTHMA

Definition: Respiratory disorder.

Possible Causes: Allergic reaction. Sensitisation to bacteria responsible for chronic or repeated infections e.g. tonsillitis and sinusitis. Allergies to pollen, cats and dogs. Occupational exposure to chemicals. Stress and hereditary factors may contribute. May be prone to eczema.

General Signs and Symptoms: Difficulty breathing due to muscle spasm in the bronchi (small passages in the lungs). Intermittent wheezing, coughing and restlessness. Raised blood pressure and pulse rate. Can panic and turn pale during an attack.

Primary Target Areas:
Lungs
Bronchi
Diaphragm
Heart

See 'Safety/Precautions'.

Areas of Assistance:
Digestive system (zonal and organic)
Adrenals (organic)

Holistic Advice: Practitioners should be fully trained to deal with asthmatic attacks before treating patients with asthma. During an attack, always calm and reassure the person. Sit them in fresh air, leaning forward, resting on their arms. Seek medical advice if the condition worsens or persists. Yoga and gentle exercise can help keep the whole body in balance, thus helping it to cope with asthma.

BACK PAIN

Definition: Acute or chronic pain in the back that can seriously affect mobility.

Possible Causes: Direct injury from an impact or a fall. Lifting incorrectly and over-stretching. Abnormal muscular tension caused from an injury, or due to anxiety. Misaligned intervertebral disc. Car seats and the working environment can greatly affect our posture and can therefore be significant factors.

General Signs and Symptoms: Symptoms can vary in locality and intensity. The pain may range from a mild ache to sharp shooting pains down into the legs. There can be pins and needles in the limbs or even complete paralysis. Mobility depends on the site and severity of the condition.

Primary Target Areas: Spine	Areas of Assistance:
Repeatedly treat the whole spine area.	

Holistic Advice: Prevention is always the best course of action. Exercise regularly to strengthen the back. Maintain correct posture at all times. If sport is played, warm up and cool down properly, using appropriate stretches. There are many complementary therapies to consider such as chiropractic, osteopathy, massage, acupuncture and the Alexander Technique. Self-help is important. Look into life style and the working environment to identify factors that may be aggravating the condition.

BELL'S PALSY

Definition: Paralysis of the muscles on one or both sides of the face.

Possible Causes: Damage to the facial nerves as a result of inflammation or a direct wound. Fracture to the base of the skull. Apoplexy (stroke).

General Signs and Symptoms: Inability to smile, close the eye, blink or show the teeth on the affected side. The eye is often dry. Drooping of the affected side.

Primary Target Areas:	Areas of Assistance:
All facial areas	Cervical spine (structural and neural) Neck related areas (structural and organic)

Holistic Advice: Gentle massage concentrating on the back of the head and neck may help. Consult a qualified massage practitioner. Acupressure or acupuncture may be useful in the initial stages.

BLURRED VISION

Definition: Unclear eyesight and the inability to focus.

Possible Causes: Stress, tiredness, migraine or a direct injury to the eye. Blurred vision can also be indicative of a serious disorder such as concussion or a cerebral haemorrhage.

General Signs and Symptoms: Possible dizziness accompanied by the inability of the eyes to focus. Watery and painful eyes.

Primary Target Areas:
Eyes

Areas of Assistance:
Cervical spine (neural)
Kidneys (zonal and organic)

Holistic Advice: The cause of the condition needs to be established. If there is doubt as to the cause, refer the patient to their General Practitioner or Optician for a diagnosis. If the condition is due to stress, then address the cause of the stress. If the blurred vision is due to tiredness, try to introduce a regular sleep pattern.

BRONCHITIS

Definition: Inflammation of the mucous membrane within the bronchial tubes.

Possible Causes: Bacterial or viral infection. Exposure to cold and damp or sudden changes in the atmosphere. Inhalation of dust or vapours. Can be a symptom of chronic asthma.

General Signs and Symptoms: Bronchitis can be acute or chronic and the symptoms will vary according to the severity of the attack and the extent of the inflammation. At first the symptoms can be similar to those of a common cold and then a fever may develop. This is followed by a short, dry, painful cough with fast wheezes of respiration. The chest becomes painful and tight and, as the disease progresses, expectoration begins.

Primary Target Areas:	**Areas of Assistance:**
Lungs	Digestive system (zonal and
Bronchi	organic)
	Adrenals (organic)

Holistic Advice: Bronchitis in the acute or chronic forms can be very serious, even fatal. Medical advice must be sought. Do not smoke. Take advice on breathing exercises. Vitamin C can be beneficial. The use of a vaporizer with eucalyptus oil can help to ease the breathing.

CANCER

Definition: Term used to describe malignant disease, such as malignant tumours, carcinoma, sarcoma or leukaemia.

Possible Causes: Causes are still undefined. It is thought that there may be various triggers, such as stress, injury, environmental pollution, cigarette smoking, viral infections, hormonal influences and hereditary factors. There may be psychological factors involved too. Some believe that people who bottle up their feelings are at greater risk. Depression, grief and severe mental stresses may also affect vulnerability.

General Signs and Symptoms: These vary according to the location of the tumour e.g. cancer of the stomach may cause dyspepsia; cancer of the bowel may produce diarrhoea or constipation; cancer affecting the jaw may cause neuralgia. In cases of breast cancer, lumps can usually be felt in the breast tissue. Skin cancers may be seen as hard swellings on the surface that may break down and ulcerate.

Primary Target Areas: Solar plexus Avoid the site of the tumour. See 'Safety/Contra-indications'.	**Areas of Assistance:**

Holistic Advice: Patients concerned that they may have cancer should be encouraged to see a General Practitioner immediately. When identified quickly, many forms of cancer can be successfully treated. Medical diagnosis and support is essential. Many complementary therapies may be of some assistance, although permission to treat should be obtained from the General Practitioner first. Psychotherapy may be beneficial to allow emotions to be expressed and a positive attitude maintained.

CATARRH

Definition: Irritation and inflammation of the mucous membranes, particularly those of the air passages, associated with a copious secretion of mucus.

Possible Causes: Prevalent in damp, cold weather. Infection due to colds and flu or, in the case of hay fever (summer catarrh), to the allergic reaction to pollen or dust.

General Signs and Symptoms: Often starts with episodes of sneezing, a sore throat and possibly a fever. As these symptoms abate, the catarrh discharged from the nose and chest becomes thicker and purulent (pus like).

Primary Target Areas:	**Areas of Assistance:**
Sinuses	Digestive system (organic) Adrenals (organic)

Holistic Advice: Diet plays an important part. Dairy products and wheat aggravate the condition and, in some cases, it may be white flour, white sugar or food additives. Some of these may have to be excluded from the diet on a permanent basis. A balanced diet of fresh fruit and vegetables with vitamin C and garlic supplements may be beneficial. Drink plenty of water and hot, fresh lemon and honey.

CHILBLAINS

Definition: Inflamed condition of the skin on the hands or feet, sometimes even the ears.

Possible Causes: Under feeding, poor circulation, poor clothing and tight boots. People who suffer with chilblains generally suffer from chills and head colds and are in poor health.

General Signs and Symptoms: The skin on the little toe and outer side of the foot or inner side of the hand becomes purple and very itchy. Blisters containing a thin yellow fluid form on the discoloured area, which becomes very painful. These blisters break and leave behind an ulcerated surface that is very difficult to heal.

Primary Target Areas: Heart Use plenty of relaxation techniques.	**Areas of Assistance:** Lumbar spine (neural)

Holistic Advice: Prevention is best. Good food, warm clothing and regular exercise may help. Avoid anything tight around the leg that restricts the circulation (even socks that leave a mark should be avoided). Wear wide boots and thick wool socks in the winter. Take a good quality garlic capsule on a daily basis to help reduce the viscosity of the blood.

COLDS AND FLU

Definition: Viral infection of the nose and throat that can lead to respiratory conditions.

Possible Causes: Viral infection by one of approximately 30 different strains. This often gives rise to secondary infections e.g. sinusitis and earache.

General Signs and Symptoms: High temperature, runny nose, cough, congestion, shivers and lethargy.

Primary Target Areas:	Areas of Assistance:
Spleen Lungs Bronchi Sinuses	

Holistic Advice: Take plenty of fresh air but keep warm. Garlic and vitamin C supplements can be beneficial. Drink plenty of fluids, especially water. Eat a light diet containing plenty of fresh fruit and vegetables. Avoid reflexology treatments if the infection is severe (see 'Safety/Contra-indications').

COMPRESSION OF SPINAL NERVES

Definition: A spinal nerve under abnormal pressure.

Possible Causes: Direct injury. Skeletal misalignment due to factors such as bad posture or a slipped disc. Muscular spasms may also compress certain nerves.

General Signs and Symptoms: Tingling, numbness, pain and, in extreme cases, possible paralysis.

Primary Target Areas:	**Areas of Assistance:**
Whole spine Pay particular attention to the spinal area related to the site of the symptoms e.g. tingling in the arms and hands relates to the cervical spine.	

Holistic Advice: Any cases of numbness and/or tingling, if persistent, should be referred to a General Practitioner for diagnosis. Try to maintain a good posture, especially when lifting heavy objects. Chiropractic and osteopathy may be beneficial in realigning the skeleton.

CONSTIPATION

Definition: The infrequent or incomplete emptying of the bowel which leads to hard faeces.

Possible Causes: A diet lacking sufficient fibre or fluids. Lack of exercise. Can also be symptomatic of an underlying disease.

General Signs and Symptoms: The faeces are hard, difficult to expel and passed in small amounts. The straining involved in this may cause haemorrhoids. Bloating, colic and headaches can be experienced due to the pressure of accumulated faeces in the rectum. Periods of diarrhoea may be experienced as the bowel overflows.

Primary Target Areas:
Small and large intestines

Areas of Assistance:
Liver (organic)
Gall bladder (organic)
Lumbar spine (neural)

Holistic Advice: Try to prevent the condition by drinking plenty of water and eating a healthy, low fat but high fibre diet. Porridge, fresh fruit (especially prunes) and brown whole meal bread are beneficial. Try to adopt a routine of opening the bowel at the same time every day. Take regular exercise and reduce stress to help the functioning of the digestive system.

CRAMP

Definition: Sudden painful contraction of a muscle, commonly in a limb.

Possible Causes: The cause normally resides in the nervous system. Alternative causes include an accumulation of lactic acid in the muscle, poor circulation, swimming in cold water, lack of salt or other minerals, over-tiredness and tension.

General Signs and Symptoms: Painful contraction of muscle, commonly in the calf. Lack of mobility. Cramp can last just a few seconds or a few hours. A general ache is often left in the muscle after the contraction has ceased.

Primary Target Areas:	**Areas of Assistance:**
Heart	Lumbar spine (neural)

Holistic Advice: Possible useful supplements: vitamin E, calcium, zinc and garlic capsules. Some General Practitioners prescribe quinine. For night cramp, keeping the feet warm can help, so use bed socks or place the feet on a feather pillow (which holds body heat and does not go cold like a hot water bottle). A regular massage is a great help as it stimulates the circulation and lymphatic system, releasing tension and waste products from the muscles.

CYSTITIS

Definition: Inflammation of the bladder.

Possible Causes: Bacterial infection. Irritants (such as crystalline deposits) in the urine.

General Signs and Symptoms: Pain in the bladder and in the small of the back. Frequent desire to pass urine. Unpleasant odour, white sediment and burning sensation on urinating. Acute cystitis often produces a high temperature and shivering. Some individuals have recurring cystitis and can become very depressed with the condition.

Primary Target Areas: Bladder	**Areas of Assistance:** Kidneys (organic and structural) Ureters (organic and structural) Lumbar spine (neural) Solar plexus (neural)

Holistic Advice: If there is blood or pus in the urine, or a fever, consult a General Practitioner immediately because cystitis can quickly become a serious kidney infection. Avoid synthetic underwear, tights and close fitting trousers. Drink plenty of water and cranberry juice. Garlic is also a good supplement. Avoid food containing vinegar, citrus fruits and animal protein e.g. eggs, fish, meat and cheese, as these make the urine more acidic and painful to pass. Eat good quality live yoghurt.

DEPRESSION

Definition: Moods of sadness and despondency.

Possible Causes: Life events such as bereavement, divorce, illness and stress. Hormonal imbalance.

General Signs and Symptoms: Moody, sad, restless, irritable, fatigued, lethargic and, in extreme cases, suicidal, with no sense of purpose.

Primary Target Areas:	**Areas of Assistance:**
Solar plexus	Endocrine system (organic) – if the cause is hormonal

Holistic Advice: Listening skills are very important. Often being able to unload problems helps to lift the mood. If in any doubt about the person's safety, refer them to their General Practitioner. Recommend professional counselling, psychotherapy or psychiatry, depending on the severity of the problem.

DIABETES

Definition: The deficiency or reduced effectiveness of insulin, resulting in a disorder in which the ability of the muscles and other tissues to utilize sugar is greatly diminished or lost.

Possible Causes: The failure of the pancreas to produce the hormone insulin due to maturity, viral infection, hereditary factors or stress.

General Signs and Symptoms: Deposits of sugar in the urine. Loss of weight, extreme thirst, increased urination, dehydrated skin, constipation, muscle weakness and poor circulation. Due to the poor vitality of the tissues, various skin complaints can occur. As the disease advances there is a risk of gangrene of the feet, beginning with the toes. A diabetic coma can lead to unconsciousness and death.

Primary Target Areas: Pancreas Take care during a treatment not to tear the delicate skin on the feet. See 'Safety/Precautions'.	**Areas of Assistance:** Heart (organic) Eyes (organic) Kidneys (organic)

Holistic Advice: Medical advice must be sought. Depending on the severity of the condition, it can be controlled by diet, tablets or insulin. A high fibre, low fat, low sugar diet with a garlic supplement is advised. Information cards should be carried or a bracelet worn if prone to unstable blood-sugar levels.

DIARRHOEA

Definition: Looseness of the bowels, usually symptomatic of some form of bowel disease.

Possible Causes: Serious bowel disease, cholera, dysentery, typhoid fever, tuberculosis, ulceration of the intestine, indigestible food, nervous excitement, shock, chill, change in the weather, micro-organisms, food poisoning or drugs (e.g. arsenic and mercury).

General Signs and Symptoms: Stomach pains and having to rush to the toilet at frequent intervals. Presence of loose watery stools, often with an offensive odour. Maybe dehydrated. Catarrhal diarrhoea is the ordinary form. It causes the intestinal mucous membrane to be congested, inflamed and swollen (much the same as the nasal mucous membranes appear during a cold).

Primary Target Areas:
Small and large intestines

Areas of Assistance:
Lumbar spine (neural)

Holistic Advice: Personal hygiene is paramount. Care must be taken when buying, storing and cooking food. Remember that diarrhoea is a symptom, so a full case history must be taken to eliminate any serious diseases. If in any doubt refer immediately to a General Practitioner.

DYSMENORRHOEA

Definition: Painful menstruation.

Possible Causes: Anaemia, chills and exhaustion. Inflammation of the uterus, ovaries or fallopian tubes. There is a psychological factor believed to be due to lack of sex education, fear or mental and domestic disharmony.

General Signs and Symptoms: Pain and spasms felt in the abdomen, pelvis and lower back. Uterine colic. Mainly appears in the beginning of menstrual life (girls in their late teens or early twenties).

Primary Target Areas:
Uterus
Ovaries
Fallopian tubes

Areas of Assistance:
Pelvis (organic)
Lumbar spine (neural)
Coccyx (neural)
Sacrum (neural)

Holistic Advice: Sometimes bed rest is necessary, however the healthier the body the less likely it is to have this discomfort. A balanced diet and plenty of exercise are good preventative measures, as are supplements of evening primrose oil and vitamin B6.

ECZEMA

Definition: A reaction of the skin to a wide range of stimulants or irritants, both physical and emotional. Can be acute or chronic.

Possible Causes: Allergy to chemicals, dust, detergents, soap and cosmetics. Stress. Poor diet. Family history of allergies. Detoxifying through the skin. Often linked to asthma.

General Signs and Symptoms: Itching, redness, dryness, scaling and weeping of the skin, crusts and secondary skin infections.

Primary Target Areas:
Lungs
Bronchi
Diaphragm
Heart

Areas of Assistance:
Digestive system (organic)
Adrenals (organic)

Holistic Advice: Ensure a good balanced diet of fresh fruit and vegetables. Drinking plenty of water can help to keep the skin hydrated. Hypoallergenic moisturisers may be of benefit.

ENDOMETRIOSIS

Definition: The presence of endometrium cells (the cells that line the interior wall of the uterus) in other parts of the body, commonly in the muscle of the uterus.

Possible Causes: Not known for definite, but may be due to an hormonal imbalance.

General Signs and Symptoms: Menorrhagia (excessive menstrual flow), dysmenorrhoea (painful menstruation) and pelvic pain.

Primary Target Areas: Reproductive system	**Areas of Assistance:** Endocrine system (organic) Pelvis (organic)

Holistic Advice: Medical advice must be sought, as often the only treatment is to remove the affected area. Relaxation exercises can be useful to help to cope with the pain.

FACIAL NEURALGIA

Definition: Nerve pain (neuralgia) in the face.

Possible Causes: Mental overload, stress, exposure to cold and damp, diseased bone, local inflammations (in which the nerves are implicated), scar tissue and the bruising of a nerve due to an impact. Can be hereditary.

General Signs and Symptoms: Localised pain that may then spread beyond the area in which it first occurs. Pain is often periodic and varies in intensity. There may be a loss of feeling, paralysis, wasting of muscle and whitening of hair.

Primary Target Areas:
All facial areas

Areas of Assistance:
Cervical spine (neural)
Neck related areas (structural and neural)

Holistic Advice: Diagnosis of the cause is important before treatment commences.

FEMALE INFERTILITY

Definition: Difficulty or inability to become pregnant.

Possible Causes: Hormonal imbalance, too little progesterone, irregular or failed ovulation. Obstruction in the fallopian tubes. Abnormalities in the uterus - the most common being fibroids and endometriosis. Stress, smoking and excess alcohol may also play a part in preventing pregnancy.

General Signs and Symptoms: Inability to conceive.

Primary Target Areas:	**Areas of Assistance:**
Reproductive system (if physical cause) Endocrine system (if hormonal cause)	Solar plexus (neural) Lumbar spine (neural) Reproductive system (if hormonal cause) Endocrine system (if physical cause)

Holistic Advice: Relax and let nature take its course. Adopt a balanced diet and take regular, gentle exercise. Try to eliminate any stress. Make sure that both parties are relaxed and leave plenty of time for the relationship. Allow some time for any previously taken oral contraceptives to be cleared from the system. If infertility continues to be a problem, seek medical advice to establish if there is a medical problem.

FEVER

Definition: A condition characterized by a rise in temperature. It accompanies many diseases.

Possible Causes: Usually secondary to, and symptomatic of, the disorder with which it is associated. Primary or specific fevers include typhoid fever, scarlet fever and diphtheria. These diseases are caused by the growth of bacteria in the blood or tissues of the body. The activity of these organisms creates toxins.

General Signs and Symptoms: The onset of a fever is usually marked by shivering, either slight or violent, with various feelings such as back pain, headache, sickness and thirst. The shivering then turns to the febrile stage where the skin feels hot and dry and the temperature is high. There could be an increase in the pulse rate, quickness of breath, furred dry tongue and loss of appetite. Urine is scanty and may contain a large quantity of solid matter. The bowels are often constipated. Sleeplessness and delirium are common.

Primary Target Areas: Pituitary gland If the fever is caused by an infectious disease, do not treat. See 'Safety/Precautions'.	Areas of Assistance:

Holistic Advice: Bed rest. Drink plenty of water. Take regular but short cool baths and sponge down until the temperature lowers. Alternatively, sponge specific parts of the body (e.g. forehead or feet) to help to reduce the temperature. It is important to consult a General Practitioner to establish the cause of the fever. Hand reflexology is helpful in this instance as treating the hand, rather than the foot, is more suitable if the patient is in bed.

FROZEN SHOULDER

Definition: A chronic condition in which the shoulder joint is stiff and its mobility is considerably affected.

Possible Causes: Inflammation of the tendons or of the fibrous capsule of the joint. Swelling of the soft sac that cushions the joint.

General Signs and Symptoms: There is considerable pain in the shoulder and deltoid muscle. There can be a near complete lack of mobility. People between 40 and 50 years old are the most susceptible.

Primary Target Areas:
Shoulder

Areas of Assistance:
Hip (zonal and structural)

Holistic Advice: Keeping the joint as active as the pain will allow may prevent the stiffness becoming worse or spreading into the neck area. Massage and soft tissue manipulation can help the pain and muscle energy techniques can aid mobility. The Bowen Technique claims good results with this condition. Looking after the whole body is important, as other muscles can tire as they compensate for the shoulder. This is a very frustrating condition and the stress it creates should also be treated.

GLUE EAR

Definition: Inflammation of the middle ear. Also known as secretory otitis media.

Possible Causes: Infection as a result of a cold, tonsillitis or sinusitis. Glue ear is often associated with large adenoids.

General Signs and Symptoms: Inflammation and the persistent presence of a sticky secretion in the middle ear.

Primary Target Areas:	Areas of Assistance:
Ears	Cervical spine (neural)
	Digestive system (organic)
	Kidneys (zonal and organic)

Holistic Advice: Never put anything into the ear – even cotton buds. Keep the outer ear clean. Seek medical advice as antibiotics or surgery may be required.

HEADACHE

Definition: Pain in the head.

Possible Causes: Stress, tension, tiredness, sinusitis, concussion, head injury, alcohol abuse and eating problems. Build up of toxins. In extreme cases, brain tumour or meningitis.

General Signs and Symptoms: Tension in the muscles of the scalp, neck and shoulders. Pain and throbbing in the head. Possibly blurred vision.

Primary Target Areas:
Brain

Areas of Assistance:
Cervical spine (neural)
Neck areas (structural, organic and neural)
Liver (organic)

Holistic Advice: If headache persists or frequently recurs, consult a General Practitioner. Drink plenty of water. Avoid eating cheese and chocolate. A light massage of lavender essential oil on the temples may help to relieve the pain.

HEART ATTACK

Definition: Insufficient blood supply for the myocardium (heart muscle) to function, causing destructive changes in the muscle tissue. Also called myocardial infarction.

Possible Causes: Disease of the coronary arteries, high blood pressure, smoking, high cholesterol levels, obesity, stress and hereditary factors.

General Signs and Symptoms: Severe pain in the front of the chest, often radiating down the abdomen and into the left arm. Rapid pulse and difficulty breathing. Pale, cold, sweating skin. May suffer nausea and vomiting. Usually a rise in temperature.

Primary Target Areas:	Areas of Assistance:
Heart	Thoracic spine (neural)
Chest	Solar plexus (neural)
Ribs	
Liver	
See 'Safety/Precautions'.	

Holistic Advice: Post heart attack, the patient should take very gentle exercise. Stop smoking. Maintain a low fat diet. Relaxation exercises can be useful. Obtain consent from the General Practitioner before commencing any treatment.

HEARTBURN

Definition: Burning sensation in the region of the heart up to the back of the throat.

Possible Causes: Excessive acidity of the gastric (stomach) juices.

General Signs and Symptoms: Burning sensation rising from the chest into the throat.

Primary Target Areas:
Stomach

Areas of Assistance:
Diaphragm (organic)
Solar plexus (neural)

Holistic Advice: Taking bicarbonate of soda or carbonate of magnesia in water can counteract the acidity. Avoid chocolate, fatty foods, tomatoes, citrus fruits, alcohol and coffee. Hot and spicy food should also be avoided. Eating too fast or too much can also overload the stomach and cause heartburn.

HIATUS HERNIA

Definition: A displacement of a portion of the stomach through the oesophageal opening in the diaphragm.

Possible Causes: Over exertion. Weakness of the diaphragm.

General Signs and Symptoms: Burning sensation in the chest area. The 'heartburn' sensation associated with a hiatus hernia is very similar to angina pectoris.

Primary Target Areas:
Stomach

Areas of Assistance:
Diaphragm (organic)
Solar plexus (neural)

Holistic Advice: Take care when lifting heavy objects. Seek medical advice as corrective surgery may be necessary.

HYPERTENSION

Definition: Higher than normal blood pressure.

Possible Causes: Cause still obscure. Possibly due to spasm of the smaller arteries, obesity, stress, excitement or symptomatic of a chronic disorder. Hereditary factors may play a part.

General Signs and Symptoms: Often there are no symptoms but a headache, dizziness and tinnitus may be present. Long term hypertension can result in kidney failure, strokes and heart disease.

Primary Target Areas: Heart Do NOT work over the adrenals. See 'Safety/Precautions'.	**Areas of Assistance:** Solar plexus (neural)

Holistic Advice: Reduce intake of animal fats, salt, tea, coffee and alcohol. Regular exercise, meditation and yoga can be very beneficial. Garlic is a good supplement.

HYPERTHYROIDISM

Definition: A form of goitre caused by an over active thyroid gland.

Possible Causes: Dysfunction of the thyroid gland.

General Signs and Symptoms: Enlarged thyroid gland. Weight loss (even though the appetite is good) as the body's metabolism speeds up. Restlessness and insomnia. There may be muscular tremors, sweating and palpitations. The eyes may protrude and appear to be staring.

Primary Target Areas:	**Areas of Assistance:**
Thyroid	Cervical spine (neural)

Holistic Advice: Seek medical advice for diagnosis.

HYPOTENSION

Definition: Lower than normal blood pressure.

Possible Causes: Can be symptomatic of a chronic disorder such as a haemorrhage. The blood pressure of an extremely fit person is usually lower than normal, due to the increased effectiveness of the heart. If extreme fitness is the cause, the general signs and symptoms below will obviously not be relevant.

General Signs and Symptoms: Prone to dizziness or even fainting. Can feel cold and tired more readily. Supply of blood to the brain may be interrupted momentarily if the pressure falls below normal.

Primary Target Areas:
Heart

Areas of Assistance:
Adrenals (organic)

Holistic Advice: Take regular exercise. Although low blood pressure is generally less serious than high blood pressure, it should be monitored in the same way. A brisk massage is a very good way to stimulate the cardiovascular system.

HYPOTHYROIDISM

Definition: A form of goitre caused by an under active thyroid gland.

Possible Causes: Dysfunction of the thyroid gland.

General Signs and Symptoms: Thyroid gland may be enlarged. Some babies are born with this condition and they have difficulty feeding and sleeping. Without treatment they would grow short and fat (used to be known as cretins). In later life hypothyroidism normally has a gradual onset. The sufferer feels lethargic, gains weight and may lose hair. The skin is generally dry and yellow but the cheeks are red. Eyes become puffy and the voice can deepen.

Primary Target Areas: Thyroid	**Areas of Assistance:** Adrenals (organic) Cervical spine (neural)

Holistic Advice: Seek medical advice for diagnosis.

INDIGESTION

Definition: Pain or discomfort in the upper part of the abdomen or in the lower part of the chest. Also called dyspepsia.

Possible Causes: Gastritis, peptic ulcer, hiatus hernia, stomach cancer, gall bladder or pancreatic disorders, heart failure and diabetes. There is also nervous dyspepsia in which indigestion is brought on by psychological or emotional causes e.g. worry, anxiety, being highly-strung, tense or excitable.

General Signs and Symptoms: Pain in the abdomen, tension, heartburn, flatulence, sweating, weakness, palpitations and insomnia.

Primary Target Areas:	**Areas of Assistance:**
Stomach	Diaphragm (organic)
	Solar plexus (neural)
	Liver (organic)
	Thoracic spine (neural)

Holistic Advice: Avoid tea, coffee, spices, pepper, fizzy drinks, fatty foods and cigarettes. Drinking herbal teas of chamomile, fennel and peppermint can help.

INSOMNIA

Definition: Sleeplessness.

Possible Causes: Noise, stress, caffeine, pain, tension, depression, worry and over-tiredness.

General Signs and Symptoms: Not able to sleep, or go to sleep immediately but wake up shortly afterwards. Tension and irritability.

Primary Target Areas: Solar plexus	Areas of Assistance:
Use plenty of relaxation techniques.	

Holistic Advice: Keep regular sleeping hours. Reduce the number of hours sleep to start with then gradually increase them. Take plenty of fresh air and exercise. Practice relaxation exercises. Ensure bedroom is well ventilated. Try a warm (not hot) bath before going to bed but do not take stimulants e.g. tea, coffee and cola drinks. Put the bedside clock out of sight. Listen to relaxing music. Note sleep patterns in a diary to try to identify any contributory factors.

IRREGULAR OVULATION

Definition: Irregular production of ova by the ovaries.

Possible Causes: Hormone imbalance, stress, anxiety, sudden weight loss or severe shock.

General Signs and Symptoms: Irregular menstruation and affected fertility.

Primary Target Areas:	**Areas of Assistance:**
Reproductive system	Endocrine system (organic)

Holistic Advice:
As emotions can affect ovulation, it is wise to address any sources of stress, anxiety or persistent emotional concerns.

IRRITABLE BOWEL SYNDROME

Definition: Bowel dysfunction, reacting to an unknown stimulus. Abbreviated to I.B.S..

Possible Causes: The cause of I.B.S. has not been firmly established. Stress may play a part and the intolerance to certain food seems a likely cause.

General Signs and Symptoms: Spasmodic pain, intermittent diarrhoea, abdominal colic and bloating, constipation, back pain, weakness and tiredness. There are usually periods of remission and relapse.

Primary Target Areas:
Stomach
Small and large intestines

Areas of Assistance:
Liver (organic)
Gall bladder (organic)
Lumbar spine (neural)

Holistic Advice: Ensure the diet includes plenty of fibre. Vitamin C and aloe vera juice can be beneficial. Provide counselling to assist with the stress. Consider herbalism and/or acupuncture.

KIDNEY STONES

Definition: Small lumps of calcium and uric acid that have crystallized in the kidneys or ureters.

Possible Causes: Bacterial infection. Urine that is too concentrated. Metabolic abnormalities. Diet and some forms of medication can be influential.

General Signs and Symptoms: Back pain in the kidney area that can spread to the abdomen and genitals. Pain (which can be extreme) on passing urine, which may sometimes contain blood.

Primary Target Areas:
Kidneys

Areas of Assistance:
Eyes (zonal and organic)

Holistic Advice: Drink up to 1.75 litres of liquid a day, especially during hot weather or when perspiring. Dehydration will increase the concentration of the urine, so increasing the risk of kidney stones and disorders such as cystitis. Empty the bladder as soon as you need to because the longer the urine remains in the body, the more likely it is that the minerals will crystallize. Reducing the intake of dairy products, animal protein, salt, rhubarb, spinach, peanuts, chocolate and tea can be beneficial.

147

LARYNGITIS

Definition: Acute or chronic inflammation of the mucous membrane of the larynx.

Possible Causes: Infection or physical injury (caused by shouting, prolonged singing, smoking and by swallowing very hot fluids). Dry air from central heating can aggravate the condition.

General Signs and Symptoms: Redness and swelling of the larynx. Hoarseness or a complete loss of the voice (the vocal cords lie in the larynx). The cough that is always present is either loud, barking, rough or husky. Inspiration and expiration can be difficult.

Primary Target Areas:	**Areas of Assistance:**
Throat	Spleen (organic)

Holistic Advice: If symptoms persist consult a General Practitioner. If laryngitis is due to an infection following a cold, cough or sore throat, then also look at boosting the immune system. Laryngitis can cause great frustration as well as discomfort, so treat the whole person.

LUMBAGO

Definition: Pain affecting the muscles in the lower back.

Possible Causes: Prolapsed intervertebral disc. Exposure to cold and damp. Injury or strain of the back muscles or ligaments.

General Signs and Symptoms: Often a severe, sudden pain in one or both sides of the back. Mobility is often restricted and painful as is breathing, coughing or sneezing. Inflammation can be present in some internal organs e.g. kidney or bowel.

Primary Target Areas:
Coccyx
Sacrum
Pelvis
Sciatic nerves
Lumbar spine

Areas of Assistance:

Holistic Advice: Local remedies can help such as a hot compress. Rest may be prescribed initially, followed by back strengthening exercises.

MASTITIS

Definition: Inflammation of the breast.

Possible Causes: The effect of a change or disturbance in the production of ovarian and pituitary hormones on the breast tissue.

General Signs and Symptoms: Swelling, tenderness or pain in the breast. It is more usual in women over the age of 30 but can occasionally occur during puberty. Occurrences during and after breast-feeding are not uncommon.

Primary Target Areas:	**Areas of Assistance:**
Breast	Lymphatic system (organic)
	Endocrine system (organic)

Holistic Advice: It is advised that a General Practitioner should look at all breast lumps. Reducing salt can help with the water retention in the fatty tissue. Eat plenty of fresh fruit and vegetables. Vitamin B6 can help with water retention and may restore the oestrogen balance. Cut down on caffeine and animal fats. Try soya bean products. Swimming the breaststroke can help to strengthen the chest muscles. Maintain a good posture.

MENOPAUSE

Definition: The natural cessation of the menstrual cycle at the end of reproductive life.

Possible Causes: The natural end of a woman's reproductive life, when no longer ovulating. The menopause usually occurs between the ages of 45 and 50, but rarely before 40.

General signs and symptoms: Gradual cessation of menstrual flow (although excessive flow can occur during the process), hot flushes, tiredness, sleeplessness, irritability, lack of concentration, palpitations, aching joints, vaginal irritation and possible loss of libido. The menopause can be disturbing psychologically as well as physically.

Primary Target Areas:	Areas of Assistance:
Pituitary gland	Solar plexus (neural)
Ovaries	Lumbar spine (neural)

Holistic Advice: This is a natural process. Regular exercise, a balanced diet and a strong positive mental attitude will help. Natural remedies available include evening primrose, Chinese herbs, homeopathic remedies and vitamin/mineral supplements. Aromatherapy massage can be one of the most powerful holistic treatments for menopause related problems.

MENORRHAGIA

Definition: Excessive menstruation.

Possible Causes: Menopause (can cause both excessive and irregular menstrual flow), polypi, fibroids and other tumours. Displacement or inflammation of the uterus, tuberculosis and miscarriage.

General Signs and Symptoms: Excessive menstrual flow. Can be irregular and painful, accompanied by feelings of exhaustion and depression.

Primary Target Areas:
Ovaries
Pituitary gland

Areas of Assistance:
Solar plexus (neural)
Lumbar spine (neural)

Holistic Advice: Any prolonged menstrual problem must be checked by a gynaecologist to make sure that no serious condition exists.

MIGRAINE

Definition: Recurring intense headaches.

Possible Causes: Anxiety, irregular meals, prolonged lack of food, diet, alcohol, pre-menstrual days, over-exertion, physical and mental fatigue, changes of routine, late rising (too much sleep), fluorescent lights, changes in weather and very hot baths.

General Signs and Symptoms: Pain in the head. Tension in the muscles of the scalp, neck and shoulders. Nausea, vomiting and blurred vision. Light may cause discomfort. Possibly tunnel vision.

Primary Target Areas:	Areas of Assistance:
Brain	Liver (organic)
	Cervical spine (neural)
	Neck areas (neural)
	Endocrine system (organic)

Holistic Advice: A regular massage can be a very good preventative treatment to release stress and tension. Keep a diary of food eaten to see if diet is the cause. Cheese, chocolate and red wine are the most common dietary triggers.

MULTIPLE SCLEROSIS

Definition: A disease of the brain and spinal cord in which the insulating sheaths of the nerves break up and patches of excessive connective tissue form. Abbreviated to M.S..

Possible Causes: Not known.

General Signs and Symptoms: This condition can have a slow onset and can remit and relapse. Symptoms depend on the site and extent of the lesions. Numbness and tingling in the extremities commonly occur in the early stages. There can be temporary stiffness or paralysis of a limb. There may be paralysis of the eye muscle, causing double vision. General weakness and tremors are common upon exertion. Visual defects and speech problems may be experienced.

Primary Target Areas:	**Areas of Assistance:**
Brain	
Spine	

Holistic Advice: Take regular exercise. Yoga can be beneficial to help relaxation and deepen the breathing, as well as stretching the muscles. Massage can help to aid muscle tone. There are many support groups for sufferers of M.S.. Joining a local group can give support to the sufferer and his/her family.

MUSCULAR FATIGUE

Definition: Tired and heavy muscles.

Possible Causes: Over exertion, influenza, glandular fever, multiple sclerosis and myalgic encephalomyelitis.

General Signs and Symptoms: Pain and discomfort. Muscular weakness and dysfunction.

Primary Target Areas:
Whole body, particularly urinary and digestive systems.

Areas of Assistance:

Holistic Advice: Take gentle, regular exercise. If symptoms persist consult a General Practitioner for a diagnosis.

MYALGIC ENCEPHALOMYELITIS

Definition: Post viral fatigue. Abbreviated to M.E..

Possible Causes: Failure to recover from a viral infection. Changes in the immune system. Physical or emotional stresses may also be contributory factors.

General Signs and Symptoms: Generally feeling unwell. Extreme fatigue, sore throat, swollen glands, headaches, giddiness and mood swings. Inability to concentrate.

Primary Target Areas: Whole body	**Areas of Assistance:**
Give short, light treatments.	

Holistic Advice: Take plenty of rest and avoid stress of any kind. Maintain a balanced diet. When feeling weak, find an activity that can still be undertaken e.g. a jigsaw. Try relaxation exercises or a massage. Exercise regularly at whatever level can be managed.

NAUSEA

Definition: A feeling of sickness.

Possible Causes: Concussion, migraine, pregnancy, motion shock, vertigo or food poisoning. Over indulgence in food or alcohol. Nausea may be a symptom of general illness and may be experienced as a reaction to certain drugs. Anaesthetics and chemotherapy treatments can create nausea as a side effect.

General Signs and Symptoms: Stomach aches and pains. A headache and possibly a lightheaded feeling may be experienced. The feeling of nausea may develop into vomiting.

Primary Target Areas:
Stomach

Areas of Assistance:
Diaphragm (organic)
Solar plexus (neural)

Holistic Advice: Avoid over indulgence in food and alcoholic drinks to prevent self-inflicted occurrences of nausea. Avoid food for 24 hours and sip water. Keep taking fluids to ensure that the body does not dehydrate. Acupressure can be beneficial for motion sickness. Excessive vomiting can be serious and medical advice must be sought if the symptoms persist or become violent.

OEDEMA

Definition: Excess fluid retention in any body tissue, cavity or organ except bone.

Possible Causes: Hormonal disturbance, heart failure, kidney failure, shock, local injury, drugs, steroids and protein deficiency.

General Signs and Symptoms: Presence of fluid, usually in a limb. Ankles are especially prone, as they are the furthest large joints from the heart. Fluid can gather if standing all day because the circulation is not good enough to cope with the force of gravity. Ankles can swell on a long flight and during pregnancy.

Primary Target Areas:
Lymphatic system
Heart
Kidneys

Areas of Assistance:

Holistic Advice: Eat fresh fennel and celery. Drink plenty of water. Ensure balanced diet with restricted salt. Take sensible, regular exercise depending on the current standard of fitness. Keep legs in raised position when relaxing. Oedema can be a symptom of a serious condition, so a formal diagnosis is needed.

OVARIAN CYSTS

Definition: Hollow tumours containing fluid or soft material located on one or both ovaries.

Possible Causes: Not known.

General Signs and Symptoms: Intermittent pain in the lower abdomen often during menstruation. Pain also may be felt during sexual intercourse. In severe cases the cysts become very large and can rupture or bleed causing severe pain and sickness.

Primary Target Areas:
Ovaries

Areas of Assistance:
Endocrine system (organic)
Lumbar spine (neural)

Holistic Advice: Medical attention must be sought. Treat any stresses in life style.

PALPITATIONS

Definition: Abnormal awareness of the heartbeat, which may feel forceful or irregular.

Possible Causes: Sudden over excitement of the nervous system in times of emotion such as fear, anger, stress or anxiety. Stimulants such as coffee, tea, tobacco or alcohol. May be experienced during puberty or the menopause. Palpitations may also be felt during acute fevers, dyspepsia and anaemia.

General Signs and Symptoms: A fluttering of the heart, pounding sensation or a feeling that the heart is missing a beat.

Primary Target Areas:
Heart

Areas of Assistance:
Stomach (zonal and organic)
Solar plexus (neural)

Holistic Advice: Palpitations are not generally a symptom of serious disease but obtain medical advice if symptoms persist or if there is any accompanying dizziness, chest pains, breathlessness or nausea. Learn to relax both mentally and physically. Massage can help to relieve stress. Moderate exercise is advantageous. Consider yoga for stretching and breathing exercises. Avoid smoking and restrict the intake of tea, coffee and alcohol.

PANIC ATTACKS

Definition: Periods of feeling out of control, anxious and fearful.

Possible Causes: Direct result of certain trigger situations.

General Signs and Symptoms: Palpitations, hyperventilation, sweating, nausea, lack of co-ordination and confusion.

Primary Target Areas: Heart Solar plexus Use plenty of relaxation techniques.	Areas of Assistance:

Holistic Advice: The trigger needs to be identified and addressed. Any treatment should be aimed at lessening the severity and number of attacks. The sufferer needs to learn how to begin to take control. Any reduction in stress will help. Breathing exercises and regular exercise may be of benefit.

161

PARKINSON'S DISEASE

Definition: A progressive disease characterized by tremors, rigidity and impairment of voluntary movement.

Possible Causes: Degenerative changes in the ganglia (collections of nerve cells) at the base of the cerebrum. This results in a deficiency of neurotransmitters (chemicals that normally either excite or inhibit the adjacent muscle cells). Dopamine is a neurotransmitter whose deficiency seems to play a part in Parkinson's disease.

General Signs and Symptoms: Increased rigidity in the muscles. The face looses its natural movement. The voice alters due to the muscles of the larynx, tongue and lips changing. Limbs become stiff and rigid and may then develop muscular tremors that cease during sleep.

Primary Target Areas:
Brain
Spine

Areas of Assistance:

Holistic Advice: There are many drugs that help to keep the condition under control, although none offer a cure. Yoga can be beneficial to counteract the stiffening process. Vitamin E, in high doses, may slow the process.

PREGNANCY

Definition: The human gestation period.

Cause: Fertilization of the female's ovum by the male's sperm.

General Signs and Symptoms: Amenorrhoea, morning sickness, weight gain, breast enlargement and possible cravings for odd food.

Primary Target Areas:	Areas of Assistance:
See 'Safety/Contra-indications'.	

Holistic Advice: It is recommended that reflexology treatments are avoided during the first three months. Experienced reflexologists may then choose to treat as normal. If there is a history of miscarriage, avoid treating during the first three months and then, if you decide to treat, take extreme care. Gentle, regular exercise should be taken. Avoid alcohol and cigarettes. Eat plenty of fresh fruit and vegetables.

PRE-MENSTRUAL TENSION

Definition: Varying symptoms in the time leading up to menstruation.

Possible Causes: A change in the balance of female hormones. Low levels of progesterone. Lack of vitamin B6 and essential fatty acids such as linoleic acid.

General Signs and Symptoms: Can be mild or severe. Physical symptoms can include water retention, swollen joints, weight gain, skin problems, weakness, headaches and food cravings. There can also be psychological disturbances such as poor concentration, insomnia, tearfulness, irritability, depression and decreased sex drive. During this pre-menstrual period judgement can also be affected and women may be more accident-prone.

Primary Target Areas:	**Areas of Assistance:**
Reproductive system	Endocrine system (organic)
	Solar plexus (neural)

Holistic Advice: Regular aromatherapy treatments, including massage, can help balance the hormones and relieve tension. Supplements of evening primrose capsules and vitamin B6 may help. Chamomile tea is calming and diuretic which can help relieve the water retention. Maintain a good, balanced, fresh food diet, cutting down on saturated fats, sugar, salt and caffeine. Take regular exercise and try to stay stress free.

PROSTATITIS

Definition: Inflammation or enlargement of the prostate gland.

Possible Causes: Young men may suffer from prostate infections that cause the prostate gland to become inflamed. In later life this gland can enlarge for no apparent reason. It is a common site for cancer in the male.

General Signs and Symptoms: Pain in the lower abdomen, back and testes or in the perineum (area between the scrotum and anus). Body temperature may be raised and the urine may be cloudy or bloody with a strong aroma. In later life the sufferer passes urine more frequently and has a lack of control afterwards, with a feeling that the bladder is not completely empty. Pain when urinating and difficulty in passing urine are also common symptoms.

Primary Target Areas:
Prostate gland

Areas of Assistance:
Lumbar spine (neural)

Holistic Advice: Antibiotics can be prescribed for infections. Operations can be performed to allow the urine to pass more freely. Cancer of the prostate is curable if detected in the early stages.

RAYNAUD'S DISEASE

Definition: Circulation suddenly becomes obstructed in the extremities of the body.

Possible Causes: Nervous influences, various diseases involving the blood vessels and the spasm of small arteries in the part affected. The majority of the cases occur before the age of 40 years. Mainly affects women.

General Signs and Symptoms: 'Dead' fingers, toes, ears or nose that become white, numb and waxy looking. The circulation can be reduced so much that the part would not bleed if it received a prick or small cut. May last a few minutes or several hours. In severe cases, which are very rare, repeated attacks can lead to gangrene.

Primary Target Areas:
Heart

Areas of Assistance:

Holistic Advice: Eat plenty of onions and fresh garlic and take garlic supplements. Ginger may help. Cut down on coffee and tea - try herbal teas such as cinnamon or orange. Regular massage to stimulate the circulation and nervous system is a useful preventative measure.

SCIATICA

Definition: Pain originating from the sciatic nerve.

Possible Causes: Lumbago, spinal injury, prolapsed disc and nerve disorders.

General Signs and Symptoms: Pain in the back and buttock that travels down the back of the thigh and outside of the leg, often going into the outside of the foot.

Primary Target Areas: Sciatic nerve	**Areas of Assistance:** Lumbar spine (neural)

Holistic Advice: Finding the cause is paramount. If it is due to a spinal problem, consider chiropractic or osteopathy. Look into general posture and the work/home environment e.g. height of chairs, desks and VDU. The shortening of the piriformis muscle can often cause sciatic pain, so soft tissue manipulation (including muscle energy techniques) can also be beneficial.

SEASONAL AFFECTIVE DISORDER

Definition: A type of depression. Abbreviated to S.A.D..

Possible Causes: The lack of daylight in winter. High levels of melatonin (a hormone produced by the pineal gland).

General Signs and Symptoms: Depression, lethargy, loss of libido, anxiety, irritability, mood changes and a craving for carbohydrates.

Primary Target Areas: Pineal gland	Areas of Assistance: Solar plexus (neural)

Holistic Advice: Light therapy can be beneficial. Counselling can also help to deal with the depression.

168

SINUSITIS

Definition: Inflammation of a sinus.

Possible Causes: Cold, hay fever, catarrh and infection in the nasal mucous membranes.

General Signs and Symptoms: Pain, headache (especially when the head tips forward), chronic dull ache around the cheekbone and possibly a raised temperature. Excessive nasal mucus.

Primary Target Areas:
Sinuses

Areas of Assistance:
Digestive system (organic)
Adrenals (organic)

Holistic Advice: Take garlic supplements and fresh garlic. Avoid dairy and wheat products as they provoke excessive formation of mucus. Consider regular massage to boost the immune system. Facial massage, concentrating on the sinus points, can help to clear the congestion. Acupuncture may be beneficial.

STRESS

Definition: Stress and stress related illnesses are when the mental and physical health of an individual are unbalanced.

Possible Causes: Stress factors may be physical, mental, emotional and environmental e.g. accident, injury, financial worries, relationship problems, pollution and work concerns.

General Signs and Symptoms: Depressed immune system. Sense of being out of control. Physical complaints such as headaches, muscular pain and lethargy. Long term stress may lead to a depleted immune system and loss of general vitality.

Primary Target Areas:
Solar plexus

Give a thorough treatment, incorporating plenty of relaxation techniques.

Areas of Assistance:
Lymphatic system (organic)

Holistic Advice: The origin of the stress needs to be identified and addressed. Time should be allocated for relaxation and exercise. Yoga may be of benefit. Regular massage treatments can also act as a preventative therapy. Stress management/counselling courses are available in most areas. Any treatment to boost the immune system may be beneficial.

STROKE

Definition: A sudden event affecting the blood supply to the brain. Also called apoplexy.

Possible Causes: Cerebral haemorrhage (rupture of a blood vessel in the brain). Blockage or clot (embolism) in one of the blood vessels in the brain. Sufferers of heart disease are at risk of a clot forming in the valves or cavities of the heart and being transported to the brain. High blood pressure.

General Signs and Symptoms: Attacks vary. Sudden lack of consciousness and voluntary motion. There may be complete paralysis down one side. Other symptoms may include numb limbs, blurred vision, inability to speak, headaches, vertigo, confusion and incontinence. A stroke can lead to death.

Primary Target Areas:	**Areas of Assistance:**
Brain	Spine (neural)
Heart	Solar plexus (neural)

Holistic Advice: Call an ambulance immediately if you suspect a stroke – some cases can be fatal. Keep the person quiet and comfortable. Post stroke physiotherapy may help to regain movement. Nothing must be given or done to further raise the blood pressure.

TENNIS ELBOW

Definition: Pain in the elbow.

Possible Causes: Playing tennis or similar games. Repetitive strain injury.

General Signs and Symptoms: Inflammation in the tendon and muscles that extend or straighten the joint. Restricted and painful mobility.

Primary Target Areas:
Elbow

Areas of Assistance:
Cervical spine (neural)

Holistic Advice: Warm up and warm down before and after exercise to help prevent this condition. Ice packs may help to reduce any swelling. Special elbow supports can be worn.

TENSION

Definition: Mental strain or excitement, or the state of muscles primed for action.

Possible Causes: Nature intended that tension in muscles should always have a quick release. But, due to the strains and stresses of the modern world, an immediate physical outlet is not always possible. Tension therefore builds up affecting the body physically and mentally.

General Signs and Symptoms: Headaches, back pain, neck pain, high blood pressure, digestive disorders and irritability.

Primary Target Areas: Whole body	**Areas of Assistance:** Solar plexus (neural)
Give thorough treatment using plenty of relaxation techniques.	

Holistic Advice: Prevention is always best. Take regular exercise and maintain a balanced diet. A regular massage may help to relieve tension. Relaxation exercises can help to release both mental and physical tension.

THRUSH

Definition: Fungal infection.

Possible Causes: Candida albicans fungus, stress, unbalanced diet, steroids, long term use of oral contraceptives and a reaction to antibiotics. Can accompany diabetes, pregnancy, auto-immune deficiency syndrome (AIDS) and leukaemia.

General Signs and Symptoms: Thrush thrives in warm, moist areas. The inflammation, itching and white flaky patches can affect the mouth, vulva, skin folds, groin, armpits and the skin under the breasts.

Primary Target Areas:
Uterus

Areas of Assistance:
Lumbar spine (neural)

Holistic Advice: Avoid sugary foods, yeast, starches and mushrooms. Avoid wearing tights and nylon underwear (cotton is better). High dosage of vitamin C can be of benefit. Natural yoghurt can be taken orally and used externally. Eat plenty of fresh garlic and take garlic supplements.

TINNITUS

Definition: Ringing, hissing or buzzing heard in the ear but without any external cause.

Possible Causes: Can be caused by excessive ear wax, blocked or impaired eustachian tube or damage to the inner ear. Tinnitus has also been linked with the use of certain drugs and with exposure to persistent, loud noise, smoking and shock. It frequently accompanies deafness.

General Signs and Symptoms: Ringing, hissing or buzzing in the ear.

Primary Target Areas:
Ears

Areas of Assistance:
Cervical spine (neural)
Neck related areas (organic)
Kidneys (zonal and organic)

Holistic Advice: As this can be a permanent, chronic condition it can cause much frustration and stress. Therapies that aid relaxation may help. Some hearing aids can have a 'masker', which can help to suppress the noise.

ULCER

Definition: A sore or break in the skin or in the membrane lining a body cavity, which usually takes a long time to heal.

Possible Causes: Damage to the surface of the body that is slow to heal. Poor blood supply (diabetics are therefore prone to ulcers). Internally, peptic ulcers (i.e. gastric (stomach) and duodenal ulcers) may possibly be caused by abrasions, the acidity of the gastric juices or stress.

General Signs and Symptoms: Peptic ulcers cause dull abdominal pain. Appetite is usually normal but fear of pain from indigestion predominates. Peptic ulcers can perforate and bleed, demanding immediate medical attention. Leg ulcers take a long time to heal and need medical attention.

Primary Target Areas:	**Areas of Assistance:**
Area affected by the ulcer	Solar plexus (neural)

Holistic Advice: Medication has limited effectiveness. Surgery often is the only resort. Remission is possible in some cases.

VARICOSE VEIN

Definition: Dilated or swollen vein.

Possible Causes: Poor circulation, weak valves in veins, prolonged standing, poor nutrition, obesity, faulty genes or pregnancy.

General Signs and Symptoms: Swelling in the area with aching, itching and pain. Varicose veins mainly occur in the legs, especially the calves, or in the lower area of the bowel (haemorrhoids).

Primary Target Areas:
Heart

Areas of Assistance:
Intestines (organic)
Lumbar spine (neural)

Holistic Advice: Fresh garlic and garlic supplements are good blood purifiers. Vitamins C and E can also be of benefit. Take regular exercise such as swimming and walking. Raise the legs above the heart when resting to aid blood flow. Support stockings can be beneficial to those who have to do much standing. Chinese herbal medicine can help, even in advanced cases.

VERTIGO

Definition: Giddiness and inability to balance oneself.

Possible Causes: Physical or locational disturbance of the body that affects the fluid in the inner ear. Meniere's disease (a condition in which there is a loss of function in the labyrinth of the inner ear). Haemorrhage in the semicircular canals of the inner ear. Removal of wax from the ear or syringing of the ear. Refractive eye defects, some stomach conditions, migraine, overstrained nervous system, mild attack of epilepsy, lack of blood to the brain and, in extreme cases, brain tumours.

General Signs and Symptoms: Feeling of dizziness or imbalance, sometimes accompanied by a headache, nausea and vomiting.

Primary Target Areas: Ear	**Areas of Assistance:** Cervical spine (neural and structural) Kidneys (zonal and neural)

Holistic Advice: While the attack lasts, lay still in a quiet, dark room. A diagnosis is important.

Questions (Answers: Page 370)

1. In which condition is menstruation absent?

    a. dysmenorrhoea
    b. menorrhagia
    c. amenorrhoea

2. Mrs Hitchcock is suffering from anxiety. To which reflex area would you pay particular attention during a reflexology treatment?

3. Which condition is defined as the inflammation of one or more joints?

    a. osteo-arthritis
    b. rheumatoid arthritis

4. Which type of arthritis is caused by auto-immune disease affecting the synovial membranes around a joint?

5. True or False?

    For both osteo and rheumatoid arthritis, the primary target area is that of the affected joint.

6. Name one of the primary target areas for asthma.

7. The adrenals are areas of assistance for asthma. What type of link exists?

    a. zonal
    b. structural
    c. neural
    d. organic

8. The digestive system is an area of assistance for asthma. One of the links is that irritation in the digestive tract can give rise to excess mucus that can settle in the lungs. What type of link is this?

    a. zonal
    b. structural
    c. neural
    d. organic

9. What condition is described below?
    Paralysis of the muscles on one or both sides of the face, caused by damage to the facial nerves or a stroke. There is an inability to smile, close the eye, blink or show the teeth on the affected side.

10. Which part of the spine is an area of assistance for blurred vision?

    a. cervical
    b. thoracic
    c. lumbar
    d. sacral

11. True or False?

    Asthma and bronchitis both have the same areas of assistance.

12. What is the primary target area for catarrh?

13. Chilblains may be caused by poor circulation. What is the primary target area?

14. There are four primary target areas for colds and flu. Three of these are the lungs, bronchi and sinuses. What is the other?

15. True or False?

    The area of the spine that corresponds to the location of the symptoms of spinal nerve compression should receive particular attention.

16. The primary target areas for constipation are the small and large intestines. What area of assistance has a neural link?

17. What condition is defined as the inflammation of the bladder?

18. The solar plexus is the primary target area for depression. Which body system is the area of assistance?

    a. cardiovascular
    b. lymphatic
    c. endocrine
    d. reproductive

19. Diabetes is caused by the deficiency or reduced effectiveness of insulin. What is the primary target area for this condition?

20. Which spinal area is an area of assistance for diarrhoea?

    a. cervical
    b. thoracic
    c. lumbar
    d. sacral

21. What is dysmenorrhoea?

    a. absence of menstruation
    b. painful menstruation
    c. excessive menstruation

22. True or False?

    The primary target areas for asthma and eczema are the same.

23. What is the primary target area for endometriosis?

    a. endocrine system
    b. reproductive system
    c. cardiovascular system
    d. lymphatic system

24. What term literally means nerve pain?

25. Which gland is the primary target area in cases of fever?

26. What is the area of assistance for a frozen shoulder?

27. What is the common name for secretory otitis media?

28. Which organ, involved in the detoxification processes, is an area of assistance for headaches?

29. What is the primary target area for heartburn?

30. Through which muscular structure does the stomach protrude in a hiatus hernia?

31. Which reflex areas must be avoided if the patient is hypertensive?

32. Which condition is defined as a form of goitre and is caused by an overactive thyroid gland?

33. The primary target area for hypotension is the heart. What areas of assistance associated with this condition can be worked to help to stimulate the body?

34. What is the primary target area for insomnia?

35. What condition is abbreviated to I.B.S.?

36. Not surprisingly, the primary target areas for kidney stones are the kidneys. What is the area of assistance for this condition?

37. Which organ of the endocrine system has a part to play in maintaining the body's immunity and is an area of assistance in cases of laryngitis?

38. What is the primary target area for mastitis?

39. Menorrhagia is defined as excessive menstrual flow. The primary target areas are the ovaries and the pituitary gland. What part of the spine, along with the solar plexus, is an area of assistance for this condition?

    a. cervical
    b. thoracic
    c. lumbar
    d. sacral

40. What condition is defined below?
    A disease of the brain and spinal cord in which the insulating sheaths of the nerves break up and patches of excessive connective tissue form.

    a. muscular fatigue
    b. Parkinson's disease
    c. multiple sclerosis
    d. myalgic encephalomyelitis

41. What condition is known as post viral fatigue?

    a. muscular fatigue
    b. Parkinson's disease
    c. Raynaud's disease
    d. myalgic encephalomyelitis

42. What term means excess fluid retention in any part of the body tissue, cavity or organ except bone?

43. The primary target area for palpitations is the heart. The stomach and the solar plexus are areas of assistance. Which of these areas of assistance has a zonal link with the heart?

    a. stomach
    b. solar plexus

44. What progressive disease, characterized by tremors, rigidity and impairment of voluntary movement, is caused by degenerative changes in the ganglia at the base of the cerebrum?

45. What term is given to the inflammation of the prostate gland?

46. What is the primary target area for Raynaud's disease?

47. Which nerve is commonly the cause of pain in the back and buttock that travels down the back of the thigh and outside of the leg, often going into the outside of the foot?

48. Sinusitis, the inflammation of a sinus, is characterized by excessive nasal mucus. A diet containing dairy and wheat products can increase the formation of mucus. What body system is therefore an organically linked area of assistance for this condition?

49. What is the primary target area for stress?

50. What term is given to a sudden event affecting the blood supply to the brain?

51. Tension affects the whole body, so there is no specific primary target area. What is the area of assistance for tension that, when worked, can have a calming effect on the body?

52. What condition can be caused by the Candida albicans fungus, stress, unbalanced diet, steroids, long term use of oral contraceptives and a reaction to antibiotics?

53. What is the primary target area for tinnitus?

54. What is the primary target area for varicose veins?

55. What organ is usually responsible for attacks of vertigo?

This page has intentionally been left blank.

Hand Reflexology

This page has intentionally been left blank.

Reflexology is based on the principle of the feet and hands mirroring the body. However, it is usually the feet that are used for the treatment. This is because the feet are more **sensitive** than the hands. They are also **bigger** and **mirror** the body more closely. The reflex areas are therefore larger, easier to locate and easier to work.

For these reasons, the results obtained by treating the hands are not usually as significant as those produced by treating the feet.

Despite these limitations, hand reflexology does have its uses. The hand can be used as a **substitute** for the foot. This is obviously necessary should the recipient not have a foot, or if a foot condition exists that prevents the treatment being performed. More commonly, however, it is used for **self-treatment** as few people are sufficiently flexible to comfortably reach their own feet.

Like the foot, **guidelines** are used to divide the hands into the **main sections**. These sections assist in the location of the specific reflex areas.

Three of the five guidelines that are used on the foot can also be found on the **hand**. The three hand guidelines are shown here.

The **diaphragm line** is located in the palm just below the joints of the phalanges and the metacarpals.

The **waist line** runs across from the base of the thumb.

The **pelvic line** runs across the bottom of the hand.

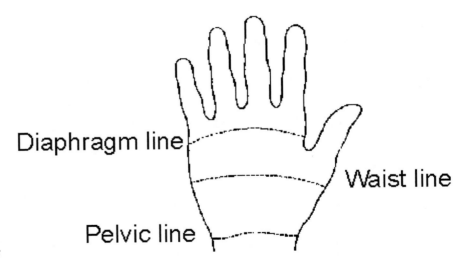

These guidelines are literally guides. They divide the hand into sections, which mirror the body, to assist in the location of the specific reflex areas.

The locations of the reflex areas are shown on the **hand charts**. For this package we'll look at the charts created by Ann Gillanders, Founder of the **British School of Reflexology**. Let's take a look at them now.

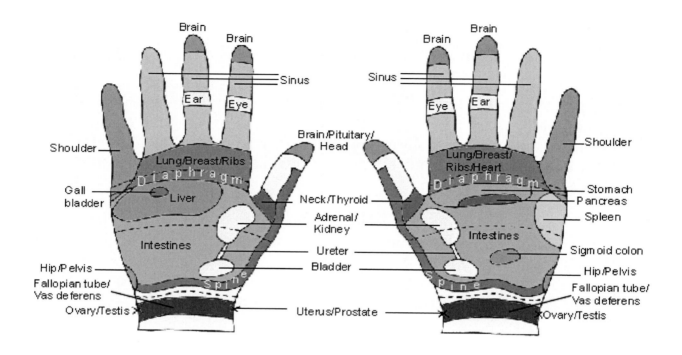

This is the **palmar** view. You can see that the spinal reflex area runs down the thumb edge and continues across the base of the hand. The locations of the reflex areas are fundamentally the same as on the feet. To allow you to compare the hand charts to the foot charts, we'll display them together.

192

Palmar aspect of the right hand

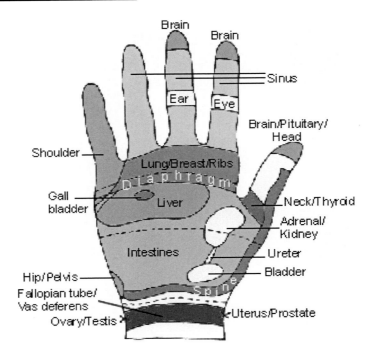

Plantar aspect of the right foot

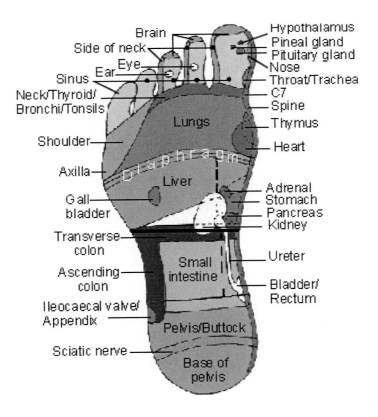

193

Palmar aspect of the left hand

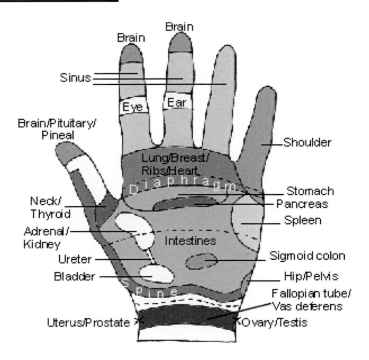

Plantar aspect of the left foot

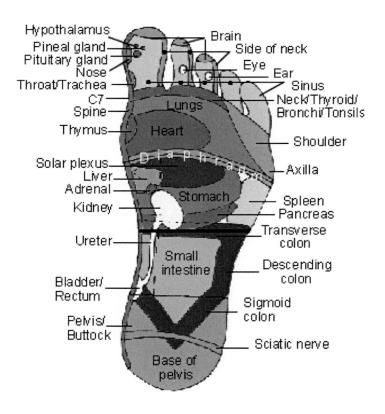

194

This is the **dorsal** view. Notice that there are some reflex areas here, relating to major organs, which only appear on the plantar aspect of the feet.

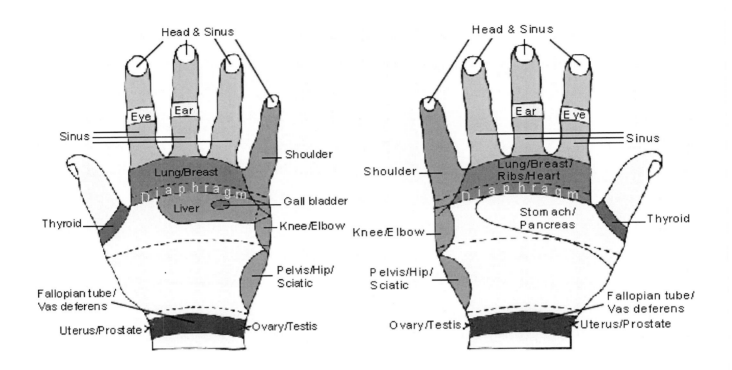

As before, to help you to compare the charts, we'll display the dorsal view of the hand and foot together.

Dorsal aspect of the right hand

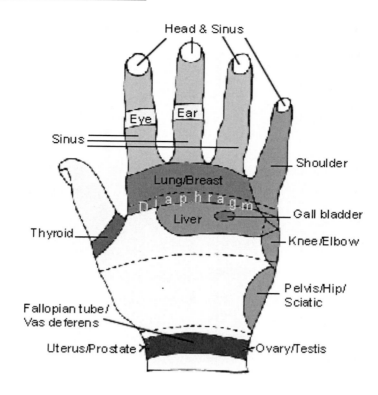

Dorsal aspect of the right foot

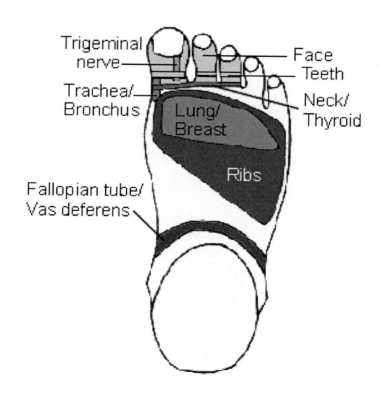

Dorsal aspect of the left hand

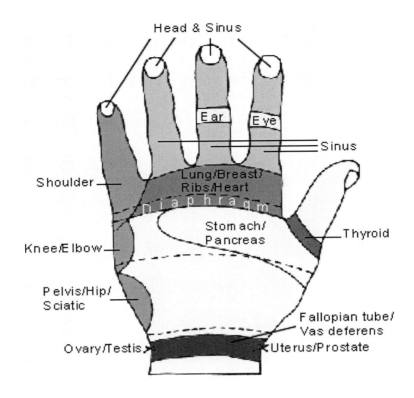

Dorsal aspect of the left foot

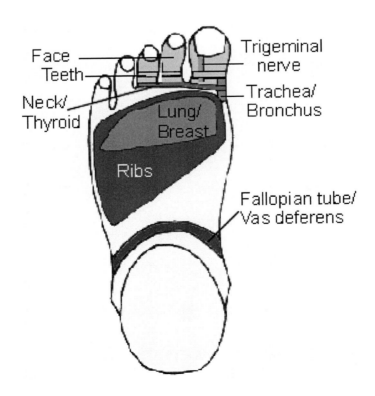

As we have mentioned, because the hands are not as big as the feet, the **reflex areas** on the hand are proportionately **smaller**. This makes the areas more **difficult** to work. The creeping thumb movement is used to cover as many reflex points as possible. However, particularly with self treatments, compromises inevitably have to be made for **comfort** and **accessibility**. Ideally, the areas are worked in the same direction(s) as on the feet (see your own school's guides).

Summary

➢ Hand reflexology is **not generally as effective** as foot reflexology.

➢ Hand reflexology is of use if, for whatever reason, it is **not possible to treat the feet**.

➢ The main use is for **self-treatment**.

➢ The **diaphragm**, **waist** and **pelvic guidelines** divide the hand into the main sections.

➢ The **hand charts** show the locations of the reflex areas.

➢ The **creeping thumb** movement is used to cover as many reflex points as possible.

➢ When possible, the **reflex areas** should be worked in the **same way** as on the foot.

Developing Professional

This page has intentionally been left blank.

To successfully practice reflexology, a professional image must be portrayed at all times.

Professionalism is reflected in the image, conduct, knowledge and ethical behaviour of the practitioner, the environment in which the treatment is carried out, the efficiency of the business and, last but by no means least, the way in which the client's diverse needs are met.

This section outlines some of the factors involved in trading as a professional reflexologist.

The information is available under the following headings:

> The Professional Practitioner
> Employed or Self-Employed?
> Setting Up Your Own Business
> Client Care
> Nutrition
> Counselling Skills

The Professional Practitioner

The first credential for a professional reflexologist is to be **qualified**! We hope that Essential Reflexology will help you with this criterion!

You may also need to apply for a **licence** to trade from your local authority. Some authorities only require registration if the treatment involves skin piercing (e.g. acupuncture), others require all practitioners to register so you will need to make inquiries.

You must also be familiar with the **code of ethics** for your own Association or Training Establishment, as well as those of the Association of Reflexology (AOR) and the British Complementary Medicine Association (BCMA). Codes of conduct for the AOR and BCMA can be obtained from the addresses below:

AOR
27 Old Gloucester Street
London
WC1N 3XX

BCMA
Kensington House
33 Imperial Square
Cheltenham
GL50 1QZ

Before you begin to practice you need to take out **insurance** policies.

1. **Public Liability Insurance** – this covers you should someone injure themselves (e.g. trip over) whilst on your premises. It also provides protection should you cause accidental damage whilst on another's premises.

2. **Personal Indemnity Insurance** – this covers you should a client claim that the treatment given was inappropriate or caused an adverse effect.

    These certificates must be displayed at your place of work.

Health and Safety Acts clearly set out the responsibilities that the business owner or employer has to ensure the safety of others.

You have a legal obligation to abide by these regulations so ensure that you are familiar with them.

Many health and safety issues come down to **common sense**. Here are a few pointers:

> ➤ ensure the comfort and safety of the patient before, during and after the treatment
> ➤ if necessary, help the patient to and from the working area
> ➤ provide support for the patient's legs and back during the treatment so as not to create new problems
> ➤ ensure a safe working environment, free from loose, torn or ill-fitting floor carpets or obstacles such as trailing wires
> ➤ allow adequate ventilation and natural light into the premises
> ➤ cleanliness is vital, so use clean, fresh towels for each treatment

Once you have started trading, there is a **legal obligation** to maintain full **written records** of all clients, the treatment given and the result. There is a legal requirement to keep these records for a minimum of **6 years** (even after you cease to trade). All patient and treatment details are private and confidential and should be kept locked away. Information on how to take a case history can be found under 'Client Care'.

As members of a **professional** body, reflexologists should look and act as such at all times. **Image** is very important. You are not only portraying how you approach your own work but you are also representing a profession which is seeking to become more accepted and credible in the eyes of the public and the medical profession alike.

Practitioners should wear a white coat or some other form of professional **uniform**. These clothes should be suitable for the job, allowing freedom of movement, but with a semi-clinical appearance. Short sleeves are best. Membership **badges** should be worn.

The practitioner's **hands** should be free from cuts, rough skin or infected areas. Fingernails must be cut short with no rough edges or nail varnish. With the exception of a fob watch, **avoid** wearing **jewellery**. Rings and bracelets can interfere with hand and wrist movement and even simple rings can rub.

Personal hygiene is obviously very important.

The practitioner should wash their hands before and after every treatment. Long hair should be tied back so that it does not dangle on the patient. Avoid odiferous foods such as garlic, onions, curry etc. prior to treatments and remember that these foods can continue emitting odours for some time after consumption!

The **relationship** between the practitioner and the client can be very powerful. It is not unusual for a client to confide more in a practitioner than friends or family. This privileged position should never be abused and **confidentiality** must be strictly maintained. Never gossip or inadvertently discuss another patient's details even if you are questioned by one of their inquisitive friends!

The professional practitioner listens to their patient's problems, understands, does not judge or make assumptions, gives sound holistic advice but guards against any emotional involvement with the client. The client should receive **undivided attention**, feel at ease to either remain quiet or talk, but should not be used as a sounding board for the therapist's own personal problems! This isn't easy and can be very stressful!

It is important to keep striving to **develop** your expertise in reflexology and to increase your knowledge of other **associated** subjects e.g. chiropractic, aromatherapy, acupuncture and homeopathy.

Nutrition is of particular importance, so there is some general information for you in this section.

Advertise your skills. Hang all your appropriate certificates on the wall of your business premises. Display leaflets containing information about other complementary therapies and recommended therapists. The more information you can acquire, the better placed you are as a professional reflexologist to offer valuable, informed, **holistic** advice.

Even the best researched reflexologist in the world still doesn't know it all! One of the most important factors in maintaining a professional image is to **know your limitations**. Always remember that it is **not** the role of a reflexologist to **diagnose**, neither should a reflexologist **profess to cure**. These are definitely **not** in the job description!

When a client has a condition outside of your scope of knowledge **refer** the client to an appropriately qualified practitioner. This isn't a sign of weakness - it is a sign of professionalism.

Being a professional practitioner isn't easy. Here is a **summary** list of some of the **attributes** and **qualities** that need to be developed.

The professional practitioner:

- ➢ has a thorough understanding of the theory and practice of reflexology
- ➢ keeps skills up to date and expands knowledge whenever possible
- ➢ has an understanding of all the legal requirements involved in running a business
- ➢ provides a safe environment for the patients
- ➢ is patient, calm and empathic
- ➢ is trustworthy with sensitive information and personal details
- ➢ can quickly gain another's trust and confidence
- ➢ is a good listener and communicator
- ➢ shows compassion, understanding and caring
- ➢ keeps personal problems to his or her self
- ➢ knows the limit of his or her own ability, training and competence

205

Employed or Self-employed?

As a qualified reflexologist, you have the choice of:

> ➢ becoming an employee for a company or individual that is already trading

OR

> ➢ becoming self-employed and setting up your own business.

This is a very important decision and there is no right or wrong outcome. What is important is that you make the decision based on your **own circumstances** and what is right for **YOU.** Let's look at the options.

Employed

Employed reflexologists enjoy the benefits of **regular hours** and **regular pay**, and will not usually be responsible for finding their own clients. There are no account issues to worry about as salaries are usually paid net of Income Tax and National Insurance under P.A.Y.E. (Pay As You Earn). They tend to work in close proximity to other therapists, which allows **social** and **professional interaction** and the exchange of ideas. At the end of each working day the employee can go home and not think about work again until they return.

Some see working for another as a disadvantage. Employees are never in complete control of their own destiny and do not always have a say in the running or direction of the business. This is only a disadvantage to those who actually WANT this level of involvement.

Self-Employed

To become a successful self-employed reflexologist, the first criterion is to really **want** to be one! It involves a **lot of work** and **responsibility**. As much time will be spent working to attract clients and maintaining the smooth running of the business as actually performing treatments.

Whether you choose to trade from fixed premises or as a mobile practice, you will need to be **self-motivated**, able to work on your own and be prepared to learn new skills and make decisions.

There is a substantial initial **monetary outlay** (see 'Setting Up Your Own Business'). A regular salary cannot be guaranteed as the availability of the money will be dependent on the business making a profit. You will also be responsible for keeping the business **accounts** and tackling issues such as

Income Tax, National Insurance and possibly V.A.T.. Unless you are experienced in this area we strongly recommend that you use an **Accountant**.

This all sounds a little daunting, and it is, but the personal satisfaction and freedom of 'being the boss' can far outweigh the disadvantages – if that is what you want to do!

There are three ways in which a self-employed person can trade:

1. Sole Trader

This is the **simplest** way. As the title implies, this method is only an option for an **individual** trading alone. The business itself is inexpensive to run with few legal formalities. There is no requirement for the accounts to be audited or published. Capital can be easily introduced and withdrawn from the business.

The disadvantage of this method is that there is **unlimited liability**. In other words the individual is personally liable for all actions and financial affairs of the business, and so all personal property and possessions are at risk. There can also be problems raising finance and any profit ploughed back into the business is taxable.

2. Partnership

A **minimum of two** people is required for a partnership. The advantages of this method are the same as for a sole trader, with the additional advantages of **shared** decision making and shared risks.

A disadvantage of this method is that **unlimited liability** still applies and each partner is responsible for the actions of the other(s). Partners are **jointly and severally liable** so, whilst on the face of it liability is **shared**, if a partner defaults the other(s) becomes totally liable. There is a need for a partnership **agreement** to be drawn up, preferably by a Solicitor.

3. <u>Limited Company</u>

A minimum of two people is required for a limited company. The main advantage is that the business is seen in law to be a **separate legal entity**. **Liability** is therefore **limited** to the value of the business, so the individuals' personal property and possessions are not at risk (except sometimes in cases of fraud or negligence). A limited company also has a perceived credibility and there are tax advantages to ploughing profits back into the business.

Most of the disadvantages of this method of trading are due to the **Companies Act**. The business must be **registered** and the accounts must be annually **audited** and **disclosed**. The operating costs of a limited company are therefore higher than those of a sole trader or partnership.

As you have seen, there are many factors to consider. Our best advice is to **take your time** making this decision. Ensure that the route you take is the one that is best suited to your own personal and financial circumstances and business aspirations.

Whatever you decide - good luck!

Setting Up Your Own Business

When setting up as a self-employed reflexologist, you have a choice of obtaining and maintaining appropriate business **premises** or setting up a **mobile practice** to treat patients in their own homes.

There are **advantages** and **disadvantages** associated with both of these options. A mobile practice may initially appear favourable. The set up costs and overheads are generally lower and a mobile practice can cater for patients unable to travel. However, valuable trading time is lost travelling from site to site, the treatment may have to take place in an unsuitable environment and the cost of purchasing and keeping a vehicle on the road is usually high.

Finding suitable premises can be tricky. You may have a suitable room in **your house**. If you choose this option you will have to accept the invasion of privacy as you welcome strangers into your home. Also be prepared for the difficulty of separating your working life from your personal life.

If you have to look for premises be prepared to **compromise**. It is extremely rare that you will find the perfect room in a perfect building in a perfect location. Here are a few tips of what you should look for.

The Perfect Room

Ideally the room will have easy access, preferably without steps. It will be clean, spacious, warm, light, airy and decorated using calming colours.

The Perfect Building

The building will be structurally sound with water, toilet facilities and heating.

The Perfect Location

The building will be located in a quiet area, with car parking facilities and easy access to public transport systems.

Once you have found your site the **purchase**, **lease** or rent has to be negotiated. You may also need to obtain **planning permission** if you intend to change the structure or the usage of the property (refer to your local council for information relevant to your own area). Seek professional advice from a **Solicitor** to ensure that **all** contracts you enter into are legally sound.

When estimating the **overheads** of your business always overestimate to allow a little leeway for the unexpected. Don't forget to include any mortgage, rent, business rates, vehicle maintenance fees, travelling expenses, heating, lighting, water, cleaning and laundry. Staff costs should be included too – hopefully you will be able to draw a salary!

As well as the regular overheads there will be some **one-off purchases** to be made. For example:

> - adjustable, raised foot-stool (for patient) or massage couch
> - low stool (for reflexologist)
> - towels and towel rack
> - pillows
> - desk and chair
> - filing cabinet
> - telephone/answer-phone
> - music system
> - waste bin
> - water jug and glasses
> - coat rack/hook
> - first aid kit

To attract customers to your new business you will need **advertising material** such as brochures, business cards, flyers and price lists. You may also want to consider advertising in local magazines or papers.

None of this comes cheap. Always shop around to get the best deal and negotiate every purchase - you will be amazed how much money this can save!

Once you have your premises and your clients have started to arrive, further costs will be accrued. **Consumable** items such as stationery, sterilizing fluid, antiseptic foot wipes, tissues and paper towels will need to be ordered on an on-going basis. Again you should **negotiate** deals with companies that supply these items.

Running your own business **isn't easy**. Just keeping up with the **accounts** can be a headache. Don't try to be a 'Jack of all Trades'. Stick at what you are good at. If you are not experienced at handling issues such as National Insurance, V.A.T. returns and Income Tax assessments - EMPLOY AN ACCOUNTANT. Professional expertise can be expensive, but the peace of mind obtained is well worth the cost. As well as freeing up some of your time, a good Accountant can even save you money!

Client Care

The way in which the client is cared for obviously reflects on the professionalism of the therapist.

From the moment the client is in your care he or she should be treated **politely**, **courteously** and with **empathy**. The client should be put at ease so that a trusting relationship can develop, and both you and the client should enjoy the treatment and benefit from it. The entire treatment should be carried out with a quiet air of efficiency, without interruptions, rush, hustle or bustle.

To successfully treat the client, you must obtain as much information as you can by employing all your senses.

When you meet the client and shake hands, pay attention to the strength of the **contact**. Is the client timid or aggressive?

Listen to what the client is telling you. Don't just simply listen to what is being said, listen to how it is being said. Is the client confident, hesitant, loud or quiet?

Observe the client's body shape and posture when walking, standing and sitting. Try to tune in to the wealth of information that body language can supply. Notice also the colour of the skin and the eyes, and the respiratory rate. The more information you can glean the better placed you will be to provide a truly **holistic** treatment.

Much information is obtained by taking a comprehensive **case history**. Allowing the client to mark sites of pain on a picture of the human anatomy can also be very useful. Maintaining client records is a **legal requirement** and you are obliged to keep these written records for a minimum of **6 years**.

Taking a case history involves obtaining a **lot** of detailed information. Using a **pre-printed case history sheet** not only looks **professional**, but acts as a **memory prompt** so that you don't forget some of the questions.

Here are the main headings under which most of the information falls, along with a list of prompts to help you obtain the information you require.

General Details
- name
- address
- date of birth
- telephone number
- sex (m/f)
- children
- left or right handed
- occupation
- hobbies/sports
- name and address of doctor
- next of kin

Current Medical Condition
- any current conditions
- GP diagnosis
- taking medication
- reason for coming/referral
- blood pressure
- headaches
- dizziness/fainting
- sleep pattern
- smoker
- alcohol intake
- caffeine intake
- epileptic
- pregnant

General Medical History
- family history
- hospitalisation
- x-rays
- operations
- other treatments
- previous manipulations
- dental treatment
- allergies
- accidents

Cardiovascular
- palpitations
- chest pains
- cold hands and feet
- varicose veins
- swollen ankles
- pains when walking
- coughs/colds
- breathing difficulties

Genito-urinary
- normal continence
- pain during urination
- blood in urine
- prostate problems
- kidney stones
- kidney infections

Skin
- skin problems
- eczema
- eruptions
- shingles
- athlete's foot

Nervous System
- sense of smell
- eyes
- ears
- sense of taste
- any tingling or numbness
- muscular tremors

Digestive System
- weight loss/gain
- appetite
- wind
- gas/heartburn
- diarrhoea
- constipation
- vomiting/nausea
- abdominal pain
- haemorrhoids
- jaundice

Endocrine system
- thyroid problems
- diabetes

Menstruation
- hysterectomy
- menopause
- painful periods
- regularity of periods
- excessive flow
- tender breasts
- discharge
- pre-menstrual tension
- hormone replacement therapy

As well as taking a comprehensive case history you are also **legally** required to document relevant **details** pertaining to **each visit**. These details must include the date, results of any previous treatment, the treatment given, the reasons for the treatment and the amount paid.

A vital part of client care is **communication**. Always explain the proposed treatment carefully and simply to the client.

Never be tempted to **diagnose**, even if you feel confident in your understanding of the underlying cause or condition. You must refer your patient back to their General Practitioner for a formal diagnosis.

Let the client know what you hope to achieve but never make claims to a miracle cure! Giving false hope is unethical and proclaiming to provide a cure is also misleading, especially since you cannot provide a diagnosis from which to base a cure. It is better that the client is pleased and gains confidence by a modest improvement than being disappointed because a major benefit hasn't occurred!

After the treatment offer the client a glass of **water** and encourage them to drink plenty later too. Try not to rush the client out of the door in 'production-line style'. Remember that you are treating the person as a whole in a holistic manner. Their symptoms are unique to them and you are often meeting them at their time of need.

Let the client know if you anticipate any **side effects** and advise the best way to deal with them. For example if, after a treatment, you expect the client to develop symptoms such as tiredness, headaches and even diarrhoea as the body expels toxins – tell them! Advise that drinking 4-6 pints of fresh water for a couple of days will help to flush the toxins through. The client should also be advised to avoid long distance driving, spicy foods, alcohol, coffee and tea for 12 hours.

As a holistic therapist you are expected to be able to give sensible, **practical advice** on issues such as diet, relaxation and exercise. The client will also often require **emotional advice** on subjects such as relationships, handling grief and stress, and caring for dependants. This is a harder area to cope with and it is strongly advised that reflexologists take a **general counselling skills** course (a few tips can be found in 'Counselling'). Just creating a professional, safe environment in which the client has the space to think and talk freely often acts as the facilitator for the beginning of self-awareness and self-healing.

<u>Nutrition</u>

Many recipients of holistic therapies have an interest in promoting their own health. The importance of what we eat is receiving more and more media attention, with food scares becoming everyday news. Views on what foods should and should not be eaten seem to change as often as the weather! Despite this, the basic information about what nutrients the body needs to remain healthy generally remain the same.

As a holistic therapist, the reflexologist is often asked about dietary needs. It is useful therefore to have a good knowledge of nutrition so that dietary advice can be offered to support the treatment.

This is **not** a nutrition training course, but here is some basic information for you. Additional nutritional advice relating to specific disorders is included in the 'Conditions' section. Support this information by reading books and news articles on the subject so that your knowledge expands and remains up to date.

We are what we eat. The maintenance of life depends on the **quality** and **quantity** of the food we ingest. As a society, we are becoming more aware of the food we eat, where and how it was grown and its nutritional value.

More and more emphasis is being placed on achieving a **balanced** diet. This is not always easy given some of the low-nutritional convenience foods that are on the market.

Let's look at the main components of a balanced diet.

<u>Water</u>

The human body is about 62% water. It is therefore essential that the body is **re-hydrated** by drinking plenty of liquids. Liquids play a major part in all the major metabolic processes and help toxins to be eliminated from the body.

Apart from the obvious source of dietary liquids such as water, juices and milk, liquids are also derived from sources such as fruits and vegetables.

<u>Carbohydrates</u>

Carbohydrates make up just 1% of the human body, but they provide our main source of **energy**. Carbohydrates that are not broken down during the digestive process to produce energy play an important part in maintaining a healthy digestive tract. This food category includes both **sugars** and **starches**, and a lack of these leads to the break down of body fats.

Foods high in sugar include honey, bananas, grapes and beets. Foods high in starch include wheat, rice, potatoes and yams.

Proteins

Proteins occur in every living cell and make up about 17% of the human body. They are involved in nearly all the vital functions of life. Proteins are essential for the **growth** and **repair** of tissues and protein deficiency results in retarded growth in children, hunger, lack of energy and loss of weight.

The best sources of protein include lean meat, fish, eggs, milk, cheese and yoghurt.

Fats

Fats generally make up about 14% of the human body. They are mainly used as a **store** of **energy** that can be called upon when required. Fats **insulate** against the cold and **cushion** delicate organs. An insufficient supply of fats will result in hunger, lack of energy and some loss of weight.

Sources of fat include full cream milk, cream, cheese, butter, soya beans, fatty fish, bacon and eggs.

Roughage

Roughage gives **bulk** to the diet and is necessary for healthy and active bowels.

Good sources of roughage include skins and pulp of fruit and vegetables, and the husks of grains.

Minerals

Approximately 4% of the human body is made up of minerals. Without minerals the body is unable to function. The correct balance of minerals ensures that we do not dehydrate or drown in our own fluids and that the nerves and muscles work well. Minerals are incorporated in bones (calcium, magnesium and phosphorous), nerves (calcium and magnesium) and cells (sodium, potassium and chlorine).

Minerals are derived from various food sources. Familiarize yourselves with these.

<u>Vitamins</u>

Vitamins are necessary in small quantities for the normal functioning of the body. A normal balanced diet will usually provide an adequate vitamin supply. A deficiency in a vitamin will usually lead to a metabolic disorder, or deficiency disease, which can be remedied by the sufficient intake of that vitamin.

Find out the sources, functions and effects of deficiencies of the main vitamins.

To ensure a good **balance** between these components, it is generally recommended that 34% of the diet is fruit and vegetables, 29% is bread, cereals and potatoes, 15% is milk and dairy foods, 14% is meat, fish and their alternatives and 8% of the diet is foods that contain fat and sugar. It is also generally recommended that at least 2 litres of water are consumed each day.

A balanced diet will contain sufficient quantities of the main food groups to fulfil the body's nutritional requirements and give energy that is proportional to the **individual's** level of activity.

The requirement of each food group will therefore vary from individual to individual, and an individual's requirement will vary during their lifetime. Clearly the nutritional requirements of a newborn baby, growing child, active teenager, adult, expectant mother and elderly person will vary enormously.

Nutrition is a huge subject of great importance to the general well being of all. We hope that this general information has been of use to you and urge you again to study this subject to bring a further dimension to your holistic treatment.

Counselling

Reflexology is a powerful **holistic** treatment, involving direct physical contact, which has been shown to be capable of inducing **emotional responses**.

The patient is always in a position that is conducive to **speech**, and **eye contact** with the practitioner is usually possible. It is not surprising, therefore, that the reflexologist is often used as a sounding board for their patients' problems and concerns.

Counselling is a skill in itself and a general counselling course is recommended for all reflexologists. However, much good can be done by simply learning to **listen.**

Be willing to listen to the patient and **pay attention** to what is being said. Try not to keep interrupting and resist the temptation to flip the conversation to your own current dilemmas or experiences.

Providing a **safe environment** in which the patient feels secure enough to talk about their problems can be therapeutic in itself. Listening and giving attention in this simple way can help the patient to feel more accepted by others and therefore more acceptable to themselves.

When people are very confused, anxious, emotional or upset, they may be a little **incoherent** and their speech may be difficult to follow.

It can be embarrassing and aggravate the situation further should you find yourself unable to answer the patient's questions because you have no understanding of their problem. This situation can be very discouraging for the patient too, as it can appear as if you were just not paying attention.

If you find yourself struggling to understand the situation, ask the patient to **clarify** what he or she is trying to say. **Admit** to being confused and ask for the main points again. Never blame your confusion on the patient's inability to communicate and never appear to be critical. Instead, state that YOU are having difficulty in understanding and ask for the relevant information again.

Once you have grasped the problem, it is useful to show that patient that you have been paying attention. You can do this by **summarising** the main points. As well as proving that you have been listening, it often helps the patient to hear the problem in someone else's words.

Another way of 'reflecting' the information is to **re-state** the patient's **feelings**, for example "So you feel angry". Offering back the information for the patient's consideration in this way can be beneficial in the understanding and acceptance of the problem.

Listen for **repeated words**. They may be very relevant to the patient's feelings.

Listen for **powerful statements** that are just thrown into the conversation and then seemingly ignored.

In both cases it may be productive to offer the information back to the patient for consideration.

Remember, when dealing with your clients, that everyone has a hunger for physical touch, mental stimulation, recognition and acknowledgement. Every human interaction is capable of generating **positive** or **negative** responses to these needs. People will grow used to receiving negative feedback if that is all that is on offer. Sadly, negative feedback is usually considered better than no feedback at all.

The practitioner is in a powerful position, capable of giving unconditional, positive feedback to the patient in many ways. To maximize this potential, further your counselling skills so that you can develop this aspect of your chosen holistic therapy.

Anatomy and Physiology

221

This page has intentionally been left blank.

A sound knowledge of the anatomy (structure) and physiology (function) of the human body is vital to any reflexologist. Knowing how the body is structured and how it functions enables the practitioner to understand what happens to the body when it is injured, diseased or placed under stress.

Let's begin by looking at the various levels of **structural organization**.

The human body consists of several levels of structural organization:

1. Chemical Level
This is the **lowest** level. It includes all **atoms** (e.g. carbon, hydrogen, oxygen, nitrogen, calcium, potassium, sodium) and **molecules** essential for maintaining life.

2. Cellular Level
Molecules combine to form **cells**. Cells are the **basic** structural and functional **units** that make up the body. There are **many types**, e.g. nerve cells, blood cells and muscle cells. Each type of cell has its own specialised structure and function but they all have some general features.

This is a typical cell. The cell is surrounded by a cell membrane. There are a number of components within the cell membrane that serve a particular function. These structures are called **organelles**.

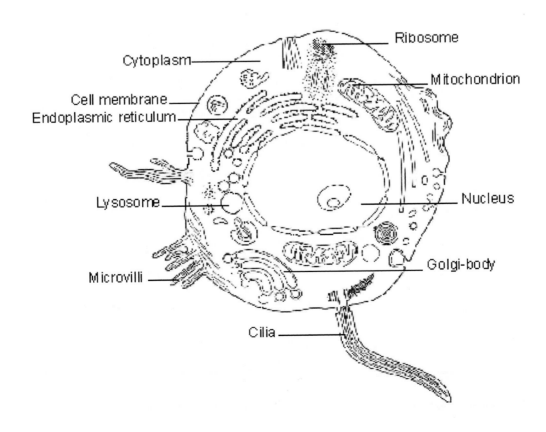

Here's a short description for each of the main components of a typical cell.

Cell membrane: The outer lining that forms the barrier between the cell and the extracellular fluid (fluid outside the cells).

Cytoplasm: Semi-fluid within the cell membrane that surrounds the organelles.

Endoplasmic reticulum: A network of channels running through the cytoplasm. It performs many roles including intracellular transport and support. Ribosomes are attached to it, and it is here that most of the cell's enzyme activity takes place under the influence of ribonucleic acid.

Cilia: Tiny hair like structures that protrude from the cell membrane. They aid movement and absorption.

Mitochondrion: A large double-membraned organelle, also known as the 'powerhouse'. It is responsible for producing the majority of the cell's adenosine triphosphate (ATP), which is the energy-carrying molecule, used to capture and store energy.

Nucleus: Literally means 'central part'. In a cell, the nucleus is the oval-shaped organelle that contains the chromosomes (the hereditary factors). The fluid within the nuclear membrane is called nucleoplasm.

Golgi-body: A structure looking similar to a stack of plates. Its functions include processing proteins and lipids (fats) and controlling the enzyme activity of the endoplasmic reticulum.

Lysosome: A single membraned organelle that contains digestive enzymes. Lysosomes break down metabolic substances, foreign particles and worn out cell parts.

Ribosome: An organelle in the cytoplasm that may attach to the endoplasmic reticulum. It contains ribonucleic acid (RNA) and proteins. Ribosomes are the site of protein synthesis.

Microvilli: Finger-like projections of the cell membrane that increase the surface area for absorption.

3. Tissue Level

Many **cells** of the **same type** make up tissue e.g. muscle cells make up muscle tissue. There are four main types of tissue:

Epithelial tissue - forms glands and the outer part of the skin. It lines the blood vessels, hollow organs and passages that lead out of the body.

Connective tissue - binds, supports, connects and holds the organs of the body in position.

Muscle tissue – capable of expanding and contracting due to its elongated cells.

Nervous tissue – capable of initializing and transmitting nerve impulses.

4. Organ Level

Tissues of **varying type** make up an **organ**. The stomach, for example, is an organ as it consists of varying tissue type. The outer layer of the stomach is comprised of connective tissue, the middle layer is muscle tissue, and the inner layer is epithelial tissue. Organs have specific functions and usually have distinctive shapes.

5. System Level

Several related **organs**, with a **common function**, make up a **system**. For example, the cardiovascular system, responsible for circulating the blood around the body, consists of the heart, veins, arteries and capillaries – all of which are organs, as they all comprise of more than one tissue type.

6. Organism Level

All parts of the body (from the chemicals to the cells, tissues, organs and systems) are structured to function together to make up the **organism**, or the **living individual**. This is the **highest** level.

Questions – Structural Organization (Answers: Page 376)

1. What is the lowest level of structural organization?

2. What name is given to the central part of the cell that contains the chromosomes?

3. What organelle is responsible for producing the majority of the cell's energy-carrying molecule, adenosine triphosphate (ATP)?

    a. mitochondrion
    b. golgi-body
    c. lysosome
    d. ribosome

4. What is formed when cells of the same type combine?

5. What type of tissue forms glands and the outer part of the skin, and lines blood vessels, hollow organs and passages that lead out of the body?

    a. epithelial
    b. connective
    c. muscle
    d. nervous

6. What term is given to a structure that comprises of more than one tissue type?

7. True or False?

    Several related organs, with a common function, make up an organism.

Now that you are aware of the structural organization within the body, we'll look at the main body systems and structures.

Skeletal System

The human skeletal system consists of **206 bones**, **cartilage**, **bone marrow** and the **periosteum** (the membrane around the bones).

The skeleton is divided into the **axial skeleton**, consisting of the skull, spine, ribcage and the sternum (breastbone), and the **appendicular skeleton**, consisting of the shoulders, arms, hands, pelvis, hips, legs and feet.

The skeleton has a number of functions:

> - It **supports** the body (we would be very floppy without it).
> - It provides **fixation points** for the muscles to facilitate movement.
> - It **protects** internal organs.
> - The red marrow in the bones produces **new blood cells**.
> - The yellow marrow in the bones consists of fat, which is used as an **energy store**.
> - The bones **store minerals** that can be released when required.

Let's take a look at the anterior view (from the front) and posterior view (from the back) of the skeleton.

Anterior View of Skeleton

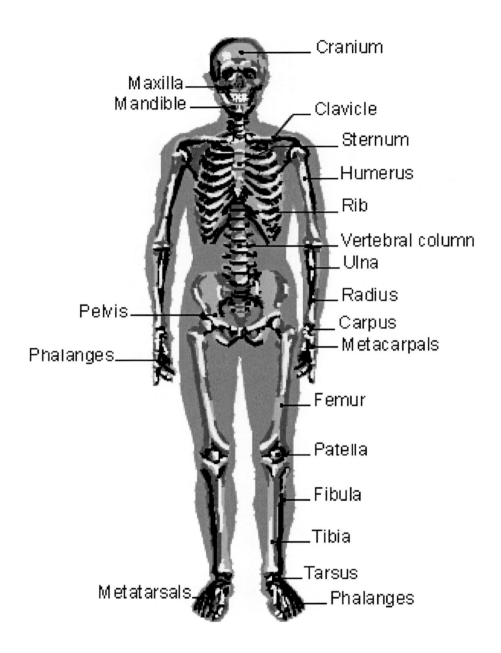

Posterior View of Skeleton

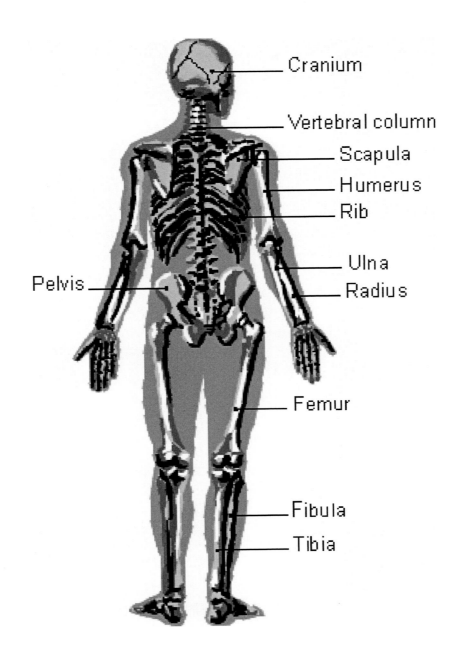

Cranium

Vertebral column

Scapula

Humerus

Rib

Ulna

Radius

Pelvis

Femur

Fibula

Tibia

As you have seen, the **vertebral column** (spine) runs from the base of the cranium (skull) down through the centre of the skeleton. The vertebral column is strong and yet it can bend forwards, backwards and to either side. It can also rotate. This mobility is possible as the adult vertebral column is made up of a series of **26** individual bones, or **vertebrae**, separated by rings of cartilage called **intervertebral discs**.

The vertebral column has **five** main areas.

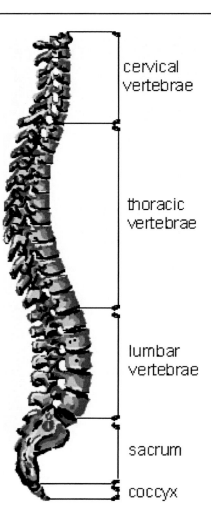

cervical vertebrae

thoracic vertebrae

lumbar vertebrae

sacrum

coccyx

Cervical Vertebrae:
The **7 cervical** vertebrae are in the **neck**. The top cervical vertebra (C1) is called the **atlas**, which permits the nodding movement. The second (C2) is the **axis**. The joint between the atlas and the axis is a pivot joint, allowing the head to rotate from side to  side. The remaining 5 cervical vertebrae (C3 – C7) are typically structured as shown here.

Thoracic Vertebrae:
 The **12 thoracic** vertebrae (T1 – T12) are located in the **chest** area. They are larger and stronger than the cervical vertebrae.

Lumbar Vertebrae:
 The **5 lumbar** vertebrae (L1 – L5), located in the **lower back**, are the **largest** and the **strongest**. Their various projections are short and thick

Sacrum:
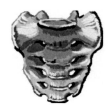 The **sacrum** is a **triangular bone**. It is formed by the **fusion** of **5 sacral** vertebrae (S1 – S5), which gradually occurs usually between the ages of 16 and 25. The sacrum provides a strong base for the vertebral column.

Coccyx:

The **coccyx** is a **triangular bone** at the very **tail** of the vertebral column. It is formed by the fusion of the **4 coccygeal** vertebrae (Co1 – Co4). This fusion usually occurs between the ages of 20 and 30.

The vertebrae, along with other structures such as ligaments, fat and fluid, protect the **spinal cord**. The spinal cord is a mass of **nerve tissue** from which **31 pairs** of spinal nerves originate and then run to all parts of the body.

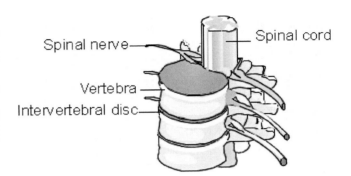

The **joints** between the vertebrae allow some **movement** in the vertebral column. **Freely moveable** joints, such as the joints in the limbs, give the otherwise rigid skeleton considerable flexibility.

Freely moveable joints are characterized by having a space between the bones. This space is called a **synovial cavity**. It is filled with a fluid known as **synovial fluid** and the ends of the articulating bones are covered in **cartilage**. Although all synovial joints share these characteristics, there are a number of different types. We'll take a look at two types of synovial joint - the ball and socket and the hinge joint.

Ball and Socket Joints

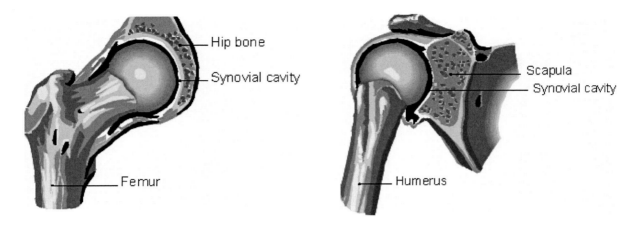

The **hip** (above left) and the **shoulder** (above right) are the only ball and socket joints in the body. They consist of the ball-shaped end of one bone fitting into a cup-shaped depression of another. Ball and socket joints give **maximum** movement. They allow the limb to move forward, backwards and to the side, and they also allow the bones to rotate.

Hinge Joints

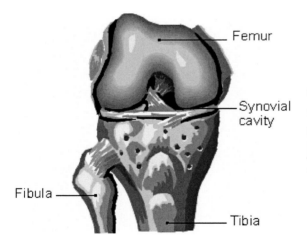

In a hinge joint, the convex surface of one bone fits into the concave surface of another. Movement is restricted to a **single** direction. Examples of hinge joints include the knee (pictured left), elbow and ankle.

The **foot** and **ankle** consist of many joints as they are made up of several bones. Let's take a look.

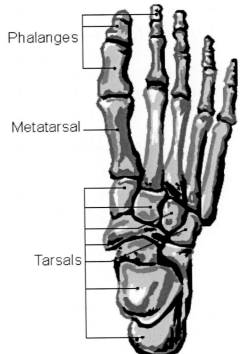

Phalanges

Metatarsal

Tarsals

The ankle is comprised of **seven** bones called **tarsals**. These bones are collectively known as the **tarsus**.

The foot has **five** long **metatarsals** that connect the tarsus to the **phalanges**.

The phalanges each have **three** bones, except for the **big toe**, that has only **two**.

The **wrist** and **hand** have a similar skeletal structure to the ankle and foot.

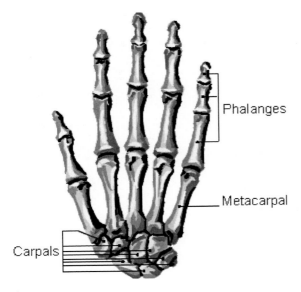

Phalanges

Metacarpal

Carpals

Eight bones called **carpals**, collectively called the **carpus**, make up the wrist.

There are **five** long **metacarpal** bones. The metacarpals connect the carpus to the **phalanges**.

There are **three** phalanges on each finger, except for the **thumb**, that has only **two**.

Common Conditions Affecting the Skeleton

The skeletal system is generally fairly robust although, as many have experienced, bones can get bruised, fractured and dislocated.

Common skeletal conditions, covered in this package, include:

> Back pain
> Compression of spinal nerves
> Frozen shoulder
> Lumbago
> Osteo-arthritis
> Rheumatoid arthritis
> Sciatica
> Tennis elbow

Questions – Skeletal System (Answers: Page 376)

1. What name is given to the skull, spine, ribcage and sternum?

    a. axial skeleton
    b. appendicular skeleton

2. Which vertebrae are located in the neck?

    a. cervical
    b. thoracic
    c. lumbar
    d. sacral
    e. coccygeal

3. Where are the 12 thoracic vertebrae located?

    a. lower back
    b. chest
    c. at the base of the vertebral column

4. Which 5 vertebrae are located in the lower back?

5. The area of the vertebral column below the lumbar vertebrae is called the sacrum. How many sacral vertebrae fuse to form this triangular bone?

    a. 2
    b. 3
    c. 4
    d. 5

6. What is the name of the triangular bone that forms the tail of the vertebral column?

7. What fluid is found in freely moveable joints?

8. Fill in the missing word:

    The elbow, knee and ankle are examples of _____ joints.

9. Name one of the two ball and socket joints.

10. What are the bones of the toes called?

    a. tarsals
    b. metatarsals
    c. phalanges

11. The ankle is comprised of 7 bones called tarsals. What collective name is given to these bones?

12. What are the long bones that connect the tarsus to the phalanges?

The Skin

The skin is a part of the **integumentary** system. The integumentary system comprises of the skin and its associated components such as the nails and hair. We will just look at the skin.

The skin is one of the largest **organs** of the body, covering the majority of the outside area of the individual. It has many functions. The skin:

> provides a **protective barrier** between the inner body and the external environment. It is the first level of immunity.

> **regulates temperature**. Sweating and increasing the blood flow to the skin cools the body. Decreasing the blood flow to the skin, and raising the hair on the surface of the skin, insulates it.

> provides **sensitivity** via the skin's nerve endings and receptors so that temperature, pressure and pain can be detected.

> allows the **secretion** of water, heat, some toxic waste and small amounts of salt.

> provides a **reservoir of blood** that can be used elsewhere if required.

> synthesizes **vitamin D** when the chemical ergosterol is stimulated by ultraviolet light.

The **top** layer of the skin is the **epidermis** (epi- = above, dermis = skin). The epidermis is actually made up of 5 layers. The deepest layer produces new cells that push up to the surface. The top layer consists of flat, dead cells that are continually shed and replaced by the new.

The epidermis varies in thickness. It is thickest on the palms of the hands and the soles of the feet. There are no blood vessels or nerve endings.

Under the epidermis is the **dermis**. This layer of the skin is thicker than the epidermis, tough and elastic. It is composed of connective tissue, collagen (a protein) and elastic fibres.

The dermis contains blood vessels, lymph vessels, nerve endings, sebaceous (oil) glands, sweat glands and ducts, hair follicles and hairs.

The deepest part of the skin is the **subcutaneous layer** (sub- = under, cutaneous = pertaining to the skin).

The subcutaneous layer connects the dermis to the underlying muscle tissue. It consists mainly of adipose tissue (a connective tissue containing fat). The adipose tissue insulates, protects and is an energy store. The subcutaneous layer also contains many blood vessels.

Common Conditions Affecting the Skin

The skin provides an excellent indication as to the state of health and fitness of the individual. The colour, pallor and dryness of the skin are affected when there is ill health or a lack of vitality.

Common skin conditions include blisters, warts, acne, boils and cysts. Common skin conditions covered in this package include:

> ➢ Cancer
> ➢ Chilblains
> ➢ Eczema
> ➢ Thrush
> ➢ Ulcer

Questions – The Skin (Answers: Page 378)

1. True or False?

    The skin is a tissue that covers the majority of the outside area of the individual.

2. What is the top layer of the skin called?

3. What layer of the skin is described below?

    A tough, elastic layer composed of connective tissue, collagen and elastic fibres, containing blood vessels, lymph vessels, nerve endings, sebaceous glands, sweat glands and ducts, hair follicles and hairs.

4. What layer of the skin connects the dermis to the underlying muscle tissue?

5. What name is given to the connective tissue containing fat that makes up the majority of the subcutaneous layer?

Respiratory System

Respiration (breathing) is a vital process to sustain human life. It is concerned with **supplying oxygen** to the cells and **removing** toxic **carbon dioxide** from the body.

During respiration:

> ➢ **oxygen** is **inhaled** into the body
> ➢ in the **lungs**, the **oxygen** is absorbed into the **blood stream** and then transported to the **cells** for use in metabolic reactions
> ➢ the cellular **metabolic reactions** create **energy** and **carbon dioxide**
> ➢ the **blood** transports the **carbon dioxide** back to the **lungs**
> ➢ in the lungs, the carbon dioxide is **extracted** from the blood then **exhaled** from the body

Respiration is therefore dependent on **two** major systems:

1. The **respiratory system** - takes in oxygen, provides the site for gaseous exchange, and expels the carbon dioxide.

2. The **cardiovascular system** - transports the gases between the lungs and the cells.

We'll look at the structure of the respiratory system next.

The upper respiratory system starts at the **nose**, through which air is taken into the **nasal cavity**. The **mucus** and the **cilia** (tiny hairs that line the nasal passages) **trap dust** particles. As the air passes through the nasal cavity, it is **warmed** and **moistened** by mucus droplets.

The warmed, moistened air then travels from the **nasal cavity** into the **pharynx** (throat). The pharynx connects the mouth and the nasal passage to the **oesophagus** and the **trachea**.

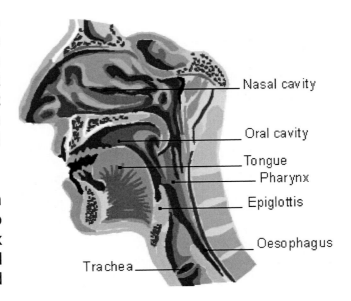

Nasal cavity

Oral cavity

Tongue
Pharynx

Epiglottis

Oesophagus

Trachea

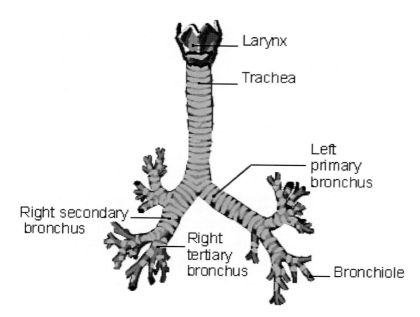

Larynx

Trachea

Left primary bronchus

Right secondary bronchus

Right tertiary bronchus

Bronchiole

At the top of the trachea is the **larynx**, or voice box. The vocal cords are folds in its lining. The larynx contains cartilage which keeps the trachea open to air. The trachea is closed off by the epiglottis during swallowing. This ensures that any food travels down the oesophagus and not into the trachea.

The trachea extends down to the level of the **5th thoracic** vertebra. The trachea then divides into the **left primary bronchus** and **right primary bronchus**, which descend into the left lung and right lung respectively. The bronchi continue to divide until, after branching into **secondary** and **tertiary** bronchi, they become **bronchioles**.

The finest bronchioles terminate in little **air sacs** called **alveoli**. It has been estimated that there are about 300 million of them in the lungs. Alveoli are moist and surrounded by a network of **capillaries**. It is here that **gaseous exchange** takes place. Oxygen is absorbed from the alveoli into the blood and carbon dioxide is taken from the blood into the alveoli.

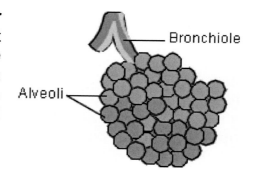

Bronchiole

Alveoli

In order for gaseous exchange to take place, 'new' air needs to be drawn into the lungs and the 'old' air expelled. This is made possible by the physical structure and location of the lungs.

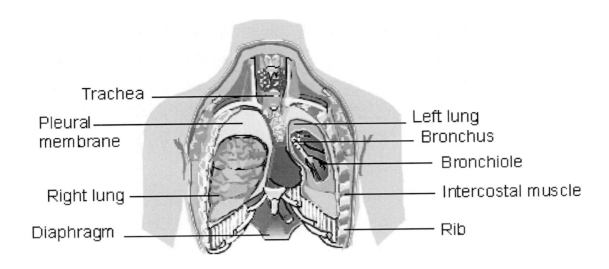

The **lungs** are located in the **upper thorax**. The right lung has three main lobes and the left lung has two.

A double **pleural membrane** covers each lung, and the lungs are further protected by the **ribcage**. The **intercostal muscles** and the **diaphragm** provide a muscular setting in which the lungs can **expand** and **relax** – a vital feature of respiration.

For air to be taken **into** the lungs, the **air pressure** in the lungs has to be **less** than the external air pressure. This is achieved by making the lungs **bigger**.

For air to be **expelled** from the lungs, the air pressure in the lungs has to be **greater** than the external air pressure. This is achieved by making the lungs **smaller**.

The **muscular** movement of the **diaphragm** is involved in increasing or decreasing the lung capacity.

During **inspiration**, the **diaphragm contracts**, causing it to flatten. This **expands** the chest, drawing the lungs out, so **increasing** the size of the lungs. This decreases the pressure in the lungs and allows air to be inhaled.

During **expiration**, the **diaphragm relaxes**, causing it to rise. This **decreases** the size of the chest, pulling the lungs in, so **reducing** the size of the lungs. This increases the pressure in the lungs and allows the air to be exhaled.

The normal breathing rate is **10-12** breaths per minute, although this increases during exercise and stress, and decreases during sleep. Each breath contains approximately **500ml** of air.

As we have already mentioned, respiration is not only dependent on the structures of the respiratory system, but also on the **cardiovascular system**. There is no point in being able to exchange gases in the lungs if there is no means to transport these gases around the body! The blood vessels involved in transporting gases to and from the lungs are the **pulmonary arteries** and the **pulmonary veins**.

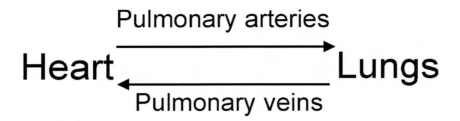

The **pulmonary arteries supply** blood to the lungs. They run from the right ventricle of the heart and contain **deoxygenated** blood (without oxygen). The blood releases its carbon dioxide and becomes oxygenated in the lungs.

The **oxygenated** blood is then **carried away** from the lungs in the **pulmonary veins**. The pulmonary veins take the oxygenated blood to the left atrium of the heart. It passes into the left ventricle from which it is **circulated** around the body.

During cellular metabolism the blood loses its oxygen and absorbs carbon dioxide. Deoxygenated blood then arrives back in the right atrium and is passed to the right ventricle for the cycle to repeat.

Common Conditions Affecting the Respiratory System

The functioning of the respiratory system is obviously vital for life to continue. Disorders of this system tend to have a knock-on effect to the whole body. An insufficient supply of oxygen to the cells causes the body to become tired and cells may begin to die. Common respiratory conditions include hayfever, pneumonia (an inflammation of the lungs), emphysema (an abnormal presence of air). Common respiratory conditions covered in this package include:

- Asthma
- Bronchitis
- Cancer
- Catarrh
- Colds and flu
- Laryngitis
- Sinusitis

Questions – Respiratory System (Answers: Page 378)

1. Respiration is concerned with supplying oxygen to the cells. What gas, produced by metabolic reactions in the cells, is removed during this process?

2. Oxygen is inhaled via the nasal cavity. Into which passage does the oxygen then travel?

   a. trachea
   b. larynx
   c. bronchus
   d. pharynx

3. The pharynx connects to the oesophagus and the trachea. Into which of these passages does oxygen pass?

   a. oesophagus
   b. trachea

4. The trachea extends to the level of the 5th thoracic vertebra. It then divides to extend into either lung. What are these two passages called?

   a. primary bronchi
   b. secondary bronchi
   c. tertiary bronchi

5. The tertiary bronchi continue to divide to form the smallest air passages in the lungs. What are these smallest air passages called?

6. What is the name of the little air sacs at the end of each bronchiole?

    a. cilia
    b. alveoli
    c. capillaries

7. Which gas is absorbed from the alveoli into the blood?

8. Which gas is taken from the blood into the alveoli?

9. What membrane covers each lung?

    a. nuclear membrane
    b. pleural membrane
    c. synovial membrane
    d. cell membrane

10. Which muscular structure contracts to draw air into the lungs, and relaxes to allow air to be expelled?

11. What blood vessels supply blood from the right ventricle of the heart to the lungs?

12. Which blood vessels transport the newly oxygenated blood from the lungs to the heart, for circulation around the body?

The Senses

Our senses exist to **provide information** about the environment.

The body receives various stimuli from the **external** environment, e.g. sight, sound, taste, touch and smell. Due to the presence of **sensory nerves**, either on the surface of the relevant organ or within its tissues, these stimuli can be received and translated into meaningful information. The body can then respond accordingly.

The body can also pick up stimuli originating in the body, such as changes in the organs or blood flow and the presence of pain or congestion. We are, however, often unaware of many **internal** changes that take place to keep the body in balance.

We will concentrate on the external senses.

Sight

The **eyes** are the organs that allow **visual** information to be received.

Each eye is a **spherical** organ, encased in a **bony cavity** on the anterior surface of the face. It is held in place by six **muscles** that allow the eye to perform many thousands of movements per day. The **retinal** arteries and veins provide the blood supply. Let's take a look at the anatomy of the eye.

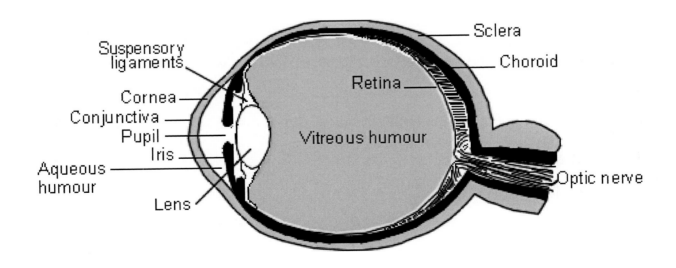

The wall of the eye consists of three layers. The **outside** layer is the **sclera**. This is tough and fibrous. The sclera is white, except at the **front** where there is a transparent area called the **cornea**. The cornea allows light into the eye and is covered by the **conjunctiva**.

The **middle** layer is the **choroid**, which contains many **blood vessels**. At the **front** of the eye the choroid forms the **iris**. The iris contains **pigment** that gives the eye its colour. The iris contains bands of **muscle**. The contraction and relaxation of these muscles causes the **pupil** to **dilate** and **constrict** respectively to regulate the amount of light that can enter the eye.

The **inner** layer of the eye is the **retina**. The retina contains the **light receptors**. At the back of the eye, **sensory neurons** lead from the retina as the **optic nerve**. The optic nerve transmits impulses generated in the retina to the **brain**.

The eye is **supported** by **aqueous** and **vitreous humour**. The **lens** is suspended in the aqueous humour at the front of the eye and is supported by **suspensory ligaments**.

As **light** enters the eye, it is **refracted** (bent) by the cornea, the front surface of the lens and the back surface of the lens, before it is **converged** on the **retina**. If this takes place successfully, the light is brought to a **point** on the retina. This allows the brain to create a **focused** and clear image from the visual stimulus.

Common Conditions Affecting the Eyes

Blurred vision maybe as a result of the inability of the eye to focus or a symptom of minor conditions such as stress, tiredness or migraine. It may, however, be indicative of a serious underlying disorder – particularly liver and kidney problems.

Common conditions of the eye include conjunctivitis (inflammation of the conjunctiva), iritis (inflammation of the iris), glaucoma (increased pressure within the eye) and cataracts (an opacity of the lens).

Questions – Sight (Answers: Page 379)

1. Which is the tough, fibrous, outer layer of the eye?

    a. sclera
    b. choroid
    c. retina

2. Which is the middle layer of the eye that contains the blood vessels?

    a. sclera
    b. choroid
    c. retina

3. What part of the eye contracts and relaxes to cause the pupil to dilate and constrict?

4. What is the name of the inner layer of the eye?

5. What structure, held in place by the suspensory ligaments and suspended in the aqueous humour, refracts the light so that it is brought to a point on the retina?

6. What nerve transmits impulses generated by the retina to the brain?

Sound

The **ears** are the organs that allow **sound** to be received. They are capable of hearing even the faintest sounds and can deal with many different stimuli at the same time.

There are **three** main parts to the ear. Only the outer part of the ear can be seen. The other two parts are buried deep within the skull. The **outer ear** is responsible for **trapping** the **sound** and passing it to the middle ear. The **middle ear** converts the sound into **mechanical vibrations**. In the **inner ear**, these mechanical vibrations **generate nerve impulses** that are transmitted to the **brain**.

Let's look at the anatomy of the ear.

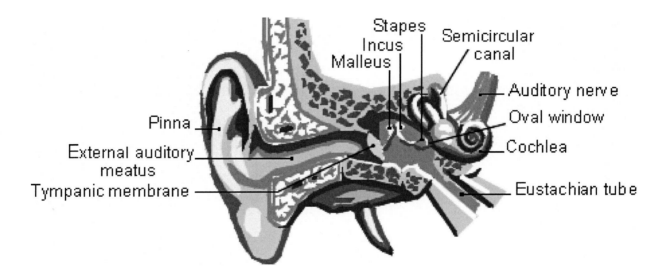

The **outer ear** consists of an external flap of skin and cartilage called the **pinna**. The pinna traps and directs the sound into the **external auditory meatus**. At the end of this passage is the **tympanic membrane** (ear-drum).

The middle ear is connected to the pharynx by the **eustachian tube**. This allows the **air pressure** on either side of the tympanic membrane to be **equalised**. The middle ear is bridged by three small bones, the malleus, incus and stapes, collectively called **ossicles**.

Sound entering the ear causes the tympanic membrane to vibrate. The tympanic membrane then vibrates the ossicles. The innermost ossicle is connected to another membrane called the **oval window**. The oval window transmits the vibrations to the inner ear.

The **inner ear** consists of a complicated series of **fluid filled canals**. The **cochlea** contains the receptors for hearing. Vibrations from the oval window cause pressure waves in the fluid of the cochlea. This causes membranes within the inner ear to vibrate, ultimately resulting in **sensory hairs** within the cochlea being moved. This stimulation of the hair cells generates **nerve impulses** that are transmitted to the **brain** via the **auditory nerve**. The brain then interprets these impulses as sound.

The inner ear is also responsible for **balance**. This role belongs to the three **semicircular canals**. The semicircular canals contain **lymph** and **sensory hairs**. As the head moves, the lymph drags the sensory hairs, stimulating sensory neurons. The nerve impulses are then passed to the brain to give information about the orientation of the head. This information is then used by the brain to co-ordinate movement and posture.

Common Conditions Affecting the Ears

Deafness can be caused by the deterioration of the nerves in the ear or by exposure to excessive loud noise.

Common conditions involving the ears covered in this package include:

➢ Glue ear
➢ Tinnitus
➢ Vertigo

Questions – Sound (Answers: Page 380)

1. Which part of the ear traps and directs sound into the external auditory meatus?

   a. outer ear
   b. middle ear
   c. inner ear

2. What is the common name for the tympanic membrane?

3. The three bones in the middle ear are called the malleus, incus and stapes. What collective name is given to these bones?

   a. semicircular canals
   b. cochlea
   c. ossicles

4. The innermost ossicle is connected to another membrane. What is this membrane called?

   a. triangular window
   b. square window
   c. oval window

5. The inner ear consists of a complicated series of fluid filled canals. What part of this structure contains the receptors for hearing?

   a. semicircular canals
   b. cochlea

6. The stimulation of the hair cells in the cochlea generates nerve impulses. Which nerve transmits these impulses to the brain?

7. What is the main function of the semicircular canals?

Taste

Taste is otherwise known as **gustatory sensation**.

Gustatory sensation is a chemical sense and so the substance needs to be dissolved before it can be tasted.

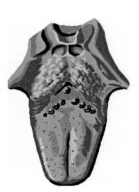

The **tongue** is the organ of **taste**. It is anchored to the back of the mouth. It contains four **taste zones**, enabling the detection of sweet, salty, sour and bitter tastes. The **receptors** for taste are located in about 10,000 **taste buds**. When the nerves in the taste buds are stimulated, they send the information to the brain where it is perceived as taste.

Common Conditions Affecting Taste

Much of what we think we taste we actually smell. Substances stimulate the sense of smell thousands of times more strongly than the sense of taste. Sufferers of colds or allergies sometimes complain that they cannot taste their food. In these circumstances it is common that the sense of taste is functioning normally but the olfactory system (responsible for the sense of smell) is not.

However, a lack of taste recognition can be due to general illness, stroke or pregnancy. It can also be indicative of a serious underlying condition.

Smell

Smell, like taste, is a **chemical sense**. It is detected by the **olfactory system**.

The olfactory system is capable of building a library of more than 10,000 odours, many of which may be linked to a memory of a person, place or event.

Olfactory bulb

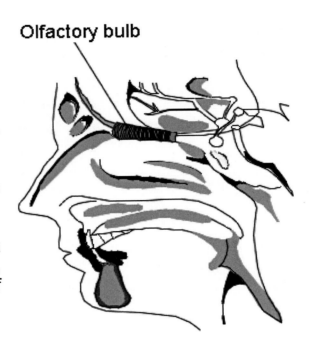

The **olfactory nerves** are located in the mucous membrane of the **nasal cavity**.

The **cilia** (hairs) of these nerve cells are stimulated by odours.

The information is sent along the nerve fibres to the **olfactory bulb**.

The information is then transmitted via the **olfactory nerve** to the **brain**, where it gives rise to the sensation of smell.

Common Conditions Affecting Smell

The sense of smell is the most immediate of the senses but it does tire. On first exposure to an aroma the perception of it is quick and sharp. After a fairly short period of time the ability to perceive it fades. This is called anosmia.

The sense of smell can be impaired by trauma, stroke, medication, infection or pregnancy. It can also be indicative of a serious underlying condition.

<u>Questions – Smell (Answers: Page 381)</u>

1. Fill in the missing word:

    Smell is detected by the _____ system.

2. What name is given to the tiny hairs on the nerve cells?

3. Where is the information from the nasal cilia sent before it is transmitted by the olfactory nerve to the brain?

Touch

The sense of touch is provided by the **nervous system**.

Sensory nerves cover every part of the skin. These nerves transmit information concerning **pressure**, **pain** and **temperature** from the periphery to the spinal cord. The information is then passed to the brain for interpretation.

Common Conditions Affecting Touch

The sense of touch becomes of particular importance in providing information about the environment when other senses fail. However, over recent years, the realization of the importance of touch in maintaining health has grown. Research has shown that the sense of touch plays a significant role in promoting healing, good health and recovery from illness.

As the sense of touch is dominated by the nervous system, there is rarely a complete loss of sensation. Conditions such as strokes, compression of spinal nerves and Raynaud's disease may temporarily affect this sense in isolated areas of the body.

Urinary System

The urinary system is primarily responsible for **eliminating urine** from the body.

Urine consists of **waste** material produced as a by-product of metabolism. It is a pale yellow fluid consisting of water, urea (a water soluble nitrogen compound) and small amounts of sodium, potassium, calcium, chloride and bicarbonate.

The components of the urinary system are the same in the male and female. We'll look at the structure of the urinary system now.

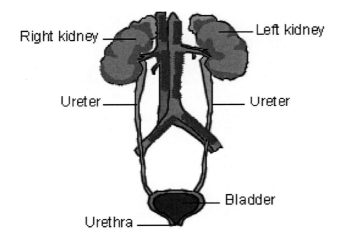

The components that make up the urine are absorbed from the blood by the **kidneys**. The urine passes from the kidneys, down the **ureters** to the **bladder**. The bladder stores the urine until it builds to a pressure that triggers the need for its release. On urinating, the urine leaves the body via the **urethra**.

The main function of the urinary system is to control the **composition**, **volume** and **pressure** of the **blood**. The kidneys are vital to this as they filter the blood by **absorbing waste** and excessive **water**. They help to regulate the blood pressure by secreting an enzyme called **renin**. The kidneys also have a part to play in producing new glucose molecules when needed, stimulating the production of red blood cells and producing an active form of vitamin D.

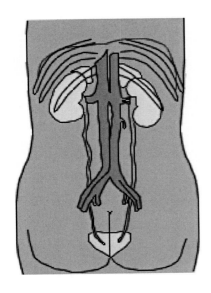

The kidneys are bean-shaped, reddish organs. They are located just **above** the **waist** at the **rear** of the abdomen.

The right kidney is located slightly lower than the left.

The kidneys receive their blood supply from the **renal arteries**. The **renal veins** drain the filtered blood away from the kidneys.

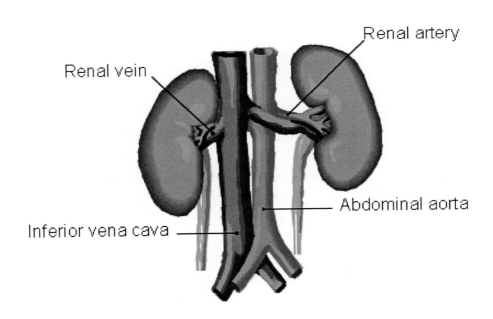

We'll look at the structure of the kidney next.

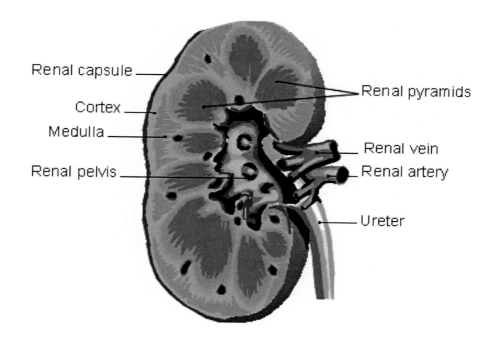

Within the **renal capsule** is the smooth, outer region of the kidney called the **cortex**.

The cortex surrounds the darker **medulla**. The cone-shaped structures in the medulla are called **renal pyramids**.

There is a large cavity in the centre of the kidney called the **renal pelvis**.

The cup-shaped extensions of the renal pelvis are involved in collecting urine from the renal pyramids and draining it into the **ureter**.

In order for the kidneys to perform their vital blood filtration processes, they have a vast **capillary network**. Situated within this network of blood vessels are numerous microscopic tubules called **nephrons**.

Nephrons are the functional units of the kidney. They extend from the renal capsule, through the cortex and medulla, to the cup-shaped extensions of the renal pelvis, absorbing excessive and unwanted substances from the blood.

Nephrons are **2-4cm** long. The cup-shaped **Bowman's capsule** encloses a small group of capillaries called the **glomerus**. It is across the walls of the Bowman's capsule that water and waste are filtered from the blood.

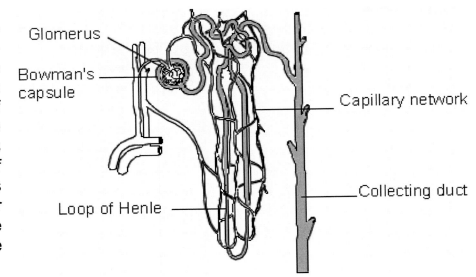

As the filtered substances pass through the tubule of the nephron, some useful substances are **selectively reabsorbed** back into the blood. The remainder passes into the **collecting duct**. It is then expelled from the kidney as urine via the renal pelvis and ureter.

Common Conditions Affecting the Urinary System

The urinary system is particularly prone to infections. Stress and the intake of alcohol and drugs also affect the functioning of the kidneys.

Common conditions of the urinary system include gout (a disorder affecting small joints, possibly caused by excessive uric acid in the blood), incontinence (the inability to control the release of urine from the bladder – in the male this tends to be due to a prostate problem). Urinary conditions covered in this package include cystitis and kidney stones.

Questions – Urinary System (Answers: Page 381)

1. What is the name of the tube that transports urine from a kidney to the bladder?

2. Which kidney is slightly lower than the other?

3. Which vessels drain the filtered blood away from the kidneys?

   a. hepatic arteries
   b. hepatic veins
   c. renal arteries
   d. renal veins

4. What is the dark region of the kidney called that contains the renal pyramids?

   a. renal capsule
   b. cortex
   c. medulla

5. What is the name of the large cavity in the centre of the kidney, involved in collecting urine and draining it into the ureter?

6. What is the name of the microscopic functional units of the kidney, that absorb excessive and unwanted substances from the blood?

   a. neurons
   b. nephrons
   c. neutrons

7. Which part of the nephron encases a small group of capillaries called the glomerus?

    a. Bowman's capsule
    b. loop of Henle
    c. collecting duct

8. True or False?

    Once water and waste have been filtered from the blood into the nephron, these substances can never return to the blood. They are all transported through the loop of Henle, passed into the collecting duct, and expelled as urine.

Reproductive System

Reproduction is the process by which new individuals are produced and the genetic information passed from generation to generation.

The male and female reproductive systems have different structures and functions to reflect their varying roles. However, there are similarities, particularly in terminology. The primary sex organs in both the male and female are called **gonads**. These are the **testes** in the male and the **ovaries** in the female. The gonads secrete **hormones**, a feature that classifies them as **endocrine** glands (see 'Endocrine system'). The gonads produce **gametes**. These are the **sperm cells** in the male and the **ova** (eggs) in the female.

We'll look at the structure of the male reproductive system first.

The **testes** are the principal structures of the male reproductive system. They descend from the abdomen into two pouches of skin called **scrotal sacs**. The testes are comprised of thousands of fine, coiled tubules in which the **sperm** are produced.

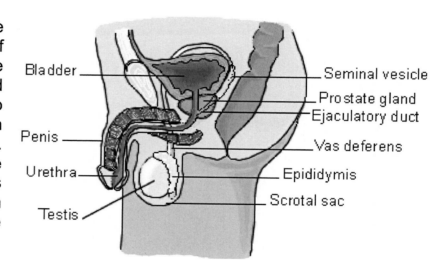

The tubules in the testis are continuous with the **epididymis**, where the sperm mature, and the **vas deferens**. The vas deferens transports the sperm from the testis and joins the **urethra** just below the bladder. During ejaculation, the muscular movement of the vas deferens and the **ejaculatory duct** aid the ejection of the sperm.

The **seminal vesicles** and the **prostate gland** secrete **fluids** during ejaculation. These fluids and the sperm make up the **semen** that is released via the penis.

The seminal fluids perform many functions including improving the mobility of the sperm, neutralizing acidity in the female reproductive tract and causing the coagulation of the semen after ejaculation.

The **ovaries** are the principal structures of the female reproductive system. They resemble unshelled almonds in size and shape.

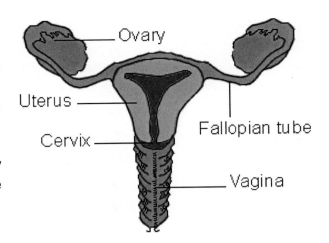

The ovaries are suspended by ligaments in the upper pelvic cavity, one either side of the **uterus**.

Each ovary contains over 200,000 **immature ova** at birth. Each immature ovum is encased in a sac and the whole structure is called a **follicle**. The follicles progressively develop, usually one at a time, in response to the various sex **hormones** until they become **primary follicles**. Once the primary follicle has matured **ovulation** takes place. The ovum breaks free and enters the fallopian tube.

The two **fallopian tubes** (or uterine tubes) connect the ovaries to the uterus. Each fallopian tube resembles a long, thin funnel that is wider at the ovary and narrower at the uterus. At the ovary end, the fallopian tube has finger-like projections called **fimbriae**. The fimbriae encourage the mature ovum to enter the fallopian tube. If fertilization occurs, it usually takes place in the wider part of the fallopian tube. The fertilized ovum, now called a **zygote**, arrives in the uterus about 7 days after ovulation.

The **uterus** is suspended by broad ligaments and is situated between the bladder and the rectum. It is a tough, muscular sac with a rich blood supply. It serves as the pathway for sperm to enter the fallopian tubes. If fertilization occurs, the uterus provides a source of **attachment** and **nourishment** for the zygote, and later expands to facilitate the developing foetus. If fertilization does not occur, the uterus lining, which thickens in preparation for the implantation of the ovum, breaks down during **menstruation**.

Menstruation is controlled by hormones. The **menstrual cycle** is usually a 28 day process with four stages:

Menstrual Phase (Days 1-5)
A reduction in oestrogens and progesterone causes the breakdown of the uterine lining, resulting in the discharge of 25-65ml of blood, tissue fluid, mucus and uterine epithelial cells. At this stage a mature follicle is being prepared.

Pre-Ovulatory Phase (Days 6-13)
Follicle stimulating hormone and luteinizing hormone stimulate the ovaries to produce more oestrogens. This encourages the re-build of the uterine lining. By the end of this phase a mature follicle is ready for ovulation.

Ovulation (Day 14)
The matured ovum is released into the fallopian tube.

Post-Ovulatory Phase (Days 15-28)
This is the time between ovulation and the period of menstrual discharge. Progesterone production by the ovaries is stimulated by luteinizing hormone to prepare the uterus to receive the fertilized ovum. If fertilization and implantation does not occur, hormonal changes initiate the breakdown of the uterine lining and the cycle continues.

Common Conditions Affecting the Reproductive System

In many cases the first indication that there is a reproductive disorder is the inability to conceive. However, this can often be due to non-physical factors such as stress. In the male, infertility may be as a result of a low sperm count, accidental injury to the testes or, a condition that is becoming increasingly common, testicular cancer. Common conditions involving the reproductive system covered in this package include:

> - Amenorrhoea
> - Cancer
> - Dysmenorrhoea
> - Endometriosis
> - Irregular ovulation
> - Female infertility
> - Menopause
> - Menorrhagia
> - Ovarian cysts
> - Pregnancy
> - Pre-menstrual tension
> - Prostatitis

Questions – Reproductive System (Answers: Page 382)

1. Which tubule transports sperm from the testis to the urethra?

    a. epididymis
    b. vas deferens
    c. ejaculatory duct

2. Fill in the missing word:

    The seminal vesicles and the _____ gland secrete fluids during ejaculation.

3. True or False?

    Every month both ovaries produce and develop an ovum.

4. What name is given to an immature ovum encased in a sac?

    a. follicle
    b. fimbriae
    c. zygote

5. In which structure is an ovum normally fertilized?

    a. ovary
    b. fallopian tube
    c. uterus

6. A fertilized ovum is called a zygote. To which structure does the zygote attach for nourishment and development?

7. What causes the breakdown of the uterine lining if the implantation of a zygote does not occur?

    a. reduction in oestrogens and progesterone
    b. increase in oestrogens and progesterone

8. What hormone, secreted by the ovaries, encourages the re-build of the uterine lining?

    a. follicle stimulating hormone
    b. luteinizing hormone
    c. oestrogen

Lymphatic System

Lymph is basically excessive or unwanted **tissue fluid**. It is termed lymph when it drains into the lymphatic vessels. The **lymphatic** system consists of **lymph,** the network of **vessels** through which it flows, **structures** that contain **lymphatic tissue** and **bone marrow**.

The lymphatic system is similar to the cardiovascular system in as much as it consists of a complete **network** of vessels. However, unlike the cardiovascular system, the lymphatic system **does not** have a **pump**. The lymph is circulated by the movement of the body's **muscles** and is also assisted by the movements involved in **respiration**.

The lymphatic system has a number of functions. It:

> allows excess fluid, waste materials and bacteria to be drained from the tissues
> transports fats and fat soluble vitamins from the digestive tract into the blood
> plays a vital role in immunity

Let's take a look at its role in immunity.

The bone marrow and lymphatic glands produce **lymphocytes**. Lymphocytes are **white blood cells** (leucocytes) that play a part in the body's natural defences and immunity against disease.

There are 2 main types of lymphocyte:

1. **B-cell lymphocytes:** These are responsible for producing **antibodies**. Antibodies are protein molecules formed within the body to **neutralize** the effect of foreign invading substances (antigens). Antibody molecules attach themselves to invading antigen molecules, rendering them inactive.

2. **T-cell lymphocytes:** These have various roles to play in immunity, including **destroying** foreign substances.

The lymphatic system is an extensive network.

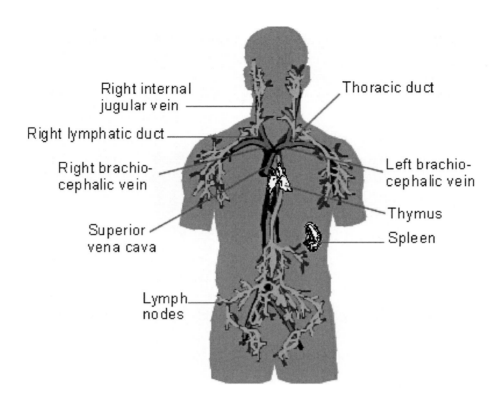

The tubes begin as closed-end vessels called **lymphatic capillaries**.

The lymphatic capillaries penetrate the spaces between the cells. The lymphatic capillaries converge to form the larger **lymphatic vessels**.

These vessels contain **valves** to prevent the back-flow of lymph. In the intestine, the lymphatic vessels are called **lacteals**. The lacteals absorb fat from digested foods.

At intervals along the lymphatic vessels, **lymph nodes** occur. These small, round bodies vary in size from a pin head to an almond. They are usually found in **clusters**, particularly in the axilla (armpit), neck, thorax, abdomen and groin. The lymph nodes are packed with **lymphocytes** and so have a valuable part to play in dealing with infection. When the lymph nodes are particularly active in this role they may swell.

Once past the lymph nodes, the lymphatic vessels unite to form **lymph trunks** and then the larger **lymph ducts**. The lymph ducts join the **cardiovascular system** and the lymph is drained into the blood.

The lymphatic system on the left of the body is served by the **thoracic duct** (or left lymphatic duct). The thoracic duct receives lymph from the left side of the head, neck and chest, the left arm and **all** of the lower body. The lymph is then drained into the **left brachiocephalic vein**.

The right of the body is served by the **right lymphatic duct**. This receives lymph from the right side of the head, neck and chest and the right arm. The lymph is then drained into the **right brachiocephalic** vein.

The brachiocephalic veins join to form the **superior vena cava**. This major vein carries the blood to the **heart**.

As well as the network of vessels, the lymphatic system also incorporates structures that comprise of **lymphatic tissue**.

The **tonsils**, located at the back of the throat, are small bodies of lymphatic tissue. They produce lymphocytes and are concerned with defence against bacterial infection. Their location makes them particularly effective in protecting against foreign substances that are inhaled or ingested.

There are also two major lymphatic glands – the **spleen** and the **thymus**.

The **spleen** is an oval shaped organ located to the left of the abdomen. It is the largest mass of **lymphatic tissue** in the body. It produces **lymphocytes** but has no connection to lymphatic vessels and so it is not involved in filtering lymph.

The spleen is highly vascular. It is connected to the circulatory system by the **splenic artery** and **splenic vein**. The spleen destroys and stores **red blood cells**, so acting as a reservoir for blood.

The **thymus** consists of two lobes located in the upper chest, between the sternum (breastbone) and the lungs. The outer layer is packed with **lymphocytes**. **T-cells**, produced in the bone marrow, migrate to the thymus for development.

The thymus is large in a child and produces lymphocytes. It reduces in size and function for adulthood, when many of its immunity functions are taken over by the spleen.

The thymus is a gland that secretes hormones, a feature that classifies it as an **endocrine** gland (see 'Endocrine System').

Common Conditions Affecting the Lymphatic System

As the lymphatic system plays a vital role in immunity, the presence of many conditions may be indicative of the inability of this system to offer sufficient resistance to infection and disease. Repeated infections and a low tolerance to stress may also suggest an immunity problem. Cancer that migrates to the lymphatic system is often terminal.

Mastitis, included in this package, and tonsillitis are conditions involving the inflammation of lymphatic tissue.

Questions – Lymphatic System (Answers: Page 383)

1. True or False?

    Lymphocytes are a type of leucocyte. They play a role in immunity.

2. Which type of lymphocyte produces antibodies?

3. What are the smallest lymph tubes called?

    a. lymph ducts
    b. lymphatic vessels
    c. lymphatic capillaries
    d. lymph trunks

4. What are formed when the lymphatic capillaries converge?

    a. lymph ducts
    b. lymphatic vessels
    c. lymph trunks

5. Which small, round structures, occurring at intervals along lymphatic vessels, are packed with lymphocytes?

6. Which of these lymphatic structures are the largest?

    a. lymph trunks
    b. lymph ducts

7. True or False?

   The left lymphatic duct (thoracic duct) drains lymph from the left side of the body into the left brachiocephalic vein. The right lymphatic duct drains lymph from the right side of the body into the right brachiocephalic vein. The brachiocephalic veins join to form the superior vena cava, which leads to the heart.

8. Which oval shaped organ is the largest mass of lymphatic tissue in the body?

9. The thymus is a lymphatic gland. Its outer layer is packed with lymphocytes. To which other body system does it belong due to the fact that it secretes hormones?

Muscular System

Muscle tissue is characterized by its ability to **contract**. There are over **600** muscles in the body, accounting for nearly half of the body weight. The muscles:

- ➤ enable **movement**
- ➤ provide a **supportive coverage** for the skeleton
- ➤ give the body **shape** and **contour**
- ➤ provide **strength**
- ➤ help to maintain body **temperature** (70% of the energy generated by the muscles is used for heat)

Muscles tend to be **narrower** at each **end** than in the middle or 'belly'. They are made up of individual muscle cells called **fibres**. Fibres are roughly **cylindrical** and vary in length. A number of fibres are bound together in **bundles**. A collection of bundles is then bound together in a **sheath**. **Nerve impulses**, generated in the brain or spinal column, stimulate their contraction.

The muscles have a **rich blood supply** to bring the necessary oxygen and nutrients. The venous return drains blood away from the muscles, removing carbon dioxide and toxins.

There are three main types of muscle tissue:

1. **Skeletal:** This type is mainly attached to **bones** (often using tendons). Skeletal muscles can **voluntarily** be made to **contract** and **relax**. As the muscle tissue contracts the muscle shortens. This creates a pull on the bone and causes movement. As the muscle tissue relaxes, the muscle returns to size and the pull on the bone is reduced. Skeletal muscle contains light and dark bands and is referred to as **striated**.

2. **Smooth:** This type is found in the **walls** of **hollow structures** such as blood vessels, the stomach and other internal organs. Smooth muscle tissue is also responsible for the ability of the hair on the skin to stand up. As the name suggests, this muscle type is **smooth** and doesn't have the bands found in striated skeletal muscle tissue. There is no conscious, voluntary control over smooth muscles. Their movement is **involuntary**.

3. **Cardiac:** This type of muscle tissue forms most of the **heart**. It is **striated** and its movement is **involuntary**.

We have said that most of the voluntary, striated **skeletal** muscles are **attached** to the skeleton. This skeletal attachment takes place at **both** ends of the muscle. One end of the skeletal muscle is attached to a bone that remains **unmoved**, or fixed, during its contraction. This is called the **origin**. The other end is attached to the bone that the muscle is **intended to move**. This is called the **insertion**.

For example, the **biceps** are the muscles that flex the arm. The biceps are attached by tendons to the scapula (shoulder blade) and the radius (a bone in the forearm). During the contraction of the biceps the scapula remains unmoved. The scapula is therefore the origin. The radius is the bone moved by the biceps. The radius is therefore the insertion.

Muscles are often categorized by the type of movement they produce. Most muscular actions can be remembered in **pairs** because one action is the **opposite** of the other. For example:

Flexors make a limb bend, **decreasing** the angle at a joint. **Extensors** have the opposite effect. Extensors cause extension, so **increasing** the angle at a joint.

Abductors move a bone **away** from the **midline**. **Adductors draw** a bone **closer** to the midline.

Levators produce an **upward** movement. **Depressors** produce a **downward** movement.

More specifically, the **supinator** moves the palm face upwards and the **pronator** turns the palm back down.

Muscular actions that do not have an opposing action include **rotators** and **sphincters**. Obviously, rotators allow the bones to rotate. Sphincters control the size of an opening.

The muscular structure of the body is very **complicated**. Muscles are often located on top of one another in **layers** or **overlap** at some point, and their origin and insertion points are usually hidden. Therefore, short of stripping them out one by one, whole muscles are rarely visible in any diagram. For the purposes of this package we'll look a few graphics showing, as far as possible, the location of the **major** muscles. We'll look at the anterior view of the body first, followed by posterior views.

Anterior View of Muscular System

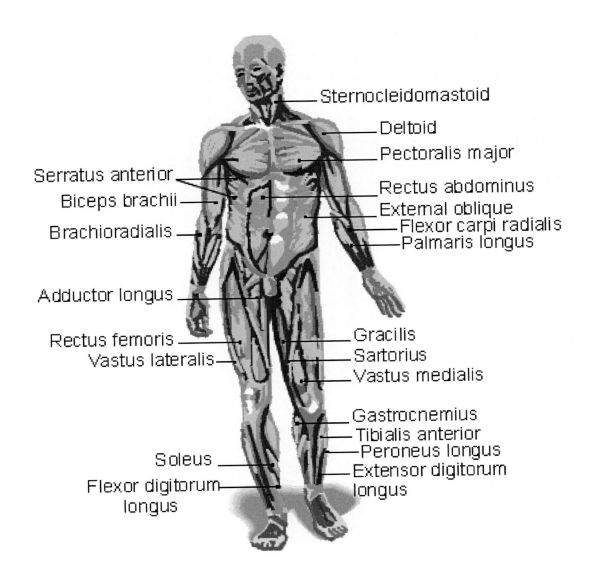

Sternocleidomastoid

Deltoid

Pectoralis major

Serratus anterior

Biceps brachii

Brachioradialis

Rectus abdominus

External oblique

Flexor carpi radialis

Palmaris longus

Adductor longus

Rectus femoris

Vastus lateralis

Gracilis

Sartorius

Vastus medialis

Gastrocnemius

Tibialis anterior

Peroneus longus

Extensor digitorum longus

Soleus

Flexor digitorum longus

Posterior View of Muscular System

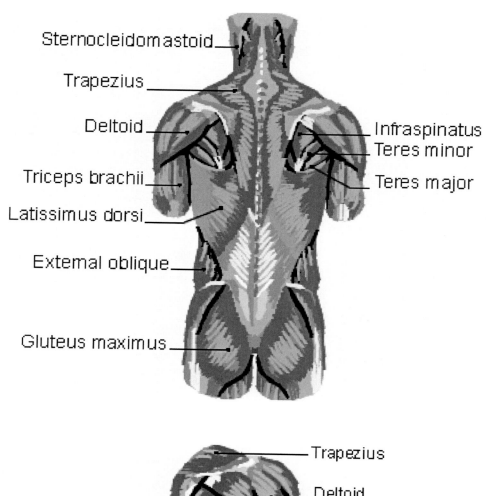

Sternocleidomastoid

Trapezius

Deltoid

Infraspinatus
Teres minor

Triceps brachii

Teres major

Latissimus dorsi

External oblique

Gluteus maximus

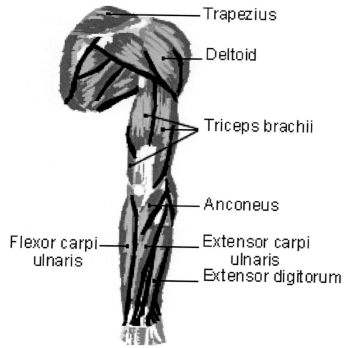

Trapezius

Deltoid

Triceps brachii

Anconeus

Flexor carpi ulnaris

Extensor carpi ulnaris
Extensor digitorum

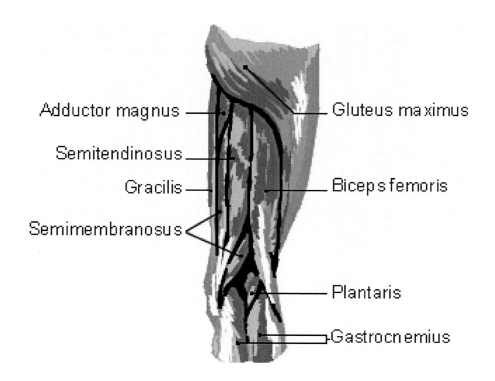

Adductor magnus ———
Gluteus maximus
Semitendinosus ———
Gracilis ———
Biceps femoris
Semimembranosus ———
Plantaris
Gastrocnemius

Common Conditions Affecting the Muscular System

In a healthy person, the muscles are very elastic and flexible. Voluntary muscles are quick to react, are accurate in movement and have sufficient strength to perform the required tasks. The muscles can lose this tone if the person's health deteriorates through injury or illness. In such cases exercises and massage can be of particular benefit as both help to increase muscle tone. Common conditions of the muscles include sprains, strains and spasms. Conditions involving the muscular system covered in this package include:

- Back pain
- Cramp
- Frozen shoulder
- Lumbago
- Muscular fatigue
- Parkinson's disease
- Tension

Questions – Muscular System (Answers: Page 384)

1. What ability has muscle tissue that distinguishes it from any other tissue type?

2. What type of muscle tissue is mainly attached to bones?

3. What type of muscle tissue is found in the walls of hollow structures?

4. Which muscle type can voluntarily be made to contract and relax?

   a. skeletal
   b. smooth
   c. cardiac

5. Where in the body can cardiac muscle be found?

6. Skeletal attachment takes place at both ends of the muscle. Which attachment is the origin?

   a. The attachment to the bone that remains unmoved during the muscular contraction.
   b. The attachment to the bone that the muscular contraction intends to move.

7. Muscle actions are often paired as they have opposing effects. Pair these actions by writing the appropriate letter alongside the opposing action.

a. flexors   adductors

b. abductors   depressors

c. levators   extensors

Cardiovascular System

The cardiovascular system is responsible for **transporting blood** to the body's tissues. The blood is pumped by the muscular contractions of the **heart** and travels around the body by means of a complicated network of blood **vessels**.

Blood is the body's transport medium, enabling substances to be carried around the body. The blood consists of:

Plasma
Over half of the blood is composed of plasma. Plasma is a straw-coloured fluid consisting of about **91% water** and **7% proteins** (including those needed for blood clotting). Plasma is responsible for transporting nutrients, salts, hormones, enzymes, gases and excretory products.

Red blood cells
Termed **erythrocytes**, red blood cells appear as bi-concave discs and are produced in the red bone marrow. Their primary function is to **transport** the **gases** of respiration. This is possible as they contain **haemoglobin**. Haemoglobin contains a protein (globin) and a pigment containing iron. Old and worn out erythrocytes are destroyed in the liver and spleen.

White blood cells
Termed **leucocytes**, white blood cells are produced in the bone marrow. There are a number of forms, including lymphocytes. They play an important role in **immunity**.

Platelets
Also called **thrombocytes**, platelets are fragments of cytoplasm (the substance that surrounds a cell's organelles) enclosed by a membrane. When they come into contact with damaged tissue they release chemicals that start a chain of reactions to form a **blood clot**.

The blood has a number of functions. It:

> - delivers oxygen and nutrients to the cells
> - removes carbon dioxide and other toxic waste from the cells
> - transports enzymes and hormones
> - transports heat
> - maintains the body's pH (level of alkalinity/acidity)
> - protects against disease
> - protects against blood loss by producing clots when necessary

The blood is only able to perform its many functions if it is pumped around the body.

The **heart** performs this role. The heart is suspended by ligaments and is located between the lungs, slightly to the left of the midline in the upper thorax. It receives its own blood supply from the **coronary arteries**.

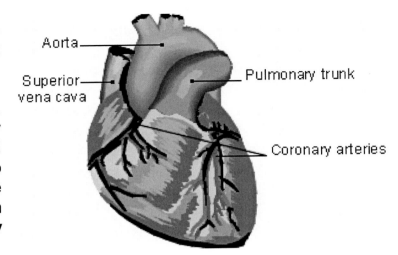

The middle layer of the heart is called the **myocardium**, or heart muscle. The specialized muscle fibres of the myocardium allow the heart to 'beat' in response to **nerve impulses**. As the nerve impulses travel through the heart, **electrical impulses** are generated which result in its **rhythmical contraction** and **relaxation**.

The heart pumps **deoxygenated** (without oxygen) blood to the **lungs** via the **pulmonary arteries**.

It receives **oxygenated** blood back from the lungs through the **pulmonary veins**.

This oxygenated blood is then pumped out of the heart from the **aorta** and circulated around the body.

The deoxygenated blood is received back from the body tissues via the **superior** and **inferior vena cava**.

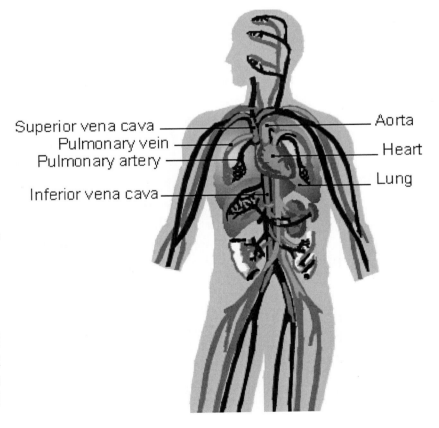

283

Internally, the heart is comprised of **four** chambers. The **upper** chambers are called **atriums**. The **lower** chambers are called **ventricles**. The **septum** divides the left and right sides of the heart, keeping the oxygenated and deoxygenated blood separate.

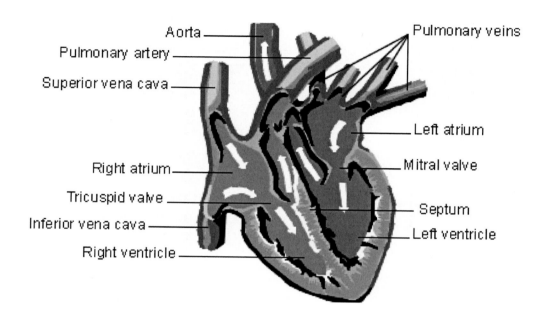

The heart receives **deoxygenated** blood from the body tissues via the superior and inferior vena cava. This deoxygenated blood enters the **right atrium** and passes through the tricuspid valve to the **right ventricle**.

The deoxygenated blood leaves the right ventricle and is transported to the **lungs** in the **pulmonary arteries**.

Oxygenated blood is brought back from the lungs in the **pulmonary veins**.

The oxygenated blood from the pulmonary veins is received in the **left atrium**. This blood passes through the mitral valve to the **left ventricle**.

The left ventricle is the largest, most muscular chamber as it is responsible for pumping the oxygenated blood around the whole body. The oxygenated blood leaves the heart via the aorta.

Blood is transported around the whole body by means of an extensive network of blood **vessels**. There are three main types:

Arteries

Arteries take blood **away** from the heart (memory hint: **A**rteries – **A**way). They have a thick middle layer consisting of smooth **muscle**. This allows them to withstand the pressures resulting from the pumping of the heart. Arteries contain **oxygenated** blood. The **exception** to this is the **pulmonary arteries**. The pulmonary arteries take deoxygenated blood from the heart to the lungs.

Veins

Veins take blood **back** to the heart. Venous blood is under **less pressure** than arterial blood. To prevent the back-flow of blood, most veins contain **valves**. Veins contain **deoxygenated** blood. The **exception** is the **pulmonary veins**. The pulmonary veins take oxygenated blood from the lungs to the heart.

Capillaries

Capillaries are **tiny**, **thin walled** vessels that make up dense networks. Arteries divide many times until they become capillaries. The capillaries allow nutrients, gases and excretory products to be **exchanged** between the blood and the tissue fluid. Capillaries merge many times until they become veins.

Common Conditions Affecting the Cardiovascular System

An adequate blood supply to the tissues is vital for maintaining health. Any disorders of the heart can obviously have serious consequences, as can any disease of the blood or its vessels. Common conditions affecting, or affected by, the cardiovascular system include angina pectoris (pain due to an inadequate blood supply to the myocardium), arteriosclerosis (hardening of the arteries) and disease of the heart valves. Conditions involving this system covered here include:

> ➢ Chilblains
> ➢ Cramp
> ➢ Diabetes
> ➢ Heart attack
> ➢ Hypertension
> ➢ Hypotension
> ➢ Oedema
> ➢ Palpitations
> ➢ Raynaud's disease
> ➢ Stroke
> ➢ Varicose veins

Questions – Cardiovascular System (Answers: Page 385)

1. What straw-coloured fluid makes up more than half of the blood?

2. What are erythrocytes?

   a. red blood cells
   b. white blood cells
   c. platelets

3. Which components of the blood transport the gases of respiration?

   a. red blood cells
   b. white blood cells
   c. platelets

4. Which components of the blood play an important role in immunity?

   a. red blood cells
   b. white blood cells
   c. platelets

5. Which components of the blood, also called thrombocytes, are involved in the blood clotting process?

6. What is the middle, muscular layer of the heart called?

7. Which arteries supply blood to the heart tissue?

8. The heart receives oxygenated blood from the lungs via the pulmonary veins. Through which major artery does the oxygenated blood leave the heart to be circulated around the body?

9. As oxygenated blood travels around the body, oxygen is absorbed from it and used by the tissues. Deoxygenated blood is then returned to the heart. Through which vessels does the heart receive deoxygenated blood?

10. How many chambers are there in the heart?

11. Which are the upper chambers of the heart?

   a. atriums
   b. ventricles

12. True or False?

   Deoxygenated blood is on the right side of the heart. Oxygenated blood is in the left side of the heart. It is kept separate by the septum.

13. Which chamber receives deoxygenated blood?

    a. right atrium
    b. right ventricle
    c. left atrium
    d. left ventricle

14. Deoxygenated blood leaves the right atrium and passes through the tricuspid valve. Into which chamber is it received?

15. Deoxygenated blood leaves the right ventricle and is taken to the lungs. Which vessels take deoxygenated blood to the lungs?

    a. superior and inferior vena cava
    b. pulmonary arteries
    c. pulmonary veins

16. Blood is oxygenated in the lungs. Which vessels bring the oxygenated blood back to the heart?

17. Which chamber receives oxygenated blood from the pulmonary veins?

    a. right atrium
    b. right ventricle
    c. left atrium
    d. left ventricle

18. Oxygenated blood leaves the left atrium and passes through the mitral valve. Into which chamber is it received?

19. Oxygenated blood leaves the left ventricle to be circulated around the body. Which major artery takes the oxygenated blood from the left ventricle?

20. Which vessels take blood away from the heart?

    a. arteries
    b. veins
    c. capillaries

21. Which vessels take blood back to the heart?

    a. arteries
    b. veins
    c. capillaries

22. Which vessels have valves to help to prevent the back-flow of blood?

    a. arteries
    b. veins
    c. capillaries

23. Which are the smallest blood vessels?

    a. arteries
    b. veins
    c. capillaries

Digestive System

The body is reliant on the intake of **food** for energy and nutrients. However, ingested food must be **broken down** both **mechanically** and **chemically** before the body can use it. The process in which food is broken down by the body is called **digestion**.

Digestion is one of the functions of the **digestive system**. The digestive system contains the organs involved in taking food into the body (ingestion), transporting it to the appropriate location, breaking it down (digestion), absorbing the required components (absorption) and eliminating waste products (elimination). Anatomically, the digestive system runs from mouth to anus, a route that is commonly called the **alimentary canal**. We'll look at this route now.

Food is taken into the body via the **mouth**. It is here that the first stage of mechanical and chemical digestion begins. Mechanically, the **teeth** and the **tongue** manipulate the food. Chemically, the three pairs of **salivary glands** secrete **saliva** into the mouth. Saliva is alkaline and consists mainly of **water** to moisten the food, but it also contains an enzyme called **salivary amylase**. Salivary amylase begins the breakdown of **starches**. The digestive processes in the mouth create a round mass of food called a **bolus**. The bolus is then **swallowed**.

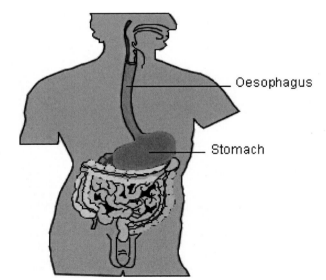

On swallowing, the bolus leaves the mouth and passes into the **pharynx** (throat). It passes the entrance to the trachea, which is covered during swallowing by the epiglottis, and moves into the **oesophagus**. Food is helped down the oesophagus by waves of muscular contraction called **peristalsis**. The oesophagus takes the bolus to the **stomach**.

The stomach is a 'J' shaped **muscular sac**, located under the diaphragm to the left of the abdomen.

It holds food received from the oesophagus for 2-6 hours before expelling it via the **pyloric sphincter** into the **duodenum**.

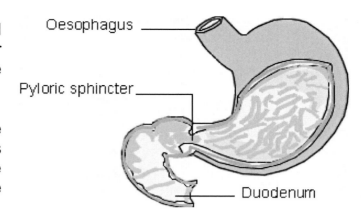

The stomach can hold about 1.5 litres and is the site of digestion, both mechanical and chemical. Mechanically, the peristaltic 'churning' of the stomach mixes the food. Chemically, the stomach is an **acidic** environment in which a number of **gastric juices** are secreted to break down the food.

The secretion of gastric juices is a **reflex action** that begins when food is in the mouth and continues when it enters the stomach. The gastric juices include:

Secretion	Action
Mucus	Protects the delicate inner lining of the stomach.
Hydrochloric acid	Kills bacteria. Neutralizes saliva. Inhibits the secretion of gastrin. Acts on pepsinogen.
Pepsinogen (enzyme)	On contact with hydrochloric acid, pepsinogen is converted to pepsin, a protein-digesting enzyme.
Rennin (enzyme)	Coagulates the milk protein casein.
Intrinsic factor	Allows the absorption of vitamin B12.
Gastrin (hormone)	Stimulates the secretion of hydrochloric acid and pepsinogen. Increases the muscular activity of the stomach. Relaxes the pyloric sphincter.

The digestive processes that take place in the stomach create a **semi-fluid** mixture of food and gastric juices called **chyme**. With the exception of some water and certain drugs (including alcohol), very few components of the chyme are absorbed from the stomach into the blood. The chyme leaves the stomach via the **pyloric sphincter** and enters the **duodenum**.

The duodenum is the first part of the **small intestine**.

The small intestine consists of a convoluted muscular passageway about 6 metres long. This passageway runs from the pyloric sphincter to the ileocaecal sphincter at the entrance to the large intestine.

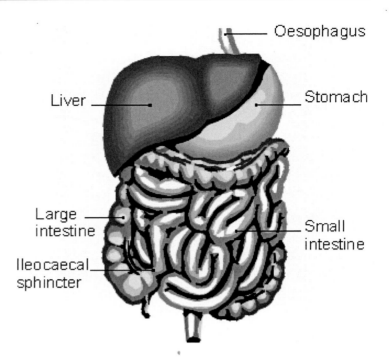

The **duodenum** is the **shortest** part. After about 25cm it runs into the **middle** part of the small intestine called the **jejunum**. The jejunum, about 2.5 metres long, then becomes the **ileum**. The ileum is the **longest** section, running for about 3.5 metres before joining the large intestine.

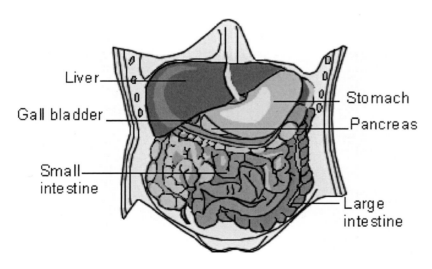

Digestion continues in the **small intestine**.

The small intestine produces alkaline intestinal juice. The epithelial cells produce **enzymes** that continue the digestive process.

However, successful digestion also depends on secretions from the **pancreas**, **liver** and **gall bladder**. We'll look at these organs next.

Pancreas

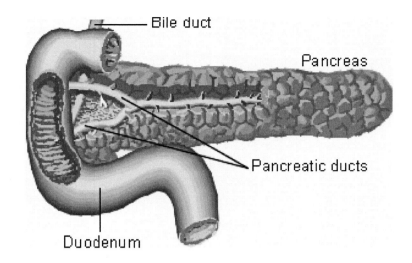

The pancreas is located below and slightly behind the stomach. It is 12-15cm long.

Digestive enzymes secreted by the pancreas are introduced into the **duodenum** via two pancreatic ducts.

Pancreatic juice is a clear liquid consisting mostly of water, some salts and several enzymes. The enzymes include **pancreatic amylase** (for digesting carbohydrates), **trypsin** (to digest proteins) and **lipase** (to digest fats).

The pancreas is made up of small clusters of glandular epithelial cells. About **99%** of these cells are arranged in clusters called **acini**. The acini are responsible for producing the **pancreatic juice**. As the pancreatic juice is secreted via a **duct** to the **epithelial** surface of the duodenum, the pancreas is classified as an **exocrine** gland.

In the remaining **1%** of the pancreas, the cells are arranged in clusters called **islets of Langerhans**. These clusters secrete **hormones** directly (not via a duct) into the **blood**. This also classifies the pancreas as an **endocrine** gland (see 'Endocrine System').

Liver

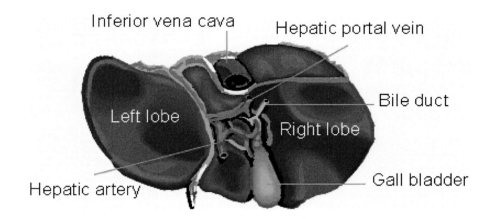

The liver is the **heaviest** gland in the body. The graphic above shows the posterior view. It is located to the right of the upper abdominal cavity, just below the diaphragm. The liver consists of two main lobes and two smaller lobes, each made up of millions of smaller lobules.

The liver is highly vascular because its main function is to regulate the composition of the blood. Its blood supply is therefore different to any other part of the body.

As you would expect, the liver receives oxygenated blood. The **oxygenated** blood is supplied by the **hepatic artery**.

The liver also receives **deoxygenated** blood from the **stomach** and **intestines**. This **deoxygenated** blood is received from the **hepatic portal vein**. Harmful substances, absorbed from the stomach and intestines into the blood, are extracted from the blood by the liver and destroyed.

The **inferior vena cava** then transports the blood from the liver back to the heart.

The liver **produces** and **secretes bile**.

Bile is partially an excretory product and partially a digestive secretion. It consists of salts, pigments, cholesterol and traces of other substances. The bile is drained from the liver and stored in the **gall bladder**.

The liver has many other functions. The liver:

> maintains the blood-sugar level
> stores and breaks down fats
> metabolizes proteins
> manufactures some of the proteins of blood plasma
> manufactures some of the blood clotting factors
> manufactures vitamin A from carotene
> stores vitamins and iron
> detoxifies or excretes drugs and poisons
> inactivates certain hormones
> destroys worn out blood cells
> produces heat

Gall bladder

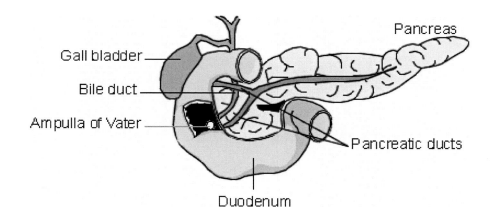

As we have mentioned **bile**, produced by the liver, is stored in the **gall bladder**. The gall bladder is a small **sac** located behind the liver. The gall bladder adds **mucus** to the bile and increases its **concentration** by absorbing some water from it.

When the bile is required, the gall bladder contracts and bile is released into the bile duct. The bile duct joins a pancreatic duct and they enter the duodenum together at the **ampulla of Vater**. Bile plays a role in the **emulsification** of **fats**, breaking down the large fat globules into smaller ones. It also helps to **lubricate** the intestines.

Let's recap on the digestive process covered so far:

In the mouth, the food is mechanically digested by the teeth and tongue, and chemically digested by the saliva. After swallowing, the peristaltic action of the oesophagus takes the food to the stomach where it is churned and chemically digested by the gastric juices. Chyme leaves the stomach via the pyloric sphincter and enters the duodenum. The duodenum is the first part of the small intestine. Here, pancreatic juice and bile are added to the intestinal secretions.

As the chyme moves through the small intestine, the digestion of many substances is completed. The molecules produced can be **absorbed** into the **blood** and used by the body.

For successful **absorption**, there must be a good **blood supply** to absorb the nutrients, and a **large surface area** to give sufficient opportunity for the process to take place. The **small intestine** is ideally suited and is the site where **most** absorption occurs.

The small intestine receives a good blood supply from the **superior mesenteric artery** and structurally it offers a large surface area. Not only is the small intestine **long**, but its inner layer extends into numerous finger-like projections called **villi**. Each villus contains a network of **capillaries** and a **lacteal** (a lymphatic vessel) to facilitate absorption. Nutrients are absorbed through the epithelial lining of the small intestine into the blood.

The small intestine leads, via the ileocaecal sphincter, to the **large intestine**.

The large intestine is about **1.5 metres** long. It is much **wider** than the small intestine and does **not** have villi.

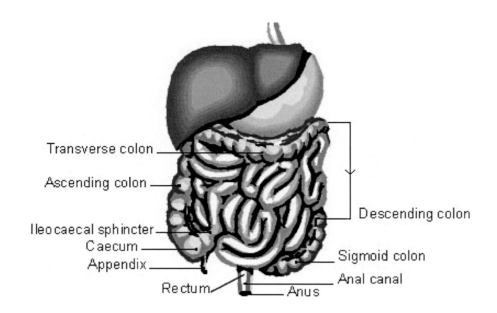

The large intestine incorporates the caecum, ascending colon, transverse colon, descending colon, sigmoid colon, rectum and anal canal. It terminates at the anus. The appendix is also a part of the large intestine but it does not perform a digestive function.

The large intestine receives the remaining chyme from the small intestine. It continues the **absorption** of water and nutrients from the digested food and prepares undigested food and waste for expulsion as **faeces**.

The large intestine secretes **mucus** but not enzymes. It does, however, contain **bacteria** that ferment any remaining carbohydrates and release **gases**. The bacteria also break down any remaining proteins. The bacterial processes produce vitamin K and some B vitamins that are required for normal metabolism. Some of the substances produced in the large intestine are **absorbed** and the rest are incorporated in the faeces.

The solid or semi-solid faeces are passed through the sphincters at the top and bottom of the **anal canal** and are expelled through the **anus**. The expulsion of the faeces completes the mouth to anus digestive process.

Common Conditions Affecting the Digestive System

The digestive system contains many differing organs. Therefore, there are a variety of conditions affecting, or affected by, the digestive system including colitis (inflammation of the colon) and Crohn's disease (inflammation of a part of the ileum). Conditions involving the digestive system included in this package include:

> ➢ Cancer
> ➢ Constipation
> ➢ Diabetes
> ➢ Diarrhoea
> ➢ Heartburn
> ➢ Hiatus hernia
> ➢ Indigestion
> ➢ Irritable bowel syndrome
> ➢ Nausea
> ➢ Stress
> ➢ Ulcer

298

Questions – Digestive System (Answers: Page 387)

1. What term is given to the digestive tract that runs from 'mouth to anus'?

    a. elementary canal
    b. digestive channel
    c. alimentary canal

2. Saliva contains the enzyme salivary amylase. Which food type does salivary amylase begin to break down?

    a. proteins
    b. starches
    c. roughage
    d. fats

3. On swallowing, the food leaves the mouth as a round mass called a bolus. Into which structure does it pass?

    a. pharynx
    b. oesophagus
    c. stomach
    d. trachea

4. Fill in the missing word:

    The food passes the entrance to the trachea, which is covered during swallowing by the epiglottis, and moves into the _____ .

5.   What type of environment does the stomach provide for digestion?

   a. acidic
   b. alkaline
   c. neutral

6.   Which of the following is NOT secreted in the gastric juices?

   a. rennin
   b. gastrin
   c. trypsin
   d. pepsinogen

7.   Through which opening does the food leave the stomach?

8.   Fill in the missing word:

   Chyme passes from the stomach, through the pyloric sphincter, into the
   _____.

9.   The small intestine runs from the stomach to the large intestine. It has
   three parts. Starting at the stomach, in which order do they occur?

   a. ileum, duodenum, jejunum
   b. jejunum, duodenum, ileum
   c. duodenum, ileum, jejunum
   d. duodenum, jejunum, ileum

300

10. All of the following are enzymes secreted in the pancreatic juice. Which pancreatic enzyme digests fats?

    a. lipase
    b. pancreatic amylase
    c. trypsin

11. Which pancreatic cells produce the pancreatic juice?

    a. acini
    b. islets of Langerhans

12. What is secreted by the islets of Langerhans?

    a. enzymes
    b. hormones
    c. gastric juice
    d. pancreatic amylase

13. Which vessel supplies oxygenated blood to the liver?

    a. hepatic artery
    b. hepatic portal vein
    c. inferior vena cava

14. Which vessel takes deoxygenated blood away from the liver to the heart?

    a. hepatic artery
    b. hepatic portal vein
    c. inferior vena cava

15. The hepatic portal vein delivers deoxygenated blood to the liver. Where does this deoxygenated blood come from?

16. What is produced and secreted by the liver and then stored in the gall bladder?

17. Bile is released from the gall bladder via the bile duct. Where does the bile duct join the small intestine?

    a. duodenum
    b. jejunum
    c. ileum

18. Which food component does bile break down?

    a. carbohydrates
    b. proteins
    c. fats

19. What finger-like projections give the small intestine a large surface area for absorption?

20. Fill in the missing word:

    The small intestine leads, via the _____ sphincter, to the large intestine.

21. True or False?

Like the small intestine, the large intestine has villi to aid absorption.

Endocrine System

The endocrine system consists of **ductless glands** that secrete **hormones** directly into the blood.

A comparison must be drawn here between endocrine glands and exocrine glands. Exocrine glands make their secretions via a duct onto epithelial surfaces such as those in body cavities. Endocrine glands secrete hormones into the spaces between the cells. This enables the hormones to diffuse directly into the capillaries to be carried away in the blood.

A hormone is a **chemical messenger**. There are over **50** hormones that control many body functions such as growth, metabolism and sexual development. Most hormones are released in short bursts. The release of hormones is stimulated or inhibited by signals from the nervous system, chemical changes in the blood or levels of other hormones.

The 'master' of the endocrine system is the **hypothalamus**. The hypothalamus is located at the **base** of the **brain**. The hypothalamus performs many functions. It:

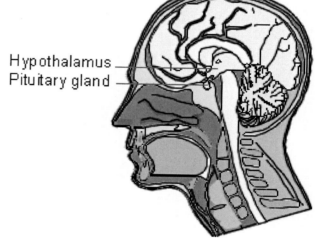

Hypothalamus
Pituitary gland

➢ controls the autonomic nervous system
➢ governs many of the body's activities
➢ governs many of the body's 'drives' (e.g. hunger, thirst and sexual behaviour)
➢ influences emotions
➢ receives sensory information from the external and internal environments

The ability of the hypothalamus to **secrete hormones** is crucial to its regulatory roles. The hormones produced by the hypothalamus travel in the blood to the **pituitary gland**. Here they are either stored and secreted as needed, or they act to release or inhibit hormones produced by the pituitary gland itself.

The pituitary gland is located just **beneath** the hypothalamus. It is the size of a large pea. It has two main portions – the **anterior** lobe and the **posterior** lobe.

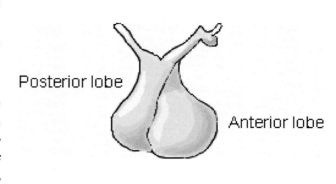

Posterior lobe

Anterior lobe

Some of the hormones secreted by the pituitary gland stimulate or inhibit the release of hormones from **other** endocrine glands. This capability of the pituitary to **control other** endocrine glands makes it a key player in the endocrine system.

The **posterior** lobe of the pituitary gland does not produce hormones. It does, however, **store** and **release** two hormones **produced** by the **hypothalamus**. They are:

1. **Oxytocin** – stimulates the contraction of the uterine muscles during birth and milk ejection after birth. During childbirth and suckling, the uterus and breasts send sensory messages to the hypothalamus. The hypothalamus then sends nerve impulses to the pituitary to release the hormone.

2. **Antidiuretic hormone** (vasopressin) – decreases urine production and causes the contraction of the arteries. Its release is triggered by dehydration. A reduced concentration in the blood is detected in the hypothalamus, which stimulates the pituitary to release this hormone.

The **anterior** lobe of the pituitary gland **produces** and releases **six** major hormones:

1. **Growth hormone** (somatotrophin) – controls body growth
2. **Prolactin** – stimulates the mammary glands to produce milk
3. **Adrenocorticotrophic hormone** – stimulates secretions from the adrenals
4. **Thyroid stimulating hormone** – controls secretions from the thyroid
5. **Gonadotrophic hormones** (e.g. follicle stimulating hormone and luteinizing hormone) – stimulate the activities of the ovaries and testes
6. **Melanocyte stimulating hormone** – stimulates the production of melanin (a pigment found in the skin and hair)

The release of these **anterior** lobe hormones is controlled by the **hypothalamus**.

The hypothalamus continually **monitors** the **blood** for **levels** of **anterior** lobe hormones. When a level **falls**, the **hypothalamus** secretes an appropriate **releasing** hormone. This hormone is **transported** to the **anterior** lobe of the pituitary, where it **stimulates** the **release** of the hormone.

The **increased** level in the blood is then **detected**. As a result, the hypothalamus secretes an appropriate **inhibiting** hormone. When it is received in the pituitary the release of the anterior lobe hormone is **inhibited** and the level in the blood **decreases**. The cycle then continues.

We'll now take a look at the other main endocrine glands: the thyroid gland, parathyroid glands, adrenals, pancreas, ovaries, testes, pineal gland and thymus.

Thyroid Gland

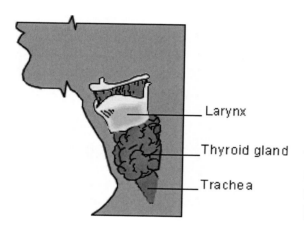

The thyroid gland is located just **below** the **larynx**. There are **two** main lobes, one either side of the trachea.

Under the influence of **thyroid stimulating hormone** (secreted from the anterior lobe of the pituitary gland), the thyroid removes iodine from the blood and produces, stores and secretes hormones. The main thyroid hormone is **thyroxine**.

The thyroid hormones regulate **growth** and **development**. They also control **metabolic rate** and the activity of the **nervous system**.

Parathyroid Glands

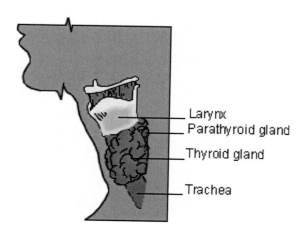

There are **four** small, oval parathyroid glands attached to the **rear** surface of the **thyroid**.

These glands produce **parathyroid hormone**. Parathyroid hormone **decreases** the blood **phosphate** level and **increases** the blood **calcium** level.

Adrenal Glands

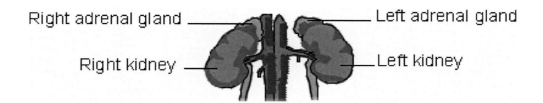

Right adrenal gland _____ _____ Left adrenal gland

Right kidney _____ _____ Left kidney

There are **two** adrenal glands, one on **top** of each **kidney**. They are sometimes called suprarenal glands (supra- = over, renal = kidney).

The **outer** layer is called the **adrenal cortex**. The **inner** layer is called the **adrenal medulla**.

The **adrenal medulla** produces the two 'fight or flight' hormones, released when the body is under **stress** to help it cope and prepare for an emergency.

1. **adrenaline** - causes an increase in metabolic rate, heart rate and blood pressure. This accounts for 80% of secretions from the adrenals.

2. **noradrenaline** - a neurotransmitter (a substance that either excites or inhibits adjacent nerve or muscle cells)

The **adrenal cortex** is rich in **vitamin C** and **cholesterol**. It secretes:

1. **cortisol** and **corticosterone** - stimulate the conversion of fats and proteins to glucose

2. **aldosterone** - controls sodium and potassium concentrations

3. **androgens** and **oestrogens** - male and female sex hormones

Pancreas

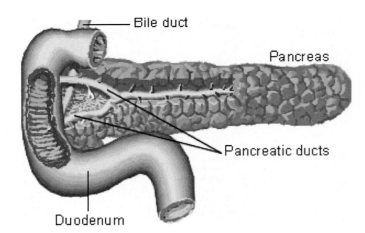

Bile duct

Pancreas

Pancreatic ducts

Duodenum

The pancreas is located below and slightly behind the stomach. It is 12-15cm long.

About **99%** of the pancreatic tissue is involved in producing **digestive enzymes** (see 'Digestive System') that are released into the digestive tract via a duct. This function classifies the pancreas as an **exocrine** gland. It is, however, also an endocrine gland…

The cells in the remaining **1%** of the pancreas are arranged in clusters called **islets of Langerhans**. These clusters secrete **hormones** into the **blood**, classifying the pancreas as an **endocrine** gland.

The pancreas secretes two hormones that are responsible for regulating the blood-glucose level:

1. **insulin** – decreases the blood-glucose level

2. **glucagon** – increases the blood-glucose level

Ovaries

The **ovaries** are the principal structures of the female reproductive system (see 'Reproductive System'). They are classified as endocrine glands as they secrete:

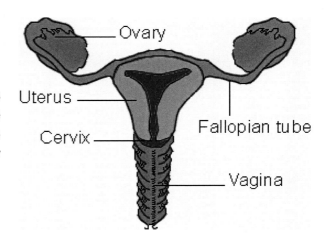

1. **oestrogen** - female sex hormone concerned with the development and maintenance of the reproductive system and the development of secondary sex characteristics.

2. **progesterone** - female sex hormone produced in the ovaries after ovulation. It helps to prepare the uterus for the implantation of the fertilized ovum, develops the placenta and prepares the mammary glands for milk secretion.

3. **inhibin** - inhibits the secretion of follicle stimulating hormone towards the end of the menstrual cycle.

4. **relaxin** - dilates the cervix and helps the pelvic girdle to widen during childbirth.

Testes

The **testes** are the principal structures of the male reproductive system (see 'Reproductive System'). They are classified as endocrine glands as they secrete:

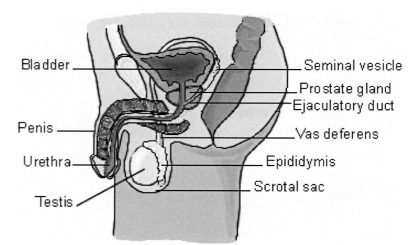

1. **testosterone** - the primary male sex hormone. It controls the growth and maintenance of the reproductive system and the development of secondary sex characteristics. It also stimulates the production of sperm and body growth.

2. **inhibin** - inhibits the secretion of follicle stimulating hormone to control sperm production.

Pineal Gland

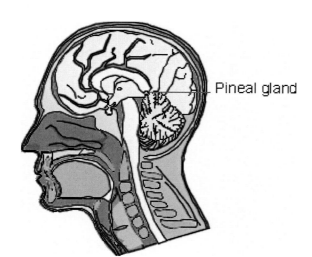

The pineal gland is attached to the roof of the third cerebral ventricle in the brain.

During **darkness**, the pineal gland secretes **melatonin**. This hormone is thought to induce sleep and inhibit sexual activity.

Thymus Gland

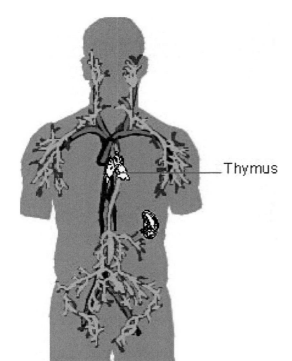

Thymus

The **thymus** consists of two lobes located in the upper chest, between the sternum (breastbone) and the lungs. It has a role to play in **immunity** (see 'Lymphatic System') as well as being an endocrine gland.

The thymus secretes a number of **thymus stimulating hormones**. As this collective name suggests, these hormones stimulate their originating gland. In stimulating itself, the thymus promotes its main role of maturating T-cell lymphocytes.

Common Conditions Affecting the Endocrine System

Conditions of the endocrine system may be as a result of hormonal imbalance or disease of an associated gland. Conditions involving the endocrine system covered in this package include:

- Amenorrhoea
- Anxiety
- Cancer
- Depression
- Diabetes
- Fever
- Hyperthyroidism
- Hypothyroidism
- Irregular ovulation
- Female infertility
- Mastitis
- Menopause
- Menorrhagia
- Ovarian cysts
- Panic attacks
- Pre-menstrual tension
- Seasonal affective disorder

Questions – Endocrine System (Answers: Page 389)

1. True or False?

   Endocrine glands are ductless and secrete hormones which pass directly into the blood.

2. Fill in the missing word:

   The hypothalamus is the 'master' of the endocrine system. Hormones secreted by the hypothalamus are released into the blood and taken to the _____ gland where they are either stored or secreted as needed.

3. Which lobe of the pituitary gland does not produce its own hormones, but stores and releases hormones produced by the hypothalamus?

   a. anterior
   b. posterior

4. Which posterior lobe pituitary hormone decreases urine production and causes the contraction of the arteries?

   a. oxytocin
   b. antidiuretic hormone

5. The anterior lobe of the pituitary gland produces its own hormones. Which of these anterior lobe hormones stimulates secretions from the adrenals?

    a. growth hormone (somatotrophin)
    b. prolactin
    c. adrenocorticotrophic hormone
    d. thyroid stimulating hormone
    e. gonadotrophic hormones
    f. melanocyte stimulating hormone

6. Which of these anterior lobe pituitary gland hormones stimulate the activities of the ovaries and testes?

    a. growth hormone (somatotrophin)
    b. prolactin
    c. adrenocorticotrophic hormone
    d. thyroid stimulating hormone
    e. gonadotrophic hormones
    f. melanocyte stimulating hormone

7. Which hormone stimulates the mammary glands to produce milk?

    a. growth hormone (somatotrophin)
    b. prolactin
    c. adrenocorticotrophic hormone
    d. thyroid stimulating hormone
    e. gonadotrophic hormones
    f. melanocyte stimulating hormone

8. The anterior lobe pituitary hormones are produced and released by the pituitary gland, but what structure controls their release?

9. What hormone, produced by the anterior lobe of the pituitary gland, stimulates the thyroid gland?

10. What is the main hormone produced by the thyroid gland?

11. How many parathyroid glands are there attached to the rear surface of the thyroid?

12. Which part of the adrenal gland produces the 'fight or flight' hormones?

    a. adrenal cortex
    b. adrenal medulla

13. Name one of the two 'fight or flight' hormones.

14. True or False?

    The adrenal cortex is rich in vitamin C and cholesterol but it does not secrete hormones.

15. True or False?

    Most of the pancreas is involved in secreting hormones.

16. Which pancreatic hormone decreases the blood-glucose level?

17. Which ovarian hormone is concerned with the development and maintenance of the reproductive system and the development of secondary sex characteristics?

18. Which ovarian hormone is produced after ovulation and helps to prepare the uterus for the implantation of the fertilized ovum?

    a. progesterone
    b. inhibin
    c. relaxin

19. Which ovarian hormone dilates the cervix during childbirth?

    a. progesterone
    b. inhibin
    c. relaxin

20. What is the primary male sex hormone produced by the testes?

21. What hormone, secreted by the ovaries in females and the testes in males, inhibits the secretion of follicle stimulating hormone?

Nervous System

The nervous system is the name given to the collection of nerve cells that receive, transmit and respond to stimuli from the external and internal environments.

The nervous system has three main functions:

1. **Senses changes** in the body or outside of the body.

2. **Analyzes** these **changes**, stores information if necessary, and decides how to respond.

3. **Responds** by either creating muscle movement or by inducing glandular secretions.

Nerve **cells** are specialized to be able to **transmit nerve impulses** and are called **neurons**. There are two types, sensory neurons and motor neurons. The main structural difference between a sensory neuron and a motor neuron is the position of the cell body (see below).

As the name suggests, **sensory** neurons transmit information **received** from the **sensory** organs. They carry information about the internal or external stimulus. They are also called **afferent** neurons.

Sensory (afferent) neuron

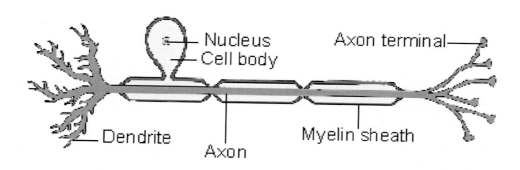

Motor neurons transmit information to the part of the body that has to **respond** to the sensory stimulus. They stimulate the muscle to contract or the gland to make its secretions. They are also called **efferent** neurons.

Motor (efferent) neuron

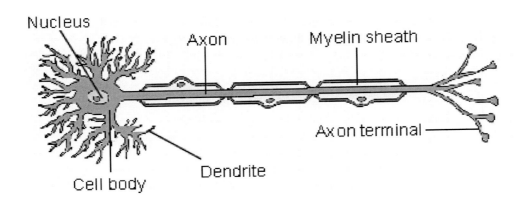

The **dendrites receive** the **nerve impulses**. The impulses are then carried away by the long **axon**. The **axon terminal** of one neuron contacts with the **dendrites** of another at a **junction** called a **synapse**. A chemical **neurotransmitter** called **dopamine** allows the nerve impulse to be **transmitted** across the synapse, so allowing the message to be conveyed.

All components of the nervous system are made up from neurons.

The **axon** of a neuron is also referred to as a **nerve fibre**. When nerve fibres occur in **bundles**, surrounded by a protective covering, they are referred to as a **nerve**.

A group of nerve **cell bodies**, usually bound by a sheath, is referred to as a **ganglion**.

317

The nervous system as a whole, consists of the **central nervous system** and the **peripheral nervous system**.

We'll look at the central nervous system first.

The central nervous system consists of the **brain** and the **spinal cord**.

The central nervous system **receives sensory** information from **all** parts of the body.

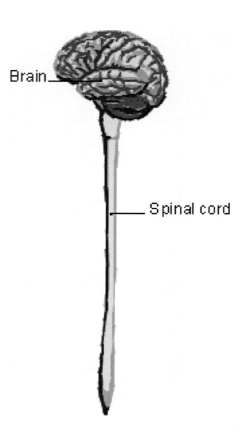

Brain

Spinal cord

On receipt of this information, the central nervous system **analyzes** the information. Thoughts, emotions and memories are generated and stored.

The central nervous system usually **responds** to nerve impulses by **stimulating** muscles or glands, so creating an appropriate **response** to the original stimulus.

The **brain** is the most highly developed part of the nervous system and is protected by the skull. The brain is surrounded by three membranes, known collectively as the **meninges**. **Cerebrospinal fluid** exists between the inner two layers to further protect and nourish the brain.

The brain is highly **vascular**. A vast network of arteries supplies the brain with blood. The main artery is the **carotid**, and the external and internal **jugulars** are the principal veins.

Twelve pairs of cranial nerves originate from the brain. Most of them supply the sensory organs and muscles in the head, but some do extend to other parts of the body. For example, the tenth cranial nerve is the vagus nerve. The vagus nerve serves the larynx, pharynx, liver, spleen, lungs, pancreas, heart and oesophagus. Please note that the cranial nerves are not a part of the central nervous system. They are included in the peripheral nervous system (see later).

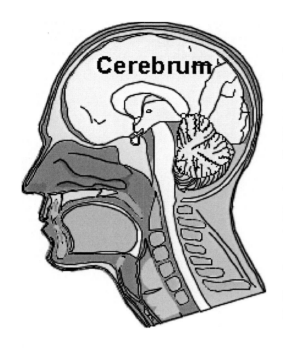

The most prominent region of the brain is the **cerebrum**.

It is the site of functions such as vision, hearing, touch, smell, voluntary muscle activity, speech and memory.

The cerebrum consists of two cerebral **hemispheres**, joined by a band of nerve fibres.

The outer layer of the hemispheres is the **grey matter**. This surrounds the inner **white matter**.

Each cerebral hemisphere has **four** lobes.

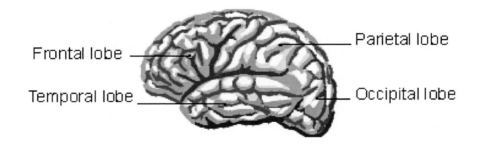

Frontal lobe: Used in the planning and execution of activities. Sends messages through the efferent nerves to the muscles. Controls facial and neck muscles, voluntary eye movement and speech.

Parietal lobe: Used for sensory reception and perception. Receives information about touch, pressure, temperature and pain. Also involved with memory.

Occipital lobe: Receives visual information from the eyes.

Temporal lobe: Associated with sensory perception. Receives information from the ears.

The rear part of the brain is called the **cerebellum**. It is partially hidden by the cerebral hemispheres.

The cerebellum monitors the position of the limbs and the tension in their muscles. It controls **fine voluntary** movements and posture by making any necessary adjustments to the messages sent out to the voluntary muscles by the cerebrum.

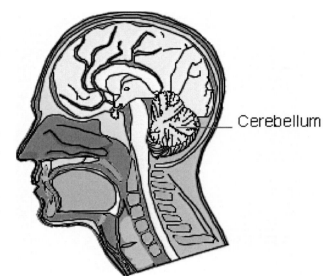

Cerebellum

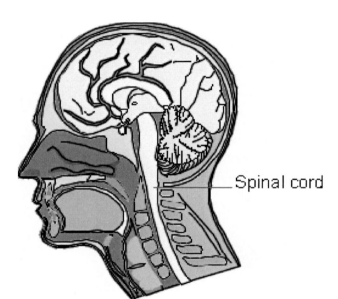

Spinal cord

The base of the brain extends into the **spinal cord**.

The spinal cord is a long **nerve tract**. It runs from the **base** of the brain, down through the vertebral column. The spinal cord allows the brain to communicate to all areas of the body. It does this using **31 pairs** of **spinal nerves**.

The 31 pairs of spinal nerves that originate from the spinal cord are not a part of the central nervous system. They are a part of the **peripheral nervous system**.

The **peripheral nervous system** includes **all** components of the nervous system **except** the **brain** and **spinal cord**.

It includes the **system of nerves**, originating at the **cranial** and **spinal** nerves, that runs to all organs and peripheral regions of the body. It also incorporates **ganglia** situated outside of the brain and spinal cord.

This system of nerves **conveys sensory** impulses from stimuli for processing by the central nervous system, and then **transmits** the consequent **motor** impulses to the muscles and glands.

Much of the peripheral nervous system is concerned with **voluntary** responses. However, the peripheral nervous system is **also** concerned with the body's many **involuntary**, **automatic** responses to stimuli.

The peripheral nervous system supplies the motor nerves to the **smooth muscle** of the internal organs, the **heart** and **glands**. This part of the peripheral nervous system is called the **autonomic nervous system**, as it deals with the body's 'automatic' responses.

The autonomic nervous system comprises of the **sympathetic** and **parasympathetic** nervous systems. They both supply motor nerves to the smooth muscle of the internal organs, heart and glands. The main **difference** is the **responses** they generate.

The **sympathetic** nervous system **increases** the heart rate, increases the respiratory rate and increases the blood pressure. It also slows down digestion.

The motor nerves of the sympathetic nervous system originate from the spinal nerves in the **thoracic** and **lumbar** regions. The nerve endings release **noradrenaline** that creates these 'fight or flight' reactions.

The **medulla** of the **adrenals** is supplied with **sympathetic** fibres. These trigger the release of **adrenaline** into the blood, so enhancing the effect of this system.

The **parasympathetic** nervous system **opposes** the sympathetic nervous system.

The motor nerves of the parasympathetic nervous system originate from **cranial** nerves (especially the vagus nerve) and a few of the spinal nerves in the **sacral** region. The nerve endings release **acetylcholine** that **decreases** the heart rate, respiratory rate and blood pressure, and promotes digestion.

Each organ receives **input** from **both** the parasympathetic and sympathetic nervous system. The **response** created depends on the **relative** stimulation received from each.

The autonomic nervous system also incorporates the **solar plexus**. The solar plexus is a **network** of nerves that is located **behind** the **stomach**. It supplies nerves to the abdominal organs below the diaphragm and regulates the functions of these organs.

When emotionally stressed or shocked, the solar plexus may give rise to a feeling of nausea stemming from the stomach.

Common Conditions Affecting the Nervous System

The nervous system is affected by all disorders. Any stress suffered by the body will stimulate responses. Conditions directly affecting the nervous system covered in this package include:

> Anxiety
> Bell's palsy
> Compression of the spinal nerves
> Cramp
> Facial neuralgia
> Migraine
> Multiple sclerosis
> Parkinson's disease
> Sciatica

Questions – Nervous System (Answers: Page 391)

1. What are nerve cells called?

2. Which type of neuron receives information from the sensory organs?

3. What name is given to the junction between the dendrites of one neuron and the axon terminal of another?

4. True or False?

    The brain and spinal cord make up the central nervous system.

5. What is the main artery that supplies blood to the brain?

6. How many pairs of cranial nerves originate from the brain?

    a. 6
    b. 12
    c. 18
    d. 31

7. Which part of the brain consists of two cerebral hemispheres, joined by a band of nerve fibres?

8. How many lobes does each cerebral hemisphere have?

9. What name is given to the rear part of the brain that is partially hidden by the cerebral hemispheres?

10. How many pairs of spinal nerves originate from the spinal cord?

    a. 6
    b. 12
    c. 31
    d. 42

11. True or False?

    All nerve cells and nervous tissue, except that of the brain and spinal cord, make up the peripheral nervous system.

12. True or False?

    The peripheral nervous system processes information received from the sensory organs.

13. What part of the peripheral nervous system deals with the body's involuntary, automatic responses?

14. The autonomic nervous system comprises of the sympathetic nervous system and the parasympathetic nervous system. Which increases the heart rate, respiratory rate and blood pressure?

    a. sympathetic
    b. parasympathetic

15. Which nervous system slows down digestion?

    a. sympathetic
    b. parasympathetic

16. Where do the motor nerves of the parasympathetic nervous system originate?

    a. spinal nerves in the thoracic and lumbar regions
    b. cranial nerves and a few of the spinal nerves in the sacral region
    c. the solar plexus

This page has intentionally been left blank.

Case Studies

This page has intentionally been left blank.

This section contains information about 20 fictitious clients/situations. Each is followed by a number of questions and you have to decide what action to take. To enable you to get the most from these, the answers follow on from the questions. We suggest, therefore, that you cover up the page with a piece of paper and then reveal the questions/answers as you progress.

Good luck!

Case Study 1

Your friend Sarah asks if you will treat her mother who has recently been diagnosed with high blood pressure. She thinks that the relaxing effect of reflexology may help.

Q1: What is the medical term for high blood pressure?

A1: Hypertension is the medical term for high blood pressure. It can be caused by obesity, stress and excitement. It can also be symptomatic of a chronic disorder.

Q2: The primary target area for hypertension is the heart. What area of assistance would you work?

A2: The solar plexus would be worked as an area of assistance.

Q3: Which reflex areas must be avoided in this case?

A3: The adrenal glands must be avoided. Working the adrenals may cause an increase in the metabolic rate, which could cause a further increase in the blood pressure.

Case Study 2

A young mother brings her 3 month old baby for a treatment because he isn't sleeping and seems irritable. You notice that the mother is very tense and seems to have little patience with her son. She says she hasn't slept properly since he was born and longs for life to return to normal.

Q1: What is your first course of action? (Options below.)

a. Treat the child while his mother has a nap in another room.
b. Refer the mother and child to her doctor to have the baby checked and to allow her to discuss the situation with a qualified medical practitioner.
c. Refer the mother to a counsellor.
d. Treat the mother while her baby is either held or placed safely near her.
e. Treat the child and suggest the mother seeks some form of support.
f. Treat the child, teach the mother how to do a few soothing techniques on the baby and suggest she seeks advice to help her sleep.

A1: Option f is correct. Reflexology may be able to help relax the baby. Teaching the mother how to perform a few techniques may allow her to take advantage of the benefits of reflexology as and when it is required. The mother clearly needs extra help with her sleep patterns.

Q2: When treating a young baby, what level of pressure would you use?

A2: A feather-light pressure is used when treating babies. The movement always starts at the heel and works towards the toes.

Q3: How would you adapt the length of the treatment to cater for such a young patient?

A3: The treatment would be reduced to last for just a few minutes.

Case Study 3

David, 32, has asked you to treat him for a neck and shoulder injury, which happened while playing rugby last weekend. He describes the incident as a "real crash" in which he heard "noises" in his neck. Since then he has been aware of stiffening neck muscles, a nagging headache and his vision has been a little blurred. The game was on Sunday and it is now Tuesday evening. He wants to go training with the team on Thursday and asks you to "make him right" for the next game this Sunday. He is not taking any medication and has not seen his General Practitioner because he isn't one for going to the Doctor.

Q1: What do you do? (Options below.)

a. Perform a full treatment and concentrate on the areas related to his condition.
b. Refer him to his General Practitioner.
c. Decline treatment and ask him to attend the Accident and Emergency department for a thorough examination of his head and neck.
d. Refer him to an osteopath.
e. Give a full treatment, advise him to take a hot bath and explain that he needs to take it easy at practice on Thursday.

A1: The correct option is c. A Doctor must see any injury that causes a disturbance in vision. X-rays may be necessary, and so by attending the Accident and Emergency department it is likely that the relevant tests and necessary treatment will be given quickly.

Case Study 4

You are invited to your local nursing home to carry out treatments on the elderly residents. One lady, Dorothy, is particularly keen to have a treatment, however she has osteo-arthritis. She is 89 and is quite deaf. She is on pain-killers and steroid anti-inflammatories which she says help.

Q1: How would you adapt the reflexology treatment to cater for Dorothy? (Options below.)

a. Use a lighter than normal pressure.
b. Use normal pressure and wait to be told it's too much.
c. Start with a lighter than normal pressure and ask for feedback.
d. Decline to treat because you would rather work on more robust feet.

A1: The correct option is c. You should use a lighter than normal pressure and always ensure that the treatment is comfortable by asking the patient how the pressure feels. Respond to the feedback by adapting the pressure accordingly.

Q2: When treating the elderly, the pressure and duration of the treatment is adapted accordingly. There is one other major safety consideration. What must you not do, particularly if you are treating an elderly person on a massage couch?

A2: The elderly (and the very young) must not, for obvious safety reasons, be left unattended.

Q3: What is the definition of osteo-arthritis? (Options below.)

a. inflammation of the connective tissue, tendons and ligaments, characterized by progressive joint destruction
b. a degenerative inflammatory disease of one or more joints

A3: Osteo-arthritis is a degenerative inflammatory disease of one or more joints.

Q4: Many commonly used drugs produce side effects. Which organ(s) are steroid anti-inflammatories known to negatively affect if taken over a long period? (Options below.)

a. kidneys
b. heart
c. brain
d. stomach

A4: The correct option is a. Steroid anti-inflammatories may cause kidney problems if used over a long term. This may be reflected by sensitivity in the kidney reflex areas.

Case Study 5

Emily, 26, is a mother of two children. She has asked you to help with her recurrent migraine. As you are taking her case history, she mentions that she struggles to eat properly and regularly because of the activities of her young children. Her sleep patterns are poor and she often feels nauseous.

Q1: What is migraine?

A1: Migraine is a recurring intense headache.

Q2: Which of the following are symptoms of migraine? (Options below.)

a. tension in the muscles of the scalp
b. tension in the neck and shoulders
c. nausea and vomiting
d. swollen ankles
e. blurred vision

A2: With the exception of swollen ankles, all of the above are symptoms of migraine.

Q3: If Emily was having an extremely bad migraine attack when she arrived for the treatment, do you think that it would be wise to treat her?

A3: No. The reflexology treatment could heighten the level of toxins in Emily's body and therefore worsen the migraine attack. It would be better if she made another appointment.

Q4: You concentrate on the reflex areas corresponding to the brain, the primary target area for migraine. Which spinal area also requires additional attention as a neural area of assistance?

A4: The cervical spine is an area of assistance for migraine.

Q5: Would Emily's condition be helped by dietary advice?

A5: Yes. Diet can affect migraine. You should advise Emily that cheese, chocolate and red wine are the most common dietary triggers. She should try to adjust her lifestyle to allow small but regular meals.

Case Study 6

Antonia has become more aware recently that her right shoulder has grown stiff and painful. She cannot lift her arm above shoulder height and reaching behind her back is impossible. Her General Practitioner has told her that she has a frozen shoulder. She thinks that this condition only affects the elderly and, at 39, she is concerned she will have this for life. Antonia suffered a severe car accident 6 months ago.

Q1: Which of the following can cause a frozen shoulder? (Options below.)

a. deterioration of the bones in the shoulder
b. exposure to extreme temperatures
c. inflammation of the tendons
d. inflammation of the fibrous capsule of the joint
e. swelling of the soft sac that cushions the joint

A1: The correct options are c, d and e. The inflammation of the tendons or the fibrous capsule of the joint, or the swelling of the soft sac that cushions the joint can cause a frozen shoulder.

Q2: What is the area of assistance for a frozen shoulder?

A2: The hip is the area of assistance.

Q3: Which two links exist between the hip and the shoulder? (Options below.)

a. neural and organic
b. zonal and structural
c. structural and neural
d. organic and zonal

A3: Option b is correct. There is a zonal and structural link between the hip and the shoulder. They are both in zone 5 and are both ball and socket joints.

Q4: Which of the following may help Antonia's shoulder? (Options below.)

a. swimming
b. massage and soft tissue manipulation
c. The Bowen Technique
d. horse riding

A4: The correct options are b and c. It is important to keep the joint active and so massage, soft tissue manipulation and the Bowen technique may help. Antonia's limited shoulder movement and the associated pain would make swimming and horse riding difficult and uncomfortable.

Case Study 7

Vivienne, a busy self-employed hairdresser, has suffered for years with various symptoms of pre-menstrual tension. She is 39 and is increasingly finding that her symptoms are interfering with her work and relationships. Specifically, Vivienne suffers with severe water retention, swollen joints, food cravings, mood swings, depression and poor concentration.

Q1: Which other symptoms are typical of pre-menstrual tension? (Options below.)

a. weight gain
b. headaches
c. allergies to certain foods
d. skin problems
e. acute hearing

A1: The correct options are a, b and d. Weight gain, headaches and skin problems are also symptoms of pre-menstrual tension.

Q2: Do you feel that reflexology can help Vivienne?

A2: Yes. Reflexology can help to balance hormones, assist in relaxation and aid fluid balance. A treatment will also give Vivienne some time to herself.

Q3: Which of the following are possible causes of pre-menstrual tension? (Options below.)

a. food intolerance
b. lack of vitamin B6 and essential fatty acids
c. a change in the balance of female hormones
d. excess thyroxine
e. low levels of progesterone

A3: The correct options are b, c and e.

More Information:

Vivienne has had three reflexology treatments and is noticing some improvement. She is keen to do as much as possible to help herself, and asks you if it is worth reviewing her diet.

Q4: What do you advise? (Options below.)

a. Tell Vivienne that there is no point reviewing her diet because it plays no part in pre-menstrual tension.
b. Encourage her to review this aspect of her lifestyle.

A4: The correct option is b. She should be encouraged to look at her diet because studies have shown that eating a good, balanced diet with plenty of fresh food can help pre-menstrual tension.

Q5: Which of the following do you suggest Vivienne reduces or removes from her diet? (Options below.)

a. saturated fats
b. sugar
c. vegetables
d. salt
e. caffeine
f. spicy food

A5: The correct options are a, b, d and e.

Case Study 8

Jane, 23, has suffered with asthma since she was a child. She tells you it is now "really bothering" her. She is on a puffer from the doctor but wants to look at different ways of treating this condition.

Q1: There are 4 primary target areas associated with asthma. The bronchi and the heart are two of them. What are the other two?

A1: The other two primary target areas are the lungs and the diaphragm.

Q2: Which of the following would serve as areas of assistance for this condition? (Options below.)

a. liver
b. spleen
c. digestive system
d. spine
e. adrenals
f. trachea

A2: The correct options are c and e. The areas of assistance for asthma are the digestive system (zonal and organic) and the adrenal glands (organic).

Q3: What additional qualification should you hold before agreeing to treat Jane?

A3: Before treating an asthmatic patient, the practitioner should take First Aid training. You must be capable of dealing with an asthmatic attack before treating an asthmatic.

Q4: What discipline, involving gentle breathing and stretching, may be of benefit to Jane?

A4: Yoga may help to keep the body in balance and therefore help it to cope with the asthma.

Case Study 9

Kristina, 45, had a bad car accident 10 months ago. She was taken to hospital immediately afterwards for a thorough examination. She was treated for whiplash, sent home, told to rest for a few days and advised to resume life as normal. She is now experiencing strong back pain, mainly on one side of the spine. She is not keen to return to the doctor and wants to try reflexology. She regularly takes pain-killers.

Q1: What do you do? (Options below.)

a. Perform a full treatment.
b. Work only on the spinal reflexes.

A1: The correct answer is a. A full treatment should be given. Reflexology is a holistic treatment and involves treating the individual as a 'whole', not just as a collection of symptoms. You would return to the spinal reflex areas to give them extra attention at the end of the full treatment.

Q2: As you perform the treatment, Kristina flinches as you work the reflex areas corresponding with the intestines. Based on her case history, would you expect this?

A2: Yes. Kristina regularly takes pain-killers, which can cause constipation. This side effect may cause sensitivity in the intestine and large bowel reflex areas.

Q3: How would you describe Kristina's condition? (Options below.)

a. acute
b. chronic

Q4: The correct option is b. Kristina's condition is chronic. It is a severe, long-lasting disorder.

Case Study 10

Iris, a 79 year old lady, awoke 3 months ago to find that one side of her face was paralysed. Her doctor has said that it may clear up on its own, but she is anxious to speed up her recovery.

Q1: Could reflexology help Iris?

A1: Yes. Reflexology could help, although recovery is best if the treatment starts as soon as possible after the incident.

Q2: What name is given to Iris's condition?

A2: Iris is suffering from Bell's palsy – the paralysis of the muscles on one or both sides of the face.

Q3: Can you assume that Iris has had a stroke?

A3: No. Stroke (apoplexy) is just one cause of Bell's palsy. It is also caused by damage to the facial nerve, localised inflammation or a fracture to the base of the skull. Bear in mind too, that it is not the role of the reflexologist to diagnose.

Q4: During the treatment you pay extra attention to the facial reflex areas, because they are the primary target areas. What areas of assistance would you use?

A4: The cervical spine and neck related areas are the areas of assistance for Bell's palsy.

Q5: Bell's palsy has a number of associated signs and symptoms. Which of the following are likely to be evident? (Options below.)

a. tinnitus
b. constipation
c. inability to smile
d. dryness of the eye
e. headaches
f. slurred speech

A5: The correct options are c, d and f.

Case Study 11

Jenny is 16 years old and is studying Health Science. She contacts you to ask a few questions about reflexology for her current project. She poses the following questions – you can answer them now:

Q1: "Who discovered reflexology?" (Options below.)

a. the Egyptians
b. the Indians
c. the Chinese
d. it cannot be traced to any one civilization

A1: The correct option is d. Reflexology cannot be traced back to any one civilization, but evidence indicates that primitive forms of reflexology were used in ancient Egypt, India and China.

Q2: "I've heard that zone therapy was an ancient belief, but who reintroduced zone therapy in the 20th century?"

A2: Doctor William H. Fitzgerald is credited with rediscovering zone therapy. It is based on longitudinal zones of energy that extend from the feet and hands to the brain.

Q3: "How many zones are there?"

A3: There are 10 longitudinal zones of energy, 5 originating on each foot.

Q4: "My Mum says that she's too old to benefit from reflexology. Is this true?"

A4: No. Age is not an issue. All ages can benefit from reflexology.

Q5: "Are all treatments the same?"

A5: No. Treatments are tailored to meet the needs of the individual.

Q6: "So, if age isn't an issue and you can tailor the treatment, can you treat anyone once you have qualified?"

A6: No. Although reflexology is basically a very safe treatment, there are certain circumstances under which the treatment must be declined. These circumstances are called contra-indications.

Case Study 12

You are asked to instruct a group of nurses. They need an overview of the main techniques. You are keen to do this, as it is quite an honour, but you need to recap on the basics of the treatment.

Q1: How is reflexology best described? (Options below.)

a. a pressure therapy
b. a foot massage

A1: Reflexology is a pressure therapy.

Q2: Where is the foot supported when working below the waist line on the plantar aspect of the foot?

A2: The foot is supported at the heel when working below the waist line.

Q3: Where is the foot supported when working above the waist line on the plantar aspect of the foot?

A3: The foot is supported at the toes, when working above the waist line.

Q4: When working on the medial or lateral edge of the foot, where do you support the foot?

A4: The foot is supported just below the toes when working on the medial or lateral edge of the foot. The foot is then angled slightly to give easy access to the appropriate edge.

Q5: Starting at the toes, what are the three main guidelines that run across the plantar aspect of the foot?

A5: The three main guidelines that run across the foot are the diaphragm line, waist line and pelvic line. The shoulder line is a secondary guideline.

Q6: What is the name of the guideline that runs down the plantar aspect of the foot?

A6: The ligament line runs down the foot. It follows the line of the ligament that can be felt under the skin when the toes are pulled back.

Case Study 13

Molly, a Solicitor aged 32, has asked you to treat her for depression. She has been working very long hours for the past few months on a particularly difficult case. This case is due to last at least a few more weeks.

340

Q1: During the treatment she seems to want to chat. What do you do? (Options below.)

a. Encourage her, hoping to hear about the case.
b. Reassure her that everything she discusses is kept strictly private and confidential and make it clear that you are willing to listen if she wants to talk.
c. Advise her that she should try to relax and avoid talking.
d. Ignore her gestures and stare intently at the feet while you work them.

A1: The correct option is b. Reflexology is a holistic therapy in which there is physical touch and eye contact. It is also carried out in a position that is conducive to speech. It can therefore induce emotional responses that the reflexologist should be prepared for and should not try to overlook. However, a reflexologist should not use their privileged position to pry!

Q2: Molly begins to confide in you as you work her right foot. After talking for a short time, she bursts into tears. What do you do? (Options below.)

a. Tell her to pull herself together.
b. Continue the treatment to ensure all the reflex areas are covered.
c. Stop the treatment, offer her a tissue, and suggest that she makes another appointment.
d. Stop the treatment, offer her a tissue, allow her time to compose herself and then ask if she would like to talk her problems through or continue with the treatment.

A2: The correct option is d. Molly should be allowed to talk if she wants to, even if this means the treatment is not completed. The patient should be dealt with sympathetically and professionally at all times.

More Information:

Molly composes herself and asks that you continue with the treatment.

Q3: What is the primary target area for someone like Molly who is suffering with depression?

A3: The primary target area is the solar plexus.

Q4: You are concerned about the depth of Molly's depression. What do you do? (Options below.)

a. Say nothing and hope that she will be OK.
b. Suggest that seeing you more frequently may help.
c. Gently advise that speaking to a counsellor or psychotherapist may help.

A4: The correct option is c. Molly should be advised to speak to someone specialised in helping sufferers of depression.

Case Study 14

James is 37 and has a longstanding problem with insomnia. He is a very stressed manager in a large company. He doesn't take much time for relaxation or exercise and he spends his night sifting through the day's problems. He has become irritable. His diet is poor.

Q1: What would be the primary target area in this case? (Options below.)

a. brain
b. solar plexus
c. stomach
d. spine

A1: The correct option is b. The primary target area for stress and insomnia is the solar plexus. The treatment should be thorough, incorporating plenty of relaxation techniques.

Q2: Which of the following would be helpful advice for James?

a. Take plenty of fresh air and exercise whenever possible.
b. Have a couple of pints of beer before going to bed.
c. Practice relaxation exercises e.g. yoga and meditation.
d. Keep regular sleeping hours.
e. Stay awake for as long as possible then sleep for as long as possible.

A2: The correct options are a, c and d.

Case Study 15

Sally is a busy sales representative. Her doctor has just told her that she is suffering from irritable bowel syndrome. She is concerned and has rung you because she has read that reflexology can help digestive disorders. You advise her that reflexology may be able to help and so she makes an appointment. Before she arrives, you decide to test your knowledge.

Q1: Which of the following are common symptoms of irritable bowel syndrome?

a. abdominal pain
b. back pain
c. numbness in the legs
d. bloating and colic
e. diarrhoea and/or constipation
f. increased appetite

A1: The correct options are a, b, d and e.

Q2: The small and large intestines are primary target areas. What is the other?

A2: The stomach is also a primary target area for irritable bowel syndrome.

Q3: Which of the following would be useful areas of assistance?

a. liver
b. gall bladder
c. kidneys
d. lumbar spine
e. adrenals

A3: The correct options are a, b and d.

Q4: Irritable bowel syndrome may be caused by intolerance to certain foods. What life style factor is also believed to play a part?

A4: Although the cause of irritable bowel syndrome has not been firmly established, stress is believed to play a part.

Case Study 16

Six weeks ago, Susan discovered she was pregnant. She has had three previous pregnancies, of which only one went the full term to produce her daughter who is now 18 months old. She is keen to have a second child but is troubled by her history of miscarriages. She has read in a magazine that reflexology can help, but has been told by a friend that she shouldn't have reflexology because of her history. Susan telephones you for information.

Q1: What do you tell her? (Options below.)

a. Reflexology can be of benefit at any stage of pregnancy, even if there is a history of miscarriage.
b. Reflexology should be avoided for the first three months of pregnancy when there is a history of miscarriage.
c. Reflexology should be avoided for the full term of pregnancy when there is a history of miscarriage.

A1: The correct option is b. Although there is no evidence to suggest that reflexology increases the likelihood of a miscarriage, it is wise to decline to treat for the first three months of the pregnancy. If you decide to treat once the first three months have elapsed, extreme care should be taken. You may choose to obtain a letter of approval from the doctor. Commonsense should be employed for peace of mind.

Case Study 17

Tina has been troubled with pain down her left leg since she slipped and fell on ice two years ago. In falling, she landed heavily at the base of her spine. Although she was stiff and felt bruised for a few weeks, she did not see her doctor. Now, occasionally, after sitting for a long period or driving for more than an hour, she starts to feel pain extending down the leg. She sometimes needs to take a pain-killer.

Q1: Although reflexologists do not attempt to diagnose, what do you think Tina is suffering from? (Options below.)

a. a broken coccyx
b. sciatica
c. a slipped intervertebral disc

A1: The correct option is b. Pain travelling down the leg is symptomatic of sciatica.

Q2: The primary target area for sciatica is the sciatic nerve. Which area of the spine is an area of assistance for this condition?

A2: The lumbar spine is an area of assistance for sciatica.

Q3: Do you think it likely that Tina's fall triggered the start of this problem?

A3: Yes, it is likely. Sciatica can be caused by an injury to the spine. Other causes include a slipped intervertebral disc, nerve disorders and lumbago.

Q4: Which of the following may help Tina by reducing the episodes of pain?

a. osteopathy
b. walking
c. massage
d. chiropractic

A4: The correct options are a, c and d. Osteopathy and chiropractic both deal with spinal problems. Massage may help, depending upon the level of muscular involvement.

Case Study 18

You are asked to be the regular practitioner at Sunnyside Nursing Home, paying weekly visits. On your initial visit you meet with some of the residents to discuss their health background. Most of the residents are mentally alert, however they suffer from various problems.

Q1: During your time at Sunnyside, you are going to be exposed to many different cases. In which of the following situations would you decline to treat?

a. the patient is in a bad mood or irritable
b. the patient is suffering from psychosis
c. you are fed up or disinterested in the treatment and/or the patient
d. the patient is sceptical about reflexology
e. the patient experiences a continued, negative reaction to the treatment
f. the patient has internal bleeding
g. the patient has a severe fever

A1: The correct options are b, e, f and g.

More Information:

Let's meet the residents of Sunnyside!

Resident 1

Mavis, 72, had a stroke some years ago. She is partially paralysed and walks with a frame.

Q1: Do you think that reflexology will significantly improve her present condition?

A1: No. As several years have passed since Mavis had her stroke, it would be very unlikely for any improvement to her present medical condition. However, reflexology may help to improve her overall health and well being and so it would be beneficial to treat on this basis.

Resident 2

Fred, 84, has recently been admitted to the nursing home due to recurrent respiratory infections and general ill health. Yesterday he started with the flu and is feeling grim. He is keen to gain some comfort and would like you to perform a reflexology treatment to help clear his chest and help his flu-related aches and pains.

Q1: Would you treat Fred on this occasion?

A1: No. Fred's treatment should be declined today. Apart from the risk of cross-infection, reflexology stimulates the detoxification processes. This causes the effects of the toxins, already high due to the infection, to become more apparent.

Resident 3

Joan, 92, has been having occasional epileptic fits over the last 6 years. Her epilepsy is generally controlled by medication and she is keen to have a reflexology treatment because she wants to see if it can help her stiff and aching back.

Q1: Would you treat Joan? (Options below.)

a. Yes, it can do no harm and she may benefit.
b. Yes, it is very safe, but I would only do so if I had a First Aid Training certificate.
c. No, epilepsy is a contra-indication.

A1: The correct option is b. It is safe to treat epileptics, but you should first ensure that you are confident to deal with an epileptic fit should one occur during the treatment.

Resident 4

Jennifer, 87, has no major health problems, however she is blind and has recurrent athlete's foot for which no medication seems to have helped.

Q1: Should you treat Jennifer? (Options below.)

a. No, athlete's foot is a contra-indication.
b. Yes, providing I wash my hands thoroughly before and after the treatment.
c. Yes, providing the affected areas can be covered with a plaster and avoided.

A1: The correct option is c. Athlete's foot need not prevent the treatment. Cover the affected areas with a plaster and avoid them. Personal hygiene is always very important.

Resident 5

Elizabeth is 86. She has been admitted to Sunnyside because she has senile dementia and mild osteoporosis. Her senile dementia is not a health threat, but the onset of osteoporosis is of concern because she is having repeated falls due to her tendency to wander outside without accompaniment.

Q1: How would you deal with Elizabeth? (Options below.)

a. Use normal pressure.
b. Perform only relaxation techniques.
c. Decline to treat.
d. Suggest she has another form of therapy.
e. Use a very light pressure, ensuring it is comfortable.

A1: The correct option is e. The treatment should be carried out carefully, using a very light and comfortable pressure. If the bones in the feet are too brittle, the treatment should be declined.

Resident 6

Teresa, 74, is waiting to go into hospital for a hip replacement. She is becoming increasingly anxious as the operation draws nearer. The in-house doctor has given consent for Teresa to have reflexology prior to the operation.

Q1: How soon do you think you should ideally commence treatment? (Options below.)

a. a few days before the operation
b. a few weeks before the operation

A1: The correct answer is b. Pre-operative reflexology has been shown to help increase resilience during the operation. The sooner it can be started before the operation the better.

Q2: Would you offer reflexology post-operatively?

A2: Yes. Used post-operatively, reflexology has been shown to reduce shock and stress, promote healing and boost the immune system.

Q3: What level of pressure would you use post-operatively? (Options below.)

a. normal
b. firmer, to encourage better healing
c. very gentle at first

A3: The correct answer is c. In the early days after an operation, a very gentle pressure is used because the body is recovering and may be in shock for a while.

Resident 7

Annie, who is generally well, has been celebrating her 90th birthday this lunchtime with her family. She has had a wonderful time and has enjoyed the champagne fully! She has returned to Sunnyside and is greatly anticipating her birthday treat – a reflexology session. She is, in her own words, "a little merry" from the champagne.

348

Q1: What do you do? (Options below.)

a. Commence the treatment as normal, wait for her to fall asleep and then stop.
b. Schedule her as your last patient and perform a very light treatment.
c. Decline the treatment for today, but try to reduce her disappointment by offering another treatment next week.

A1: The correct answer is b. As she is in good health but just "a little merry", it would be wise to let her have a rest while you treat the other patients. Treat her last, by which time she will be less affected by the alcohol. Use a very light treatment so as not to significantly increase the toxin levels.

Resident 8

Barbara is 81. She has been brought to Sunnyside as her local hospital is full. She has terminal lung cancer and is heavily medicated for pain control. She is awake and alert for a part of each day. Her family has asked if you would perform some reflexology to help Barbara rest better and perhaps ease the pain. You have sufficient experience and confidence to deal with cancer patients and permission to treat has been granted by the doctor.

Q1: Do you feel that reflexology could help to reduce Barbara's pain?

A1: Yes. It has been found that reflexology can help to reduce the pain associated with cancer and other terminal illnesses.

Q2: How would you tailor the treatment to suit Barbara's needs? (Options below.)

a. Perform a normal treatment with normal pressure.
b. Use relaxation techniques only.
c. Perform regular but shorter treatments.
d. Use a lighter pressure.
e. Pay extra attention to the liver and systems of elimination.

A2: The correct options are c, d and e. You would use a lighter pressure during more frequent but shorter treatments. Paying extra attention to the liver and systems of elimination may help the body deal more efficiently with the medication.

Q3: What reflex areas should you avoid?

A3: The site of the tumour, in this case the lungs, should be avoided.

Case Study 19

Martin, 71, is a patient that you treat in his own home. He has suffered with late onset diabetes since he was 45. He is comfortable in himself, and his medical and dietary needs are met adequately by his District Nurse, Home Help and supportive family. His diabetes, however, does cause some problems.

Q1: Which of the following are likely to occur as a result of diabetes?

a. weight gain
b. extreme thirst
c. constipation
d. increased urine output
e. flushed appearance
f. poor circulation

A1: The correct options are b, d and f. These are three of the most common symptoms of diabetes. Others include weight loss, dehydration and muscle weakness.

Q2: Why must extra care be taken when treating Martin? (Options below.)

a. His circulation may be poor and so extreme care must be taken not to nip the skin.
b. His skin may be thin and therefore susceptible to tearing.
c. He may report your actions to the District Nurse.
d. You are not insured to treat away from your own premises.

A2: The correct options are a and b. Diabetes can affect the circulation. The skin is often cold, clammy, less mobile and thinner. Damage is therefore easier to induce and may take a long time to heal. You must ensure that your insurance covers all aspects of your practice.

Q3: What serious condition, affecting the extremities of the body, are diabetics susceptible to should the skin on the feet be broken?

A3: There is a risk of gangrene when the skin is broken and the circulation is poor. In such cases medical attention is required immediately and foot reflexology is clearly not suitable.

Case Study 20

Helen, 35, is one of your regular patients. She arrives for her appointment and, during the pre-treatment chat to update your records, she tells you that she is currently menstruating.

Q1: What do you do? (Options below.)

a. Perform a treatment as normal, giving all areas equal attention and pressure.
b. Work the endocrine system a few extra times to help the body normalize after the menstrual period.
c. Perform a full treatment, but only work briefly and lightly over the uterus and ovary reflex areas.
d. Decline to treat today and ask her to come back next week.

A1: The correct option is c. It is perfectly safe to provide a reflexology treatment during menstruation. However, work the uterus and ovary reflex areas only briefly and lightly to avoid the possibility of causing an excessive menstrual flow.

This page has intentionally been left blank

Revision and Exam Tips

353

This page has intentionally been left blank

The first revision tip is "**Do Some!**" You will not do well if you do not revise (unless you are a natural genius). You will only get out what you put in.

Write a **revision timetable**. Consider:

> ➤ the order of the exams
> ➤ the time you have to revise
> ➤ the complexity of each topic
> ➤ your level of ability in each topic (you will have to spend more time on your weaker topics)

Stick to your timetable. There is nothing worse than getting behind schedule.

Revise in an **environment** that suits you. Have music playing in the background if it helps you - but don't just have it on because singing along gives you something more interesting to do!

As the exam approaches you will not have time to keep going through your vast quantity of original notes. Your notes need to be **summarised** and the important points **highlighted**. Revise from the summary, returning to your original notes only if necessary.

Essential Reflexology has done this for you. Your 'need to know' information is all here.

Don't be afraid to **test yourself**. It is better to find out now which areas you need to brush up on rather than having the examiner tell you! See if you can write down the important points after you have read them. Reading and understanding are not the same as learning.

Find out as much as you can about the **format and style** of the exam. Is there a topic on which there will definitely be a question?

If there are mandatory questions make sure that you know these topics.

If your training school has a policy of releasing **past papers**, ask to have a look at as many as you can. Read them carefully to get used to the **phraseology** of the questions. Try to break down the questions to determine what the examiner is looking for. Take these past papers under exam conditions to practice your exam technique. If you find this too stressful try to brainstorm by just writing down the main points you would put into the answer. Check to see if you are on the right track. If you are not – don't worry. Go back to the relevant section and read it again. Don't do the question again immediately, wait until later.

When it comes to the exam, **don't panic!**

Don't feel as if you have to start writing immediately. Spend the first 5 - 10 minutes **reading and planning**. This will increase your mark in the long run.

Carefully **read the exam instructions**. Find out:

> ➢ How long is the exam?
> ➢ How many questions have to be answered?
> ➢ Are there any mandatory questions?
> ➢ Do a certain number of questions have to be taken from specified sections of the paper?
> ➢ Does the answer paper have to be completed in any particular way?

Take your time at the beginning of an exam. It is so easy, in a moment of panic, to miss the instructions and so throw away many valuable marks.

Read ALL the questions slowly and carefully, underlining the key words. If you can choose your questions decide which to answer based on:

> ➢ what you know about the subject
> ➢ the question being asked (some questions are more difficult to answer than others, even though the subject may be the same)
> ➢ **YOUR ABILITY TO ANSWER THE QUESTION**

This last point is vital. You will not get marks for regurgitating everything you know about the subject. The examiner will lose the will to live! The test is whether you can **apply your knowledge** to the question. Ask yourself what points the examiner is looking for and then expand on these to show you have an understanding of the subject. Whenever possible refer to practical experience to show the examiner that you really understand the principle.

Allocate yourself an amount of **time** for each question **proportionate** to the number of **marks** available. In other words do not spend ½ hour on a question worth 10 marks and ¼ hour on a question worth 20 marks! If you know the subject it is fairly easy to get the first 50% or so of the marks. You will be able to do this well within the time. The remaining marks are much harder to get. If you are short of time it is better to start on the next question (to get that 50%) rather than continuing for perhaps another 5%.

For confidence **start with your best question**, but don't get carried away, finish when you should.

You may find it useful to start each answer on a separate piece of paper to allow space for adding any extra points if needed. There may, however, be specific instructions on how the answer paper should be completed so ensure you comply with them. As you answer a question cross it off the exam paper so you can clearly see what you have left.

Plan your essays. Write the essay plan on your exam answer paper. If you don't get to finish, the examiner will know what you intended and so you may get an extra mark. Also, if you think of another point after you have started, write it down immediately on your plan so that you don't forget to mention it in your essay.

If you are running out of time there is nothing wrong with quickly writing in note/point form the other facts you were going to mention. You will usually pick up a mark for this.

Finally, if you **prepare** for the exam and **take your time** reading the exam paper before you begin there is no reason why you should not do well. Remember, however, that exam technique is a skill in itself and like any skill it needs to be **practiced**. Therefore the importance of answering questions and taking past papers cannot be overstated.

We hope that these hints will help you to obtain the result that you deserve.

Good Luck!

This page has intentionally been left blank.

Answers

This page has intentionally been left blank.

Introduction to Reflexology

1. **b**

   Reflexology is a pressure therapy. The reflex points on the feet (and hands) are stimulated by a gentle on-off pressure.

2. **False**

   Reflexology does indeed induce a state of deep relaxation but many other benefits may be derived. These include reducing stress and tension, improving the blood supply, promoting the flow of nerve impulses, reducing inflammation, encouraging the release of toxins, reducing congestion and helping the body to regain or maintain its natural equilibrium. It is, however, widely accepted that inducing a state of deep relaxation may provide the environment necessary for these other benefits to be achieved.

3. **a**

   As the heart is mainly positioned in the left side of the body, the main reflex area associated with the heart is situated on the left foot. A small portion of the heart is on the right side of the chest. This small portion of the heart is reflected in a small reflex area on the right foot. Simply remember that, as the feet mirror the body, the left foot contains the reflex areas associated with the left side of the body and the right foot contains the reflex areas associated with the right side of the body.

4. **metatarsal**

   The metatarsal notch, a small bony protuberance situated on the lateral edge of the foot at the end of the 5th metatarsal, is used to locate the position of the waist line.

5. **2**

   The waist line is shown as line number 2. The waist line runs across the middle of the foot.

6. **1**

   The heart and lung reflex areas are situated above the diaphragm line, represented on the graphic by line number 1.

7. **shoulder line**

   Line number 5 is the shoulder line. This secondary guideline is situated just beneath the toes. The head and neck reflex areas lie above it.

8. **pelvic line**

   The pelvic line is represented by line number 3. It is located by drawing a line across the plantar aspect of the foot from one side of the ankle bone to the other. There is often a change of skin colour from lighter above the pelvic line to darker below it.

9. **ligament line**

   The ligament line runs down the foot between the first and second toes. It can be located by pulling the toes back and tracing the ligament that runs down the foot just beneath the skin. This line is useful for locating the kidney and adrenal reflex areas but should not be pulled taut when treating any of the reflex areas through which this ligament runs.

10. **diaphragm line**

    The skin also changes colour at the diaphragm line, located just beneath the joints of the phalanges and the metatarsals. The skin changes from darker above the line, to lighter below.

History

1. c

The ancient painting depicting a reflexology treatment can be found in the tomb of the Egyptian physician Ankhmahor.

2. b

The tomb of Ankhmahor is in Saqqara.

3. e

The zig-zag symbol represents power. In the painting in Ankhmahor's tomb the zig-zag is thought to represent the power of reflexology. It is believed that the owl represents wisdom, the bird represents peace and paradise, the pyramid is a symbol of energy, and the eyes depict the windows of the soul.

4. Vishnu

Vishnu is pictured reclining having his feet treated. The picture can be dated to around 1760.

5. padas

The missing word is 'padas'. The locations of the symbols on the feet shown in the painting 'Vishnu-padas', closely correspond to the positions of many reflex areas used today.

6. acupuncture

Reflexology was developed in conjunction with acupuncture in China, under Emperor Hwang, some 4,000 years ago.

7. a

This footprint is carved in the rock at Kusinara in China.

8. Dr. William H. Fitzgerald

Dr. William H. Fitzgerald rediscovered zone therapy.

9. 10

Zone therapy hinges on the belief that the body is divided into 10 longitudinal zones of energy that extend from the feet and hands to the brain.

10. zone 1

Zone 1 originates from the big toe and the thumb.

11. True

The basis of zone therapy is that any treatment performed on any site within a zone will have a healing effect on the whole zone. Therefore, if all the zones are stimulated during a full reflexology treatment, the whole body must be influenced.

12. d

Dr. Joe Shelby Riley extensively used zone therapy. He made the first detailed drawings of the reflexes on the foot. He also added 8 horizontal lines to the 5 longitudinal lines originating from zone therapy.

13. Eunice Ingham

The therapist is Eunice Ingham. Her work became more and more reflex based and, importantly, she found that not only did treatments relieve pain but they also promoted healing.

14. Hanne Marquardt

Hanne Marquardt, trained by Eunice Ingham, became the first practitioner in Germany to use pressure on the feet only. She is also credited with introducing the concept of transverse lines across the feet.

15. Dwight C. Byers

Dwight C. Byers assisted Eunice and continued her work after her death. The National Institute of Reflexology and the International Institute of Reflexology were formed, dedicated to the teaching of the Original Ingham Method.

16. Ann Gillanders

Ann Gillanders trained with Dwight Byers. She qualified in 1976 and is now considered to be one of the leading authorities and teachers of modern day reflexology.

The Principle

1. **True**
    The reflex area corresponding to the spine runs down the medial (middle or inside) edge of both feet.

2. **d**
    The pelvic reflex area is located below the pelvic line on the plantar and lateral aspects of both feet. The pelvis sits symmetrically in the body and so the corresponding reflex area is represented on both feet.

3. **left**
    As the solar plexus is located on the left side of the body, the corresponding reflex area is on the left foot.

4. **3**
    There are three reflex areas representing the brain on each foot. They are located on the end of the big toe, second toe and middle toe.

5. **False**
    Anatomically, the heart is mainly to the left of the thorax, but some of the heart is positioned on the right. Therefore there is a reflex area corresponding to the heart on the right foot, although the largest heart reflex area is on the left foot.

6. **True**
    The lungs are represented on both the plantar and dorsal aspects of the feet. The trachea/bronchi reflex areas are located on the top of the big toes and on the medial edge of the big toes.

7. **right**
    The gall bladder, ileocaecal valve and appendix reflex areas are on the right foot. Anatomically they are located on the right side of the body.

8. **right**
    The largest liver reflex area is on the right foot. Anatomically the liver is located mainly to the right of the body.

9. **left**
    The descending colon and sigmoid colon reflex areas are on the left foot. Anatomically they are located on the left side of the body.

10. False

The transverse colon runs across the body and so a reflex area is located on both feet.

11. b

The medial aspect shows the prostate/uterus reflex area. The testis (on the male) or ovary (on the female) reflex area is on the lateral aspect. The vas deferens (in the male) or fallopian tube (in the female) reflex area runs over the dorsal aspect of the foot, from the medial prostate/uterus reflex area to the lateral testis/ovary reflex area.

12. a

The ovary/testis reflex area is on the lateral aspect.

13. areas of assistance

These additional areas are called areas of assistance.

14. b

This link is organic as the palpitations are caused by a secondary body part, in this case the stomach. The heart and stomach are also in the same zone, so there is a zonal link too.

15. d

The link is neural as the condition may be caused or worsened by the impairment of the **nerves**, originating in the spine.

16. zonal

There is a zonal link between the hip and the shoulder. They are both in zone 5. Based on zone therapy, treating one area in a zone can influence all of the structures within that zone.

17. structural

There is a structural link between the ankle and the knee as there is a physical structural connection between them.

The Treatment

1. **False**

    As a holistic therapy, a reflexology treatment should, whenever possible, cover all the body systems by treating all the reflex areas. It is important to take a full case history. This helps to identify if there are any reflex areas that have to be avoided and those that need additional attention. The areas needing extra attention should be re-visited at the end of the session.

2. **aspirin (acetylsalicylic acid)**

    Aspirin can have a detrimental effect on the stomach, from minor irritations and inflammation to ulceration and bleeding in some sensitive individuals. The stomach reflex area may therefore be sensitive if the recipient is taking aspirin.

3. **kidney**

    Anti-histamines may cause sensitivity in the kidney reflex areas.

4. **liver**

    The liver can be affected by the use of these two drugs. This may cause sensitivity in the associated reflex area.

5. **c**

    Steroids is the odd group. Anti-depressants, sleeping tablets and amphetamines all may cause sensitivity in the brain reflex areas, steroids generally do not.

6. **right**

    The right foot is always treated first. This is because the treatment follows the direction of the large intestine, which originates on the right of the body. Following the flow of the large intestine helps the body to gently eliminate the toxins released as a result of the treatment. The main movement is the creeping thumb.

7. **c**

    The first movement would be from the medial edge to the lateral edge. When the area has been covered, the working hand is changed. The movement is then from the lateral to the medial edge.

8. **at the heel**

    The foot is supported at the heel when treating reflex areas below the waist line. The foot is supported at the toes when working areas above the waist line.

9. True

The initial working hand does always match the foot being worked. This allows the foot to be worked from the medial to the lateral edge. The supporting hand then changes to allow the opposite hand to work back from the lateral to the medial edge.

10. True

Supporting the foot at the base of the toes and gently angling it, makes the medial and lateral edges easy to work.

11. lateral

On the lateral edge, the working hand does not match the foot being worked. The opposite hand is used. When working the medial edge, the working hand does match the foot being worked.

Safety

1. **True**

   Reflexology is generally very safe. All ages, from tiny babies to the elderly, can benefit from it.

2. **pressure**

   The pressure applied can be reduced. For example, when treating babies the pressure applied is reduced to a feather-light touch.

3. **c**

   The treatment should be stopped immediately if the patient displays any adverse symptoms. Adverse symptoms are not common, but may occasionally be displayed by hypersensitive individuals.

4. **a**

   Infectious illness is a contra-indication. Infectious illnesses are usually contra-indicated because there is a risk of cross-infection and the treatment encourages the release of more toxins. Verrucae and menstruation do not prevent the treatment but caution is required. A verruca should be covered with a plaster and avoided. If the recipient is menstruating, the level of pressure and the time spent on the uterus and ovary reflex areas are reduced.

5. **True**

   Declining treatment eliminates the risk of the reflexologist being blamed should a miscarriage occur. When there is a history of a miscarriage, as well as declining to treat in the first three months, great care and consideration should be taken for the rest of the pregnancy.

6. **d**

   Hypertension is a circumstance under which care must be taken. The adrenal reflex areas must be avoided to prevent any possible further increase in the blood pressure. Psychosis, thrombosis and phlebitis are contra-indications and so prevent the treatment from taking place.

Conditions

1. **c**
    Amenorrhoea is the absence of menstruation. The primary target area is the reproductive system. The endocrine system is an area of assistance.

2. **solar plexus**
    The solar plexus is the primary target area in cases of anxiety. You would give a thorough treatment, using plenty of relaxation techniques. There are no areas of assistance.

3. **a**
    Osteo-arthritis is the inflammation of one or more joints. Rheumatoid arthritis is defined as the inflammation of the connective tissue, tendons and ligaments.

4. **rheumatoid**
    Rheumatoid arthritis is caused by auto-immune disease. The auto-immunity enzymes eat into the synovial membranes first and then into the cartilage. A virus or allergy can trigger this condition.

5. **True**
    The primary target area is that of the affected joint. All systems of elimination are areas of assistance.

6. **lungs, bronchi, diaphragm, heart**
    The primary target areas for asthma are the lungs, bronchi, diaphragm and the heart.

7. **d**
    There is an organic link between the adrenals and asthma. The adrenals have an effect on the condition. They produce cortisone, which helps to reduce inflammation.

8. **d**
    This is an organic link, as the digestive system may have an effect on the condition.

9. **Bell's palsy**
    This is a description of Bell's palsy. The primary target area is the face. The cervical spine and neck are areas of assistance.

10. a

The cervical spine is an area of assistance for blurred vision. Compressed or damaged nerves in this area may contribute to the condition.

11. True

The digestive system and adrenals are areas of assistance for both asthma and bronchitis.

12. sinuses

The sinuses are the primary target areas for catarrh, an inflammation of the mucous membranes associated with the copious secretion of mucus.

13. heart

The heart is the primary target area for chilblains. The lumbar spine is an area of assistance.

14. spleen

The spleen is the other primary target area for colds and flu. It has a role to play in maintaining a healthy immune system.

15. True

The spinal area that relates to the site of the symptoms should receive particular attention. For example, should tingling or numbness be present in the arms and hands, the cervical spine should receive particular attention because this is where the nerves of the arms originate.

16. lumbar spine

The lumbar spine is the area of assistance neurologically linked to constipation. Compression or damage to the nerves of the lumbar spine may lead to the disturbed functioning of the intestines.

17. cystitis

Cystitis is the inflammation of the bladder. It can be caused by bacterial infections or irritants in the urine.

18. c

The endocrine system is the area of assistance for depression. Organs of the endocrine system produce hormones that have a considerable influence on the emotional state.

19. pancreas

The pancreas is the primary target area for diabetes as this gland is responsible for the production of insulin.

20. c

The lumbar spine is an area of assistance for diarrhoea. Compression or damage to the nerves of the lumbar spine may lead to the disturbed functioning of the intestines.

21. b

Dysmenorrhoea is a condition involving painful menstruation. The primary target areas are the uterus, ovaries and fallopian tubes.

22. True

The primary target areas for both asthma and eczema are the lungs, bronchi, diaphragm and heart.

23. b

The reproductive system is the primary target area for endometriosis. This condition is characterized by the presence of endometrium cells (that naturally line the interior wall of the uterus) in other parts of the body, commonly in the muscle of the uterus.

24. neuralgia

Neuralgia means nerve pain (neur- = nerve, -algia = pain).

25. pituitary

The pituitary gland is the primary target area for fever. It secretes many hormones that control major bodily processes, including temperature regulation, and has the ability to affect other components of the endocrine system.

26. hip

The hip is the area of assistance for shoulder conditions. There is a zonal link as both the shoulder and the hip are in zone 5. There is also a structural link as both the hip and the shoulder are ball and socket joints.

27. glue ear

Glue ear is the common name for secretory otitis media. The middle ear is inflamed and has a persistent presence of a sticky secretion.

28. liver

The liver is an area of assistance for headaches. The liver plays a major role in removing toxins from the blood that may otherwise build up causing many problems including headaches.

29. stomach

The primary target area for heartburn is the stomach. Heartburn is caused by the excessive acidity of the gastric (stomach) juices.

30. diaphragm

A hiatus hernia is the displacement of a portion of the stomach through the oesophageal opening in the diaphragm. It can be caused by over exertion or a weakness in the diaphragm itself.

31. adrenals

The adrenals must be avoided in cases of hypertension (high blood pressure). Working these areas may cause an increase in the metabolic rate, which could cause a further increase in the blood pressure.

32. hyperthyroidism

Hyperthyroidism is a form of goitre caused by an over active thyroid gland. Symptoms may include an enlarged thyroid, weight loss, restlessness, insomnia, muscular tremors, sweating and palpitations. This condition may also cause the eyes to protrude.

33. adrenals

The adrenals are areas of assistance for hypotension (low blood pressure). Due to their stimulating effect on the body, they are areas of assistance for other under-active conditions too, e.g. hypothyroidism.

34. solar plexus

The solar plexus is the primary target area for insomnia. Working this nerve plexus may help to calm the body, perhaps making sleep easier.

35. irritable bowel syndrome

I.B.S. stands for irritable bowel syndrome, a condition in which normal bowel function is disrupted. Its cause is uncertain but it is believed that the bowel loses its function in response to stimuli such as stress and certain food types.

36. eyes

The eyes are areas of assistance for kidney stones. There is a zonal link, as the kidneys and the eyes are in the same zone. There is also an organic link, as the kidneys have a strong association with the eyes.

37. spleen

The spleen is an area of assistance for laryngitis. Its function is important in maintaining a healthy immune system.

38. breast/chest

Mastitis is the inflammation of the breast. The breast is therefore the primary target area. There are organic links to both the lymphatic and endocrine systems.

39. c

The lumbar spine is an area of assistance for menorrhagia. Compression or damage to the nerves in the lumbar area may lead to the dysfunction of the reproductive organs.

40. c

The statement defines multiple sclerosis. The primary target areas for this condition are the brain and the spine.

41. d

Myalgic encephalomyelitis (M.E.) is known as post viral fatigue as it often seems to be caused by the failure to recover from a viral infection. Changes in the immune system and physical and emotional stresses may be other contributory factors. The reflexology treatment should be short and light, working on all the body systems.

42. oedema

Excess fluid retention is known as oedema. Oedema can be caused by hormonal disturbances, heart failure, kidney failure, shock, local injury, drugs, steroids and protein deficiency. The primary target areas are the lymphatic system, heart and kidneys.

43. a

The stomach has a zonal link with the heart – they are both generally located in the same zones. The stomach also has an organic link with the heart. The stomach can become swollen and press on the diaphragm, thereby causing pressure on the heart and possibly palpitations.

44. Parkinson's

Parkinson's disease is described. The primary target areas are the brain and spine.

45. prostatitis

Prostatitis is the inflammation of the prostate gland. This can be caused by an infection (usually only in young men) or for no apparent reason later in life. The prostate gland is a common site for cancer.

46. heart

The heart is the primary target area for Raynaud's disease. In this condition, the circulation in the extremities suddenly becomes obstructed, causing 'dead', white, numb and waxy looking fingers, toes, ears or nose.

47. sciatic

This pain, sciatica, originates from the sciatic nerve. The primary target area is the sciatic nerve. The area of assistance is the lumbar spine.

48. digestive

The digestive system is an area of assistance for sinusitis.

49. solar plexus

The solar plexus is the primary target area for stress. Working this area may help to calm the body.

50. stroke/apoplexy

A stroke, also called apoplexy, is the sudden change in the blood supply to the brain. A stroke may be caused by a rupture or blockage of a cerebral blood vessel.

51. solar plexus

The solar plexus is the area of assistance for tension.

52. thrush

Thrush, a fungal infection that thrives in warm, moist areas, can be caused by these factors. The uterus is the primary target area and the lumbar spine is the area of assistance.

53. ears

The ears are the primary target areas for tinnitus. A ringing, hissing or buzzing in the ear, without any external noise, characterizes this condition.

54. heart

The heart is the primary target area for varicose veins. Dilated or swollen veins are often caused by poor circulation. The intestines and the lumbar spine are areas of assistance.

55. ear

Vertigo is usually caused by defects in the middle or inner ear. The ears are therefore the primary target areas. The cervical spine and the kidneys are areas of assistance.

Anatomy and Physiology

Structural Organization

1. **chemical**

   The lowest level of structural organization is chemical. This includes all atoms and molecules essential for maintaining life. Atoms and molecules combine to form cells, the basic structural and functional units of the body.

2. **nucleus**

   The nucleus is the central part of the cell. It is oval-shaped and contains chromosomes and a fluid called nucleoplasm.

3. **a**

   The mitochondrion is responsible for producing ATP. The golgi-body processes proteins and lipids. The lysosomes contain digestive enzymes and the ribosomes are the site of protein synthesis.

4. **tissue**

   Many cells of the same type make up tissue. For example, nerve cells make up nervous tissue.

5. **a**

   Epithelial tissue performs all of these functions.

6. **organ**

   A structure comprising of more than one tissue type is an organ. The skin, for example, is an organ as it is made up of a number of different tissue types.

7. **False**

   Several related organs with a common function make up a system. For example, the digestive organs make up the digestive system. All parts of the body, from the chemicals to the systems, make up an organism.

Skeletal System

1. **a**

   The axial skeleton consists of the skull, spine, ribcage and sternum. The remaining skeletal frame is called the appendicular skeleton.

2. **a**

There are 7 cervical vertebrae in the neck. The first cervical vertebra is called the atlas. This permits nodding. The second cervical vertebra is called the axis. The axis allows the head to rotate.

3. **b**

The thoracic vertebrae are located in the chest area.

4. **lumbar**

The 5 lumbar vertebrae make up the lower back. The lumbar vertebrae are the largest and strongest.

5. **d**

The sacrum is formed by the fusion of 5 sacral vertebrae. This fusion usually occurs between the ages of 16 and 25.

6. **coccyx**

The coccyx forms the tail of the vertebral column. It is formed by the fusion of 4 coccygeal vertebrae. This fusion usually occurs between the ages of 20 and 30.

7. **synovial**

Synovial fluid fills the space between the bones in freely moveable joints.

8. **hinge**

The elbow, knee and ankle are hinge joints. Hinge joints restrict movement to a single direction.

9. **shoulder and hip**

The shoulder and hip are ball and socket joints. Ball and socket joints allow the limb to move forward, backwards and to the side. They also allow the bones to rotate.

10. **c**

The phalanges make up the toes. There are three phalanges in each toe, except for the big toe that has only two.

11. **tarsus**

The tarsals are collectively known as the tarsus.

12. **metatarsals**

The metatarsals are the long bones that connect the tarsus to the phalanges.

The Skin

1. **False**

   The skin is classified as an organ because it consists of more than one tissue type.

2. **epidermis**

   The epidermis is the top layer of the skin. The deepest epidermis produces new cells that push to the surface. The cells on the surface of the epidermis are continually shed and replaced by the new.

3. **dermis**

   The dermis is a tough, elastic layer composed of connective tissue, collagen and elastic fibres.

4. **subcutaneous**

   The subcutaneous layer is located beneath the dermis.

5. **adipose tissue**

   The subcutaneous layer consists mainly of adipose tissue. Adipose tissue insulates, protects and is also an energy store.

Respiratory System

1. **carbon dioxide**

   Carbon dioxide is removed from the body during the process of respiration.

2. **d**

   The oxygen passes from the nasal cavity into the pharynx (throat).

3. **b**

   Oxygen passes from the pharynx into the trachea. Food is prevented from going into the trachea by the epiglottis that closes off the trachea during swallowing. This allows the food to pass into the oesophagus, which leads to the stomach.

4. **a**

   The trachea divides into the left primary bronchus and right primary bronchus, which descend into the left lung and right lung respectively. The primary bronchi then branch into secondary bronchi, which branch again to form tertiary bronchi.

5. bronchioles

Tertiary bronchi divide to form bronchioles, the smallest air passages in the lungs.

6. b

The bronchioles terminate in little air sacs called alveoli. A network of capillaries surrounds the alveoli. It is in the alveoli that gaseous exchange takes place.

7. oxygen

Oxygen is absorbed from the alveoli into the blood.

8. carbon dioxide

Carbon dioxide is absorbed from the blood into the alveoli.

9. b

The lungs are covered by a double pleural membrane. They are further protected by the ribcage.

10. diaphragm

The muscular movements of the diaphragm increase and decrease the size of the lungs, so allowing air to be drawn in and expelled.

11. pulmonary arteries

The pulmonary arteries supply blood to the lungs. The blood in the pulmonary arteries is deoxygenated. The blood releases its carbon dioxide and absorbs oxygen in the lungs.

12. pulmonary veins

The pulmonary veins transport the oxygenated blood from the lungs to the left atrium of the heart. The oxygenated blood is then passed to the left ventricle and circulated around the body.

Sight

1. a

The tough outer layer of the eye is the sclera. It is white, except at the front where it is transparent and called the cornea. The cornea is covered by the conjunctiva.

2. b

The choroid is the middle layer of the eye. At the front of the eye the choroid forms the iris. The iris gives the eye its colour.

3. **iris**

The iris contains a band of muscle that can regulate the amount of light that can enter the eye.

4. **retina**

The retina is the inner layer of the eye. It contains the light receptors.

5. **lens**

The lens refracts the light, already refracted by the cornea, to allow the brain to create a focused and clear image.

6. **optic**

The optic nerve transports the information from the eye to the brain.

Sound

1. **a**

The outer ear traps and directs sound. The external flap of skin involved in this is called the pinna.

2. **ear-drum**

The tympanic membrane is commonly called the ear-drum. Sound entering the ear causes the tympanic membrane to vibrate.

3. **c**

The three bones of the middle ear are collectively known as the ossicles. The vibrating tympanic membrane causes the ossicles to vibrate.

4. **c**

The innermost ossicle is connected to the oval window. This membrane transmits the vibrations from the middle ear to the inner ear.

5. **b**

The cochlea contains the receptors for hearing. Vibrations from the oval window cause pressure waves in the cochlea, ultimately resulting in sensory hairs within the cochlea being moved.

6. **auditory nerve**

The auditory nerve transmits auditory information to the brain where it is interpreted as sound.

7. **balance**

   The semicircular canals are responsible for balance. As the head moves, the fluid in these canals drags sensory hairs, stimulating sensory neurons. The nerve impulses are passed to the brain, interpreted, and then used to co-ordinate movement and posture.

Smell

1. **olfactory**

   The olfactory system can store information about thousands of odours.

2. **cilia**

   The hairs on nerve cells are called cilia. The cilia are stimulated by odours.

3. **olfactory bulb**

   The information is sent to the olfactory bulb before being transmitted via the olfactory nerve to the brain.

Urinary System

1. **ureter**

   Urine passes from a kidney to the bladder through a ureter. Urine leaves the bladder via the urethra.

2. **right**

   The right kidney is slightly lower than the left.

3. **d**

   The renal veins take blood away from the kidneys. The renal arteries provide the blood supply.

4. **c**

   The medulla is the dark region of the kidney that contains the renal pyramids. The cortex surrounds the medulla. The renal capsule forms the outer layer of the kidney.

5. **renal pelvis**

   The large cavity in the kidney is called the renal pelvis. Its cup-like extensions collect urine from the renal pyramids and drain it into the ureter.

6. b

The kidney has numerous nephrons that extend from the renal capsule to the cup-like extensions of the renal pelvis. They are situated within a vast capillary network and they absorb excessive and unwanted substances from the blood.

7. a

The Bowman's capsule encases the glomerus. It provides the site at which water and waste are filtered from the blood into the nephron.

8. False

As these substances pass through the nephron, some useful substances are selectively reabsorbed back into the blood. Only the remainder is expelled as urine.

Reproductive System

1. b

The vas deferens carries sperm from the testis and joins the urethra just below the bladder.

2. prostate

The missing word is prostate. These fluids and the sperm make up the semen that is released by the penis.

3. False

Each ovary contains over 200,000 immature ova at birth. Each is encased in a sac. They develop progressively, usually one at a time, in response to the various sex hormones.

4. a

This structure is called a follicle. When a follicle is fully mature it is called a primary follicle. Ovulation then takes place and the ovum is released.

5. b

On ovulation, the ovum is released into the fallopian tube. The fallopian tube is normally the site at which the ovum is fertilized.

6. uterus

The uterus provides the source of attachment and nourishment for the zygote. The uterus later expands to facilitate the developing foetus.

7. a
A reduction of oestrogens and progesterone causes the breakdown of the uterine lining, resulting in the menstrual phase of menstruation.

8. c
The ovaries secrete oestrogen to re-build the uterine wall. They are encouraged to do so by follicle stimulating hormone and luteinizing hormone. Luteinizing hormone also stimulates the ovaries to produce progesterone, the hormone that prepares the uterus to receive a zygote.

Lymphatic System

1. True
Lymphocytes are a type of leucocyte (white blood cell) that play a part in the body's natural defenses and immunity against disease.

2. B-cell
B-cell lymphocytes produce antibodies that attach themselves to invading antigens. T-cell lymphocytes destroy foreign substances.

3. c
The lymphatic capillaries are the smallest. They penetrate the spaces between the cells.

4. b
The lymphatic capillaries converge to form lymphatic vessels. These larger vessels contain valves.

5. lymph nodes
These structures are lymph nodes. Lymph nodes are usually found in clusters, particularly in the axilla, neck, thorax, abdomen and groin.

6. b
Lymph ducts are the largest. They are formed by converging lymph trunks. Lymph ducts join the cardiovascular system.

7. False
The left lymphatic duct drains lymph from the left side of the head, neck and chest, left arm, and all the lower body. The right lymphatic duct drains lymph from the right side of the head, neck and chest and the right arm.

8. **spleen**
The spleen is the largest mass of lymphatic tissue in the body, although it has no connection to lymphatic vessels. The spleen produces lymphocytes and stores red blood cells.

9. **endocrine system**
The thymus is a component of both the lymphatic system and the endocrine system.

Muscular System

1. **contraction**
Muscle tissue is characterized by its ability to contract.

2. **skeletal**
Skeletal muscle is mainly attached to bone (often using tendons). Skeletal muscle contains light and dark bands and is referred to as striated.

3. **smooth**
Smooth muscle is found in the walls of hollow structures such as blood vessels and the stomach. Smooth muscle does not have the striations found in skeletal muscle.

4. **a**
There is voluntary control over skeletal muscle. The movement of both smooth muscle and cardiac muscle is involuntary.

5. **heart**
Cardiac muscle forms most of the heart.

6. **a**
The attachment to the bone that remains unmoved is the origin. The attachment to the bone that the contraction is intended to move is called the insertion.

7. **b, c, a**
The pairs are: flexors and extensors (decrease and increase the angle at a joint), abductors and adductors (move away from and draw into the midline), and levators and depressors (produce an upward and downward movement).

Cardiovascular System

1. **plasma**
   Plasma makes up over half of the blood. Plasma is 91% water and 7% proteins. It is responsible for transporting nutrients, salts, hormones, enzymes, gases and excretory products.

2. **a**
   Erythrocytes are red blood cells. They appear as bi-concave discs and are produced in the red bone marrow.

3. **a**
   Red blood cells transport the gases of respiration. They are able to do so as they contain the protein haemoglobin.

4. **b**
   White blood cells, called leucocytes, play an important role in immunity. They are produced in the bone marrow.

5. **platelets**
   Platelets are involved in blood clotting. When platelets come in contact with damaged tissue they release chemicals which start a chain of reactions to form a blood clot.

6. **myocardium**
   The myocardium is the middle, muscular layer of the heart. The specialized muscle fibres allow the heart to 'beat'.

7. **coronary**
   The heart receives its own blood supply from the coronary arteries.

8. **aorta**
   Oxygenated blood leaves the heart via the aorta.

9. **vena cava**
   The heart receives deoxygenated blood via the superior and inferior vena cava. The deoxygenated blood is then pumped to the lungs, via the pulmonary arteries, where it becomes oxygenated.

10. **4**
    There are four chambers in the heart, two atriums and two ventricles.

11. **a**
    The upper chambers are called atriums.

12. True

Deoxygenated and oxygenated blood do not mix in the heart. It is kept separate by the dividing septum.

13. a

The right atrium receives deoxygenated blood. It is received via the superior and inferior vena cava.

14. right ventricle

Deoxygenated blood passes from the right atrium to the right ventricle.

15. b

Deoxygenated blood is taken to the lungs in the pulmonary arteries.

16. pulmonary veins

The pulmonary veins bring oxygenated blood back from the lungs to the heart.

17. c

The left atrium receives oxygenated blood from the pulmonary veins.

18. left ventricle

The blood passes from the left atrium into the left ventricle. The left ventricle is the largest, most muscular chamber of the heart.

19. aorta

The aorta takes oxygenated blood from the left ventricle, for circulation around the body.

20. a

Arteries carry blood away from the heart. With the exception of the pulmonary arteries, they contain oxygenated blood.

21. b

Veins carry blood back to the heart. With the exception of the pulmonary veins, they contain deoxygenated blood.

22. b

Veins have valves. Venous blood is under less pressure and so the valves help to prevent the back-flow of blood.

23. c

Capillaries are the smallest blood vessels. They make up dense networks. Arteries divide many times until they become capillaries. Capillaries merge many times until they become veins.

Digestive System

1. c
The alimentary canal runs from 'mouth to anus'.

2. b
Salivary amylase begins to break down starches. This is the beginning of chemical digestion. Mechanical digestion also begins in the mouth as the teeth and tongue manipulate the food.

3. a
The food passes from the mouth into the pharynx.

4. oesophagus
The oesophagus takes the food from the pharynx to the stomach.

5. a
The stomach provides an acidic environment for digestion. The gastric juices include hydrochloric acid.

6. c
Trypsin is not a part of the gastric juices (it is secreted by the pancreas). Rennin is an enzyme that coagulates the milk protein casein. Gastrin is a hormone that stimulates the secretion of hydrochloric acid and pepsinogen, and affects the muscular activity of the stomach. Pepsinogen, on contact with hydrochloric acid, is converted to pepsin, a protein-digesting enzyme.

7. pyloric sphincter
Food leaves the stomach via the pyloric sphincter. At this point, the semi-fluid mixture is called chyme.

8. duodenum
The missing word is duodenum, the first part of the small intestine.

9. d
The small intestine begins with the duodenum. The second part is the jejunum and then lastly the ileum.

10. a
Lipase digests fats (also known as lipids). Pancreatic amylase digests carbohydrates and trypsin digests proteins.

11. a

The acini produce the pancreatic juice. The acini account for about 99% of the clusters of glandular epithelial cells.

12. b

The islets of Langerhans secrete hormones. The islets of Langerhans account for 1% of the clusters of glandular epithelial cells. This hormonal secretion classifies the pancreas as an endocrine gland.

13. a

The hepatic artery supplies the liver with oxygenated blood.

14. c

The inferior vena cava takes deoxygenated blood from the liver to the heart.

15. stomach and intestines

The hepatic portal vein brings deoxygenated blood from the stomach and intestines. The harmful substances, absorbed by the blood from the digestive tract, are removed from the blood by the liver and then destroyed.

16. bile

Bile is produced and secreted by the liver and then stored in the gall bladder. Bile consists of salts, pigments, cholesterol and traces of other substances.

17. a

The bile duct meets the small intestine at the duodenum. The bile duct joins a pancreatic duct and they both enter the duodenum at the ampulla of Vater.

18. c

Bile plays a role in the emulsification of fats, breaking down the large fat globules into smaller ones.

19. villi

The inner layer of the small intestine extends into numerous finger-like projections called villi. Each villus contains a network of capillaries and a lacteal (a lymphatic vessel) to facilitate absorption.

20. ileocaecal

The missing word is ileocaecal. Chyme passes through the ileocaecal sphincter to enter the large intestine.

21. **False**

The large intestine does not have villi. It is also much wider than the small intestine. The large intestine continues the absorption of water and nutrients from the food, and prepares undigested food and waste for expulsion as faeces.

Endocrine System

1. **True**

Endocrine glands are ductless and secrete hormones directly into the blood.

2. **pituitary**

The missing word is pituitary. Hormones secreted by the hypothalamus are taken in the blood to the pituitary gland.

3. **b**

The posterior lobe of the pituitary gland stores and releases two hormones produced by the hypothalamus.

4. **b**

Antidiuretic hormone, also called vasopressin, decreases urine production and causes the contraction of the arteries. Oxytocin stimulates the contraction of the uterine muscles during childbirth and milk ejection after birth.

5. **c**

Adrenocorticotrophic hormone stimulates secretions from the adrenal glands.

6. **e**

Gonadotrophic hormones (e.g. follicle stimulating hormone and luteinizing hormone) stimulate the activities of the ovaries and testes (gonads).

7. **b**

Prolactin stimulates the mammary glands to produce milk.

8. **hypothalamus**

The hypothalamus controls the release of the anterior lobe pituitary hormones. Remember, hormones actually produced by the hypothalamus are stored and released by the posterior lobe of the pituitary gland.

9. **thyroid stimulating hormone**

Thyroid stimulating hormone stimulates the thyroid.

10. thyroxine

Thyroxine is the main thyroid hormone. The thyroid hormones regulate growth and development.

11. four

There are four parathyroid glands. They produce parathyroid hormone that decreases the blood phosphate level and increases the blood calcium level.

12. b

The adrenal medulla produces the 'fight or flight' hormones when the body is under stress.

13. adrenaline or noradrenaline

The 'fight or flight' hormones are adrenaline, which causes an increase in the metabolic rate, heart rate and blood pressure, and noradrenaline, a neurotransmitter that either excites or inhibits adjacent nerve or muscle cells.

14. False

The adrenal cortex does secrete hormones. It secretes cortisol and corticosterone (stimulate the conversion of fats and proteins to glucose), aldosterone (controls sodium and potassium concentrations) and androgens and oestrogens (male and female sex hormones).

15. False

Only the islets of Langerhans, which make up just 1% of the pancreas, secrete hormones. Most of the pancreatic tissue is involved in producing digestive enzymes.

16. insulin

The pancreas secretes insulin that decreases the blood-glucose level. It also secretes glucagon, a hormone that increases the blood-glucose level.

17. oestrogen

Oestrogen is the female sex hormone that performs these roles.

18. a

Progesterone is produced after ovulation to help prepare the uterus for the implantation of the fertilized ovum. It also develops the placenta and prepares the mammary glands for milk secretion.

19. c
Relaxin dilates the cervix and helps the pelvic girdle to widen during childbirth.

20. testosterone
Testosterone is the primary male sex hormone. It controls the growth and maintenance of the reproductive system and the development of secondary sex characteristics. It also stimulates the production of sperm and body growth.

21. inhibin
Inhibin inhibits the secretion of follicle stimulating hormone. In the male, this controls sperm production. In females, it reduces the secretion of oestrogen.

Nervous System

1. neurons
Nerve cells are called neurons. They are specialized to be able to transmit nerve impulses.

2. sensory neuron
Sensory neurons transmit information from the sensory organs. Motor neurons transmit information to the part of the body that has to respond to the sensory stimulus.

3. synapse
The junction between neurons is called a synapse. A neurotransmitter called dopamine allows the nerve impulse to be conveyed across the synapse.

4. True
The central nervous system consists of the brain and the spinal cord. The rest of the nervous system makes up the peripheral nervous system.

5. carotid
The carotid is the main artery that supplies blood to the brain. The external and internal jugulars are the principal veins.

6. b
There are 12 pairs of cranial nerves. Many of these serve the sensory organs and muscles to the head, but some do extend to other parts of the body. Although the cranial nerves originate from the brain, they are not a part of the central nervous system. They form a part of the peripheral nervous system.

7. cerebrum
The cerebrum consists of two hemispheres. It is the most prominent region of the brain.

8. four
Each cerebral hemisphere has four lobes – frontal, parietal, occipital and temporal.

9. cerebellum
The rear part of the brain is the cerebellum. The cerebellum controls fine voluntary movements and posture.

10. c
There are 31 pairs of spinal nerves. Although they originate from the spinal cord they are not a part of the central nervous system. They form a part of the peripheral nervous system.

11. True
Apart from the brain and the spinal cord, all structures made up of nerve cells or tissues are a part of the peripheral nervous system.

12. False
The peripheral nervous system conveys sensory impulses from sensory organs to the central nervous system. These impulses are processed by the central nervous system. The peripheral nervous system is then used to transmit the consequent motor impulses to the muscles and glands.

13. autonomic nervous system
The autonomic nervous system deals with the body's involuntary, automatic responses. The autonomic nervous system supplies motor nerves to the smooth muscle of the internal organs, heart and glands.

14. a
The sympathetic nervous system increases the heart rate, respiratory rate and blood pressure. The parasympathetic nervous system has the opposite effect.

15. a
The sympathetic nervous system slows digestion. The parasympathetic nervous system has the opposite effect.

16. b

Motor nerves of the parasympathetic nervous system arise from the cranial nerves and a few of the spinal nerves in the sacral region. Motor nerves of the sympathetic nervous system originate from the spinal nerves in the thoracic and lumbar regions.

This page has intentionally been left blank.

Foot
and
Hand
Charts

395

This page has intentionally been left blank.

Plantar Foot Charts

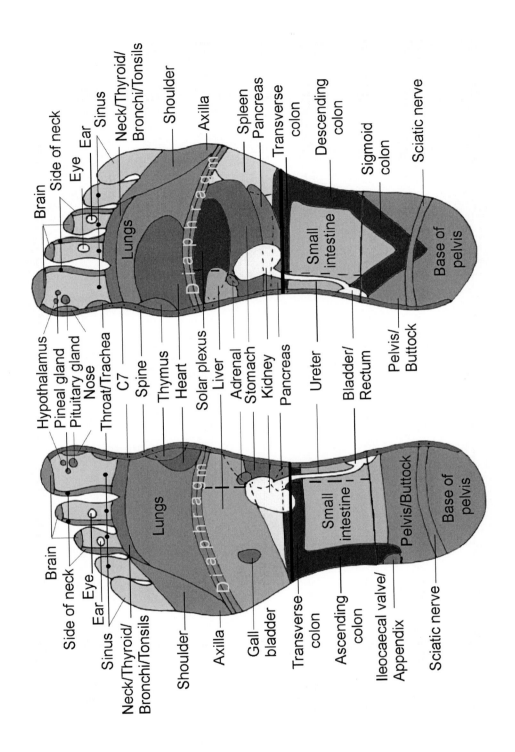

By kind permission of the British School of Reflexology.

This page has intentionally been left blank.

Dorsal Foot Charts

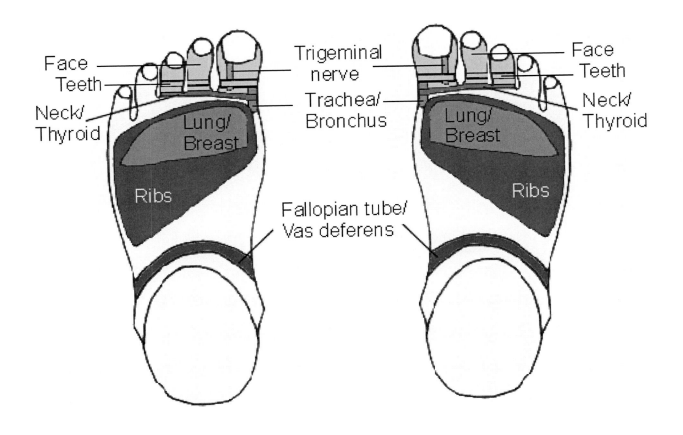

By kind permission of the British School of Reflexology.

This page has intentionally been left blank.

Medial Foot Charts

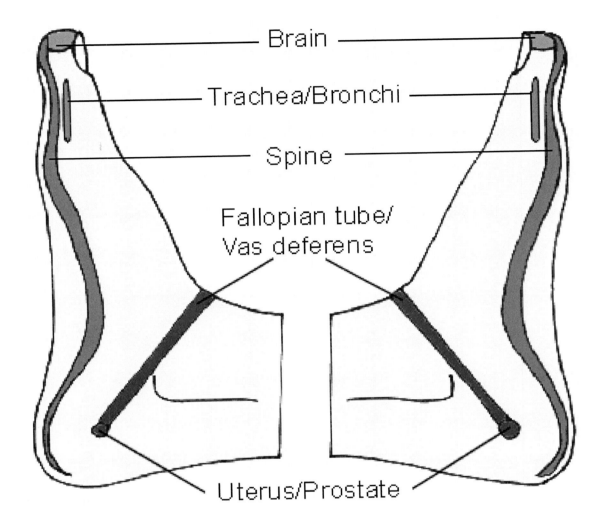

Brain

Trachea/Bronchi

Spine

Fallopian tube/
Vas deferens

Uterus/Prostate

By kind permission of the British School of Reflexology.

This page has intentionally been left blank.

Lateral Foot Charts

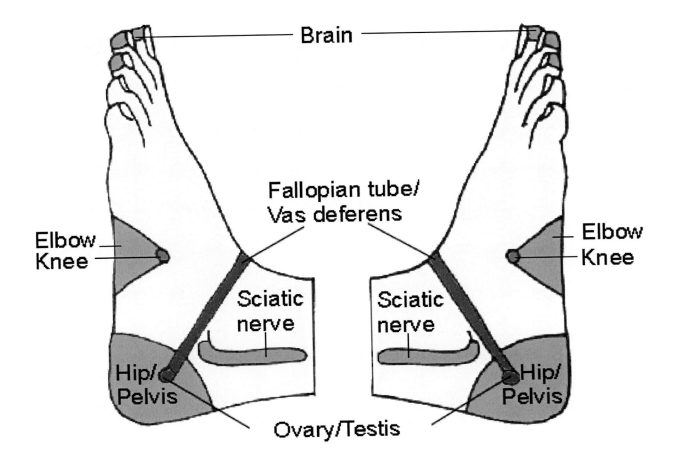

By kind permission of the British School of Reflexology.

This page has intentionally been left blank.

Palmar Hand Charts

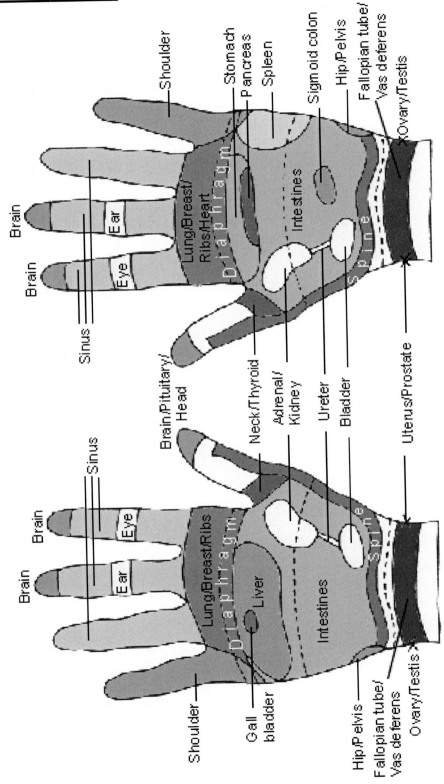

By kind permission of the British School of Reflexology.

This page has intentionally been left blank.

Dorsal Hand Charts

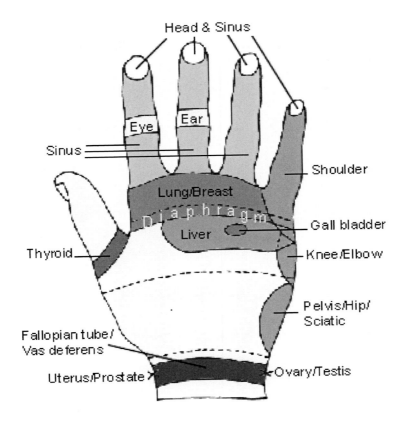

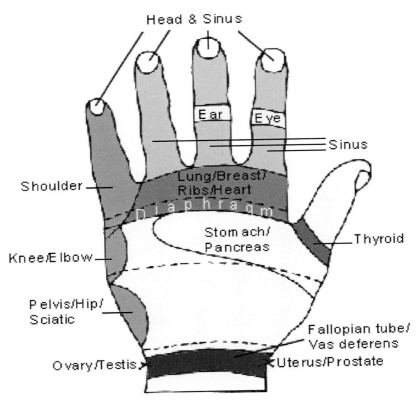

By kind permission of the British School of Reflexology.

This page has intentionally been left blank.

Glossary

409

This page has intentionally been left blank.

Acupuncture: A pressure therapy in which the pressure is applied to specific sites of the body using needles.

Acute condition: A worse than chronic disorder, possibly leading rapidly to death.

Adenoids: An overgrowth of the glandular tissue, naturally found in small amounts, on the back of the upper part of the throat.

Adrenal glands: Endocrine glands located on the top of the kidneys. They produce a variety of hormones including adrenaline.

Adrenaline: The 'fight or flight' hormone produced by the adrenal glands. It prepares the body for an emergency. Adrenaline causes an increase in heart rate, dilation of the pupils and an increase in the metabolic rate. Also called epinephrine.

Afferent: Conveys from the outer part of the body to the inner.

Alexander Technique: A technique developed by Frederick Matthias Alexander, aimed to improve posture so that the body can operate with minimum strain.

Alveoli: A cluster of air sacs found in the lungs at the end of the finest bronchioles.

Alveolus: A small opening or cavity. An air sac found in the lungs.

Anaemia: Deficiency of red blood cells or haemoglobin.

Angina pectoris: A painful sensation in the chest, usually connected with disease of the coronary arteries. It is usually due to an inadequate blood supply to the myocardium (heart muscle). The pain often extends into the left arm.

Ankhmahor: An Egyptian physician of great importance, second only to the King. In his tomb at Saqqara, a painting, dating back to 2330 B.C., appears to show a reflexology treatment being performed.

Anorexia nervosa: A severe loss of appetite, generally in women, in which the sufferer eats almost nothing and hardly sleeps. There is often a phobia about putting on weight and this usually stems from a psychological disorder. This condition often ends in a nervous breakdown and in severe cases death.

Anterior: To the front. Also called ventral.

Antibacterial: Destroys bacteria.

Antibody: A protein produced by the body to neutralize the effect of antigens.

Antidepressant: Aids to lift the mood, alleviating depression.

Antigen: A foreign, invading substance that induces the body to form antibodies.

Apoplexy: Commonly known as a stroke, apoplexy is characterized by a sudden insensibility or impairment of bodily function. This may be due to a blood clot or a diseased condition of the brain.

Appendix: A small blind tube protruding from the caecum in the large intestine. It no longer has a digestive function.

Area of assistance: An additional reflex area, away from the area in difficulty, associated with some conditions which, when treated, benefits the primary target area. For example, shoulder conditions can be eased by working on the hip reflex area. In this case the hip is the area of assistance. An area of assistance generally has a zonal, organic, structural or neural link to the primary target area.

Artery: A vessel that carries blood away from the heart.

Ascending colon: A part of the large intestine that runs up the right side of the abdomen from the caecum to the transverse colon.

Athlete's foot: Skin eruption on the foot, usually between the toes. It is commonly due to a fungal infection, such as ringworm, or simply caused by excessive sweating of the feet. The skin tends to be inflamed, moist, flaky, itchy and painful.

Atlas: The top cervical vertebra (C1), which permits the nodding movement.

Atom: The smallest and simplest matter that can take part in a chemical reaction. An atom has a nucleus (central part) containing protons (positively charged particles) and neutrons (particles with no electrical charge). The nucleus is surrounded by a number of electrons (negatively charged particles).

Autonomic nervous system: Part of the peripheral nervous system that regulates the activity of smooth muscle (found in the walls of hollow structures), cardiac muscle (found in the heart) and glands. It comprises of the sympathetic and parasympathetic nervous systems.

Axilla: Commonly called the armpit. It is the hollow underneath the arm where the arm joins the side of the chest.

Axis: The second cervical vertebra (C2). The pivot joint between C1 and C2 allows the head to rotate from side to side.

Bach Rescue Remedy: A liquid remedy, produced by infusing plant material in spring water. Dr Edward Bach, an English doctor, started producing flower-based remedies in the 1930's, mainly to treat emotional conditions or physical symptoms arising from emotional problems.

Bi-directional: Two way.

Bile: A secretion of the liver, stored in the gall bladder, which enters the duodenum via the bile duct. It consists of salts, pigments, cholesterol and traces of other substances. Bile aids digestion by emulsifying fats.

Bladder (urinary): A thin-walled muscular sac used to temporarily store urine. The urine is drained from the kidneys to the bladder by the ureters, and leaves the bladder via the urethra.

Bowen Technique: A non-manipulative, hands-on technique, pioneered in Australia in the 1950's by Mr Tom Bowen. Practitioners make a series of light, rolling movements on the muscles and tendons using their fingers and thumbs. It is said to stimulate energy flow.

Bowers, Dr. Edwin: Worked with Dr. William H. Fitzgerald. In 1917 Bowers and Fitzgerald co-wrote "Zone Therapy, or Relieving Pain at Home". Two years later they published "Zone Therapy or Curing Pain and Disease".

Bronchiole: A third or greater branch of the bronchus. The many bronchioles carry air to all areas of the lung. The finest bronchioles end in alveoli.

Bronchus (primary): One of the two large branches of the trachea. The bronchi take air into the lungs. They branch into secondary bronchi, tertiary bronchi and then into bronchioles.

Buddha: Title meaning 'Awakened One', primarily given to Gautama Siddhartha (c 563-483 B.C.), founder of Buddhism. He was born near Nepal in northern India and become enlightened under a bo (bodhi meaning wisdom) tree near Buddh Gaya in Bihar, India. It is believed that different Buddhas have appeared from time to time and will continue to do so in the future when mankind needs them.

Buddhism: A religious system and philosophy taught by the Buddha. Buddhism was founded in India in the 6th century B.C. and is based on the moral conduct of the individual, not on the authority of priests. There is no worship of a supreme God and the purpose of the Buddhist is to follow the path taken by Gautama Buddha towards enlightenment and mystical awareness. Buddhism reached China and South East Asia by the 1st and 2nd centuries A.D. and reached Japan (via Korea) by the 6th century A.D.. Western observers have been impressed with the serenity and strength of character associated with Buddhism, and it has even been suggested that the future of Buddhism lies in the West.

Byers, Dwight C.: Nephew of Eunice Ingham. Dwight Byers assisted Eunice Ingham with her work and carried it on after her death in 1974.

C7: The last (lowest) of the seven cervical vertebrae.

Capillary: One of numerous tiny blood vessels. They have thin walls that allow the exchange of gases and other substances between the blood and the tissues.

Carbohydrate: Energy producing compound of carbon, oxygen and hydrogen, e.g. starch, glucose and sugar.

Carcinoma: Malignant disease of the epithelial tissue (the tissue that forms glands and the outer part of the skin, and lines the blood vessels, hollow organs and passages that lead externally from the body).

Cardiovascular system: Responsible for supplying blood to the tissues. It consists of the blood, heart and the network of vessels.

Carotene: Orange/red substance, formed in foods such as carrots, that is a source of vitamin A.

Carpals: The eight bones that make up the wrist.

Cartilage: Thick, fibrous gristle found in a number of locations in the body, e.g. lining the end of the bones in joints, between the vertebrae, in the outer ear and at the end of the nose.

Case history: Full patient details including current and past medical history. There is a legal requirement to document this information, along with any treatment and subsequent results. These details must be kept for a minimum of 6 years.

Cells: The basic structural and functional units that make up the body.

Central nervous system: Comprises of the brain and the spinal cord. It receives sensory information from all parts of the body, analyzes the information and then responds by sending impulses to stimulate muscles or glands.

Cerebrum: The two hemispheres that make up the largest part of the brain.

Cervical vertebra: One of the seven bones that make up the neck area of the vertebral column (spine). The first cervical vertebra is called the atlas. The second is called the axis.

Cholera: A potentially fatal infection caused by the bacteria Vibrio cholerae. It is commonly spread by contaminated water but also by flies which contaminate food with infected faeces. This condition is characterized by diarrhoea, vomiting and stomach cramps.

Cholesterol: A fat derivative found in animal cells that is insoluble in water. Its presence on the inside of the walls of blood vessels is thought to contribute to hypertension and thrombosis. It can also accumulate in the gall bladder as gall stones.

Chromosome: A structure in the cell nucleus (centre) that carries the genes. Each chromosome consists of one very long strand of deoxyribonucleic acid (DNA). Humans usually have 23 pairs of chromosomes.

Chronic condition: A severe, long lasting disorder.

Cilia: Tiny hairs that line many body cavities.

Coccyx: The triangular bone at the tail of the vertebral column (spine), consisting of four fused coccygeal vertebrae.

Congenital: Existing at birth.

Connective tissue: The most abundant tissue type. It binds, supports and connects structures within the body.

Contra-indication: An aspect of the patient's condition that prevents the treatment. Contra-indications that may prevent a reflexology treatment from taking place include pregnancy, cancer, infectious and contagious illnesses, thrombosis, phlebitis, venous or lymphatic inflammations, psychosis, internal bleeding and a continued extreme negative reaction to the treatment.

Cortisone: A steroid hormone produced by the adrenal glands or synthetically. It has anti-inflammatory properties.

Cranial nerves: The twelve pairs of nerves originating in the brain.

Deoxyribonucleic acid (DNA): A complex two-stranded molecule, found in chromosomes, that contains all the information needed to build, control and maintain a living organism. It forms the basis for genetic inheritance.

Descending colon: A part of the large intestine that runs down the left side of the abdomen from the transverse colon to the sigmoid colon.

Diaphragm line: The guideline located just beneath the joints of the phalanges and the metatarsals. This line is easy to determine because the skin colour is darker above this line than it is below it. On the hand it is located in the palm just below the joints of the phalanges and the metacarpals.

Diaphragm: A dome-shaped sheet of muscle and tendon that divides the thorax from the abdomen. It plays a major role in respiration. During inspiration it contracts, drawing air into the lungs. During expiration the diaphragm relaxes, forcing air to be expelled.

Digestion: The mechanical and chemical breakdown of food into molecules that can be absorbed and used by the body.

Digestive system: The organs responsible for the ingestion, digestion, absorption and elimination of food. The digestive system runs from mouth to anus, a route often referred to as the alimentary canal.

Diphtheria: An acute infectious disease. It primarily affects the throat but can harm the heart muscle and the nerves.

Dorsal: Pertains to the back or posterior. In reflexology, the dorsal view shows the top of the feet.

Duodenum: The first and shortest part of the small intestine.

Dysentery: An infectious disease characterized by the inflammation and ulceration of the lower portion of the bowel, causing stomach cramps and diarrhoea.

Dyspepsia: Another name for indigestion, characterized by pain or discomfort in the upper part of the abdomen or the front of the chest.

Efferent: Conveys from the inner part of the body away to the outer.

Emulsification: The break down of large fat globules into smaller ones in the presence of bile.

Endocrine gland: A ductless gland that secretes hormones into the blood.

Endocrine system: The system in which ductless endocrine glands (e.g. hypothalamus, pituitary, adrenals, thymus, testes, ovaries, thyroid, parathyroids, pancreas and pineal) secrete hormones into the blood to regulate many body functions.

Enzyme: Biological catalyst produced in cells, capable of speeding up chemical reactions. Enzymes are large, complex proteins and are not destroyed during the chemical reactions that they promote.

Epiglottis: A flap of tissue that prevents food entering the trachea during swallowing, so allowing the food to pass safely into the oesophagus.

Epilepsy: A nervous condition, characterized by fits, convulsions and a sudden loss of consciousness.

Epithelial tissue: Forms glands and the outer part of the skin. It lines the blood vessels, hollow organs and passages that lead out of the body.

Eustachian tube: The passage that leads from the pharynx to the middle ear.

Exocrine gland: A gland that secretes substances into ducts that empty to an epithelial surface.

Expectoration: Bringing material up from the chest via the air passages.

Fallopian tube: One of two funnel-shaped tubes, each leading from an ovary to the uterus. The fallopian tubes transport the ova to the uterus and provide the site for fertilization.

Fat: An oily or greasy energy-providing food source. Saturated fats are derived from animal fats and dairy products. Unsaturated fats include vegetable oils (soya bean, maize and sunflower) and marine oils from fish.

Fibroid: Tumour of the womb.

Fitzgerald, Dr. William H.: (1872-1942) American physician who rediscovered the ancient belief of zone therapy. He also worked in Europe, including Vienna, Paris and London. In 1917 he wrote, in association with Dr. Edwin Bowers, "Zone Therapy, or Relieving Pain at Home". Two years later they published "Zone Therapy or Curing Pain and Disease".

Follicle stimulating hormone: Abbreviated to FSH, this hormone is secreted by the pituitary gland. It initializes the development of ova and stimulates the ovaries to secrete oestrogens (in females) and stimulates the production of sperm (in males).

Follicle: A small secretory cavity.

Gall bladder: A small sac, located behind the liver, which stores bile and secretes it into the duodenum via the bile duct.

Ganglion: A group of nerve cell bodies that lie outside the central nervous system.

Gangrene: Death and decomposition of a part of the body, usually caused by obstructed circulation.

Gastritis: Inflammation of the stomach.

Gene: Unit of inherited material located on a chromosome that, by itself or with other genes, determines a characteristic in an organism.

Gillanders, Ann: Studied reflexology with Dwight C. Byers and qualified in 1976. She is the Founder of the British School of Reflexology and is now considered to be one of the leading authorities and teachers of modern day reflexology.

Goitre: The swelling on the front of the neck, caused by the enlargement of the thyroid gland.

Glucose: A form of sugar that circulates in the blood.

Glycogen: The form in which carbohydrates are stored in the liver and muscle. They are converted into glucose as the body needs it.

Guidelines: Lines derived from the principle that the feet (and hands) mirror the body. Guidelines are used to divide the feet (and hands) into the main sections that assist in the location of specific reflex areas.

Haemorrhage: The escape of blood from a vessel.

Haemorrhoids: Commonly called piles, they consist of a varicose vein at the lower end of the bowel.

Heart: The main organ of the cardiovascular system, responsible for pumping the blood around the body.

Hinduism: An ancient religious culture dating back more than 3,000 years, dominating India. Hinduism has no founder and many of its sacred writings originate from widely different dates and places. The oldest scriptures are the Vedas, perhaps dating from 1500 or 2000 B.C.. The Supreme Being is Brahman, into whom the individual soul will ultimately be absorbed. The three chief Gods are Brahma (the creator), Vishnu (the preserver) and Siva (the destroyer). Central to Hinduism is the belief in reincarnation and karma (actions being carried forward from one life to the next, resulting in an improved or worsened fate).

Holistic: Whole, encompassing all aspects. Holistic therapies usually consider the mind, body and spirit.

Hormones: Chemical messengers, secreted into the blood by the endocrine glands. They control many body processes including growth, metabolism, sexual development and reproduction.

Humour: A fluid or semi-fluid substance in the body often used to support organs, e.g. aqueous humour and vitreous humour support the eye.

Hyperventilation: Increased respiratory rate.

Hypothalamus: Situated at the base of the brain, the hypothalamus is involved in many regulatory and metabolic activities, e.g. body temperature, hormone release, heart rate, respiratory rate, blood pressure, hunger and digestion. It also acts as an emotional regulator capable of alleviating anxiety and depression.

Ileocaecal sphincter/valve: The point at which the ileum of the small intestine meets the caecum of the large intestine.

Ileum: The final and longest part of the small intestine. The ileum joins the large intestine at the ileocaecal valve.

Ingham, Eunice: (1889-1974) Worked with Dr. Joe Shelby Riley in the early 30's. Eunice Ingham started equating areas on the feet with the anatomy of the body and drew up detailed foot charts. She found that not only did 'zone therapy' relieve pain but it also promoted healing. In 1938 she published a book entitled "Stories the Feet Can Tell" and then "Stories the Feet Have Told". Eunice Ingham is credited with coining the term 'reflexology'. The National Institute of Reflexology and the International Institute of Reflexology were formed, dedicated to the teaching of the Original Ingham Method.

Inorganic compound: Substance not containing carbon that is non-living or has never lived.

Insulin: A pancreatic secretion that enables the muscles and other tissues to utilize the sugar in the blood.

Integumentary system: Comprises of the skin and its associated components such as the nails and hair.

Intercostal muscles: Muscles located between the ribs.

Intervertebral disc: A pad of fibrous cartilage located between two vertebrae.

Jejunum: The middle part of the small intestine, between the duodenum and the ileum.

Kidney: A bean-shaped excretory organ of the urinary system, responsible for controlling the composition, volume and pressure of the blood. The kidneys absorb excessive materials and waste products from the blood and form urine.

Lacteal: A lymphatic vessel embedded in the villi of the small intestine.

Lactic acid: A colourless, syrupy, sour liquid, produced by the action of a bacterium on the sugar content of milk. It is produced in the body during muscular activity from the breakdown of glycogen. Muscle fatigue and cramp are associated with an accumulation of lactic acid in the muscles. Recovery takes place when a sufficient amount of oxygen accesses the muscles and reacts with the lactic acid, building it up once more into glycogen.

Large intestine: The part of the digestive tract that extends from the ileocaecal sphincter to the anus. It incorporates the caecum, appendix, ascending colon, transverse colon, descending colon, sigmoid colon, rectum and anal canal. The large intestine receives chyme from the small intestine. It continues the absorption of water and nutrients from the digested food and prepares undigested food and waste for expulsion as faeces.

Larynx: Voice box, situated at the top of the trachea.

Lateral: Pertaining to the side. In reflexology, the lateral view of the foot shows the little toe in the foreground. Memory hint: **Lateral = Little** toe side.

Leucocyte: White blood cell that plays a part in the body's natural defenses and immunity against disease. Leucocytes occur in the blood, lymph and elsewhere in the body's tissues. Some engulf invading micro-organisms, some kill infected cells, while lymphocytes (a type of white blood cell) produce more specific immune responses.

Leukaemia: A disease in which the number of white blood cells is permanently excessive. It is characterized by the enlargement of the spleen and the lymph glands. Changes also occur in the bone marrow. The cause is unknown.

Ligament line: A guideline that runs down the plantar aspect of the foot between the first and second toes. It follows the line of the ligament that can be felt just below the surface of the skin when the toes are pulled back.

Ligament: Tough, elastic, connective tissue that connects two bones at a joint.

Liver: The heaviest organ in the body, located to the right of the upper abdomen, just below the diaphragm. Its many functions include regulating the composition of the blood, producing bile, removing toxic substances and breaking down used blood cells. It also manufactures and stores certain substances.

Longitudinal: Running lengthwise.

Lumbar vertebra: One of the five bones that make up the lower back area of the vertebral column (spine). The lumbar vertebrae are the largest and strongest of the vertebrae.

Lung: A major organ of the respiratory system, situated in the thorax. The lungs receive 'new' air, provide the site in which gaseous exchange can take place in the blood, and expel 'old' air.

Luteinizing hormone: Abbreviated to LH, this hormone is secreted by the pituitary gland. In females, it stimulates ovulation and the production of oestrogen and progesterone. It also prepares the mammary glands for milk secretion. In males, it stimulates the production of testosterone by the testes.

Lymph nodes: Small, round bodies that occur at intervals along the lymphatic vessels. They are usually found in clusters, particularly in the axilla (armpit), neck, thorax, abdomen and groin. The lymph nodes are packed with lymphocytes and so have a valuable part to play in dealing with infection. When the lymph nodes are particularly active in this role they may swell.

Lymph: The used and excess tissue fluid that is drained from the intercellular spaces into the vessels of the lymphatic system.

Lymphatic system: A series of vessels and associated lymph nodes in which lymph is transported from the tissue fluids into the bloodstream. Lymph is drained from the tissues by lymph capillaries, which empty into larger lymph vessels. The lymph vessels lead to lymph nodes (found mainly in the neck, axilla, groin, thorax and abdomen) which process the lymphocytes produced by the bone marrow and filter out harmful substances and bacteria. From the lymph nodes the lymph is carried in larger vessels called lymphatic trunks. The lymphatic trunks join to form lymph ducts. The lymph ducts join the cardiovascular system and the lymph is drained into large veins that transport the blood to the heart. The tonsils, spleen and thymus comprise of lymphatic tissue and are included in this system.

Lymphocyte: Type of white blood cell produced in the bone marrow and lymphatic glands. Most occur in the lymph and blood and around sites of infection. There are two main types of lymphocyte; B-cell lymphocytes that are responsible for producing antibodies and T-cell lymphocytes that have various roles to play in immunity including destroying foreign substances.

Malaria: A potentially fatal, parasitic disease spread by the Anopheles mosquito. It is characterized by headaches and periodic fever.

Malignant: The term used for several diseases to indicate its severity. In the case of tumours, malignant means fast growing and spreading, eventually leading to death.

Marquardt, Hanne: Trained with Eunice Ingham and then became the first practitioner in Germany to work using pressure on the feet only. She was also credited with introducing the concept of transverse lines across the feet. Marquardt went on to train a large number of medically qualified professionals to be reflexologists.

Marrow: Soft substance in the cavities of bones. Red marrow produces blood cells. Yellow marrow consists mainly of fat.

Medial: Pertains to the middle. In reflexology, the medial view of the foot shows the big toe in the foreground. Memory hint: **M**edial = **M**iddle.

Meningitis: An inflammation of the membranes surrounding the brain and/or spinal cord.

Menstruation: The monthly menstrual flow caused by the breakdown and expulsion of the lining of the uterus, together with much bleeding. The uterine lining regenerates after menstruation in preparation for the reception of a fertilized ovum. In the absence of this, it breaks down again and the cycle continues. The monthly menstrual cycle begins with the onset of puberty and continues until the menopause.

Metabolism: The chemical reactions that take place in cells. It is metabolic reactions that keep cells alive. Metabolic reactions involve breaking down molecules to provide energy, and building up more complex molecules and structures from simpler molecules.

Metacarpals: Five bones in the hand that are situated below the phalanges (the bones that make up the fingers) and above the carpals (the eight bones that make up the wrist).

Metatarsal notch: The small bony protuberance on the lateral (outside) edge of the foot, at the end of the 5th metatarsal. It is used to locate the position of the waist line.

Metatarsals: Five bones in the foot that are situated below the phalanges (the bones that make up the toes) and above the cuboid and the three cuneiforms (four of the seven bones that make up the ankle).

Molecule: Formed when two or more atoms combine.

Mucus: A thick secretion from the mucous glands or membranes.

Muscle tissue: Characterized by its ability to contract. There are three main types: 1. Skeletal - this type is mainly attached to bones and it can voluntarily be made to contract and relax. 2. Smooth - this type is found in the walls of hollow structures such as blood vessels, the stomach and other internal organs. Its movement is involuntary. 3. Cardiac - this type of muscle tissue forms most of the heart. Its movement is involuntary.

Nervous system: All components of the body made of nerve cells (neurons). Divided into the central nervous system (comprising of the brain and spinal cord) and the peripheral nervous system that includes all other nervous tissue.

Neuron: A nerve cell.

Noradrenaline: A hormonal neurotransmitter secreted by the medulla of the adrenals and from nerve endings supplied by the sympathetic nervous system. It increases heart rate, breathing rate and blood pressure and slows down digestion.

Oesophagus: The tube that connects the throat to the stomach.

Oestrogens: Female sex hormones produced by the ovaries. Oestrogens are concerned with the development and maintenance of the reproductive system and the development of secondary sex characteristics (e.g. growth of the breasts). During the menstrual cycle, oestrogen prepares the body for the implantation and growth of the fertilized ovum.

Organ: Made up of varying types of tissue. Organs have specific functions and usually have distinctive shapes.

Organic compound: Contains carbon and forms the basis for life. All matter that is living or has once lived will consist of organic compounds.

Organelle: A structure within a cell that serves a particular function.

Osteoporosis: Brittleness of the bone caused by its increased porousness due to a lack of calcium salts.

Ovary: Principal structure of the female reproductive system. The two ovaries are suspended in the upper pelvic cavity, one either side of the uterus. They produce ova (eggs). The ovaries secrete hormones and so they are classified as endocrine glands.

Ovum: Egg cell, produced by the ovaries.

Palmar: Pertains to the palm of the hands.

Pancreas: A gland located below and slightly behind the stomach. It secretes pancreatic juice (containing digestive enzymes) via ducts into the duodenum. It also secretes hormones into the blood. It is therefore both an exocrine and endocrine gland.

Parasympathetic nervous system: A part of the autonomic nervous system. The motor nerves originate from cranial nerves (especially the vagus nerve) and a few of the spinal nerves in the sacral region. The nerve endings release acetylcholine that decreases the heart rate, breathing rate and blood pressure, and promotes digestion. This system opposes the sympathetic nervous system.

Pelvic line: A guideline on the foot derived by drawing a line from one side of the ankle bone to the other. There is often a change of skin colour from lighter above the line to darker below it. On the hand, it runs across the bottom of the hand, just below the wrist.

Peripheral nervous system: Includes all components of the nervous system except the brain and spinal cord. It is the system of nerves, originating at the cranial and spinal nerves, that runs to all organs and peripheral regions of the body. It also incorporates ganglia situated outside of the brain and spinal cord.

Phalanges: The bones that make up the toes or fingers.

Pharynx: Commonly called the throat. The pharynx connects the mouth and the nasal passage to the oesophagus and the trachea.

Phlebitis: Inflammation of a vein. Also called thrombophlebitis as blood usually clots in the inflamed part of the vein. The skin near the inflamed vein becomes red and hot. The swelling may extend beyond the affected area and tenderness and pain are experienced along the vein.

Physiology: The science of the function of living organisms and the function of their individual parts.

Pineal gland: An endocrine gland located in the roof of the third cerebral ventricle of the brain. It secretes melatonin during darkness that may induce sleep and inhibit sexual activity.

Pituitary gland: An endocrine gland located just beneath the hypothalamus at the base of the brain. The anterior lobe produces, stores and secretes 6 major hormones. The posterior lobe stores and releases hormones produced in the hypothalamus.

Plantar: Pertains to the sole of the foot.

Pleural membrane: A double membrane that surrounds the lungs. The space between the membranes (the pleural cavity) is filled with air, which helps to cushion and protect the lungs.

Polypus: General name given to a tumour which is attached to the surface by a stalk. Most polypi are simple, but some may be malignant.

Posterior: To the back. Also called dorsal.

Precaution: An aspect of the patient's condition that requires care to be taken during the treatment. Conditions that require caution include terminal illnesses, fevers, foot conditions, heart conditions, menstruation, osteoporosis, hypertension, asthma, epilepsy and diabetes. Caution should also be taken with treatments performed pre- and post surgery and with patients under the influence of drugs or alcohol.

Pressure therapy: A treatment involving the application of pressure to specific points on the body. Examples of pressure therapies include reflexology, acupuncture and acupressure.

Progesterone: A female sex hormone produced in the ovaries after ovulation. It helps to prepare the uterus for the implantation of the fertilized ovum, develops the placenta and prepares the mammary glands for milk secretion.

Proprioceptive: Relates to stimuli produced and received in a living being.

Prostate gland: A large, oval gland in males, surrounding the urethra near the point where it leaves the bladder. It produces a fluid containing various substances during ejaculation that is incorporated in the semen.

Protein: An organic compound containing carbon, hydrogen, oxygen and nitrogen. It may include sulphur and phosphorus. Proteins form an important part of all living organisms and are an essential constituent of any animal's diet. Major sources of protein are meat, egg-white, gelatin and pulses.

Protuberance: A bulge or prominence.

Psychology: Literally means the study of the mind, but can be defined more accurately as the scientific study of behaviour and experience.

Psychosis: A serious disorder of the mind, affecting the whole personality.

Pulmonary arteries: Blood vessels that transport deoxygenated blood from the right ventricle of the heart to the lungs. These are the only arteries that contain deoxygenated blood.

Pulmonary veins: Blood vessels that transport newly oxygenated blood from the lungs to the left atrium of the heart. These are the only veins that contain oxygenated blood.

Pyloric sphincter: The muscle at the duodenal end of the stomach through which the stomach content passes into the duodenum.

Reflex area: An area on the foot (and hand) that relates to a specific part of the body.

Reflex point: The position of a nerve ending.

Reflex: An involuntary response to a stimulus, possible if there is a neural pathway between the point of stimulus and the site of response.

Reflexology: A pressure therapy primarily involving the feet. It revolves around the understanding that there are reflex points on the feet (and hands) that relate to the structure and function of all parts of the body. Applying pressure to these reflexes, using a gentle on-off pressure, may influence the state of the body in many ways.

Reproductive system: The organs involved in reproduction, the process by which new individuals are produced and the genetic information passed from generation to generation. The main reproductive structures are the testes and the ovaries in the male and female respectively.

Respiratory system: The organs involved in taking oxygen from the external environment, absorbing oxygen into the blood, removing carbon dioxide from the blood and expelling the carbon dioxide from the body.

Ribonucleic acid (RNA): A nucleic acid found mainly in the cytoplasm. It works with deoxyribonucleic acid (DNA) in protein synthesis.

Riley, Dr. Joe Shelby: American physician, influenced by Dr. William H. Fitzgerald. He wrote four books, devoting much attention to zone therapy. His first book was published in 1919 and was entitled "Zone Therapy Simplified". As well as extensively using zone therapy, Dr. Riley made the first detailed drawings of the reflexes on the foot. He also added 8 horizontal lines to the 5 longitudinal lines originating from zone therapy.

Sacrum: The triangular bone at the base of the vertebral column (spine), consisting of five fused sacral vertebrae.

Sarcoma: A malignant tumour developing in the connective tissue (tissue that binds and supports) of bones, muscles etc.

Scarlet fever: An acute infectious disease, characterized by a high temperature, sore throat and a red rash.

Sciatic nerve: A large spinal nerve, originating in the lumbar region, which descends through the thigh.

Sedative: Calming, reducing functional activity.

Semen: The sperm and secretory fluids released via the penis during ejaculation.

Shoulder line: A secondary guideline situated just below the line of the toes.

Sigmoid colon: A part of the large intestine that runs from the descending colon (on the left of the abdomen) to the anal canal.

Sinus: A hollow in the bone, space or channel.

Skeletal system: In the human, the skeletal system consists of 206 bones, cartilage, bone marrow and the periosteum (the membrane around the bones).

Small intestine: Consists of the duodenum, jejunum and ileum. The small intestine runs from the pyloric sphincter at the base of the stomach to the ileocaecal valve at the entrance to the large intestine. It is the site of digestion and absorption.

Solar plexus: A network of autonomic nerves located behind the stomach.

Spleen: An oval shaped organ located to the left of the abdomen. It is the largest mass of lymphatic tissue in the body. It produces lymphocytes and destroys and stores red blood cells.

Spinal cord: A mass of nervous tissue running through the vertebral column from which 31 pairs of spinal nerves originate.

Starch: A carbohydrate obtained mainly from cereals and potatoes. It is converted to sugar under certain conditions such as the presence of heat and certain chemicals.

Steroid: The group name for compounds derived from cholesterol. Some hormones are included in this group.

Stomach: A muscular sac between the oesophagus and the duodenum. It holds food for 2-6 hours. The stomach churns food and secretes acidic gastric juices and enzymes to facilitate digestion.

Sugar: A carbohydrate containing carbon, hydrogen and oxygen. It has many forms, e.g. glucose (found in fruit and produced by the tissues), sucrose (found in sugar cane, beetroot and maple), lactose (found in milk) and maltose (produced from starch).

Symmetrical: Proportioned equally by size, shape and position either side of a dividing line.

Sympathetic nervous system: A part of the autonomic nervous system. It increases the heart rate, breathing rate and blood pressure, and slows down digestion. The motor nerves of this system originate from the spinal nerves in the thoracic and lumbar regions. The nerve endings release noradrenaline that creates these 'fight or flight' reactions. Sympathetic fibres also trigger the release of adrenaline.

Synovial cavity: The space between the bones of a synovial (fully moveable) joint that is filled with synovial fluid and lined by the synovial membrane.

System: Several related organs with a common function.

Tarsals: The seven bones that make up the ankle.

Tendon: Non-elastic, tough, connective tissue that joins muscle to bone.

Testis: One of a pair of male reproductive organs. The testes (or testicles) descend from the abdomen into two sacs of skin called scrotal sacs. The testes are comprised of thousands of fine, coiled tubules in which the sperm are produced. The testes secrete hormones and are therefore classified as endocrine glands.

Testosterone: A male sex hormone secreted by the testes. It controls the growth and maintenance of the reproductive system and the development of secondary sex characteristics. It also stimulates the production of sperm and body growth. The level of testosterone is controlled by luteinizing hormone.

Thoracic duct: Otherwise called the left lymphatic duct, this vessel receives lymph from the left side of the head, neck and chest, the left arm and all of the lower body. The lymph is then drained into venous blood via the left brachiocephalic vein.

Thoracic vertebra: One of the twelve bones that make up the chest area of the vertebral column (spine).

Thorax: The section of the body containing the heart and the lungs, divided from the abdomen by the diaphragm.

Thrombosis: The formation of a blood clot in the blood vessels or heart.

Thymus: A lymphatic gland, consisting of two lobes located in the upper chest, between the sternum (breastbone) and the lungs. The outer layer is packed with lymphocytes. T-cell lymphocytes, produced in the bone marrow, migrate to the thymus for development. The thymus secretes hormones, a feature that classifies it as an endocrine gland.

Thyroid: An endocrine gland situated just below the larynx. It secretes hormones that regulate growth and development and control the metabolic rate.

Tissue: Made up of cells of the same type, e.g. muscle tissue is made up of muscle cells only. There are four main types of tissue: epithelial, connective, muscle and nervous.

Tonsils: Small bodies of lymphatic tissue located at the back of the throat.

Toxin: Poison.

Trachea: Commonly called the windpipe. It extends from the pharynx (throat) down to the level of the 5th thoracic vertebra. It then branches to form the left and right primary bronchi.

Transverse colon: A part of the large intestine that runs across the abdomen from the ascending colon (on the right) to the descending colon (on the left).

Trigeminal nerve: The fifth cranial nerve that serves the muscles of the face, tongue and the teeth.

Tuberculosis: A general name for a group of diseases caused by the bacteria Mycobacterium tuberculosis. Pulmonary tuberculosis (or consumption) affects the lungs, but tuberculosis may affect any organ. It spreads by way of the lymphatic system and the severity of the disease depends on the organ(s) affected.

Tumour: Literally means swelling. There are three main types; 1. Simple, when the tumour is growing from a gland and is composed of gland-like tissue. 2. Hollow, when the tumour contains fluid or soft material e.g. cysts. 3. Malignant, when the tumour has imperfect cellular structure. This last group is categorized as cancer.

Typhoid fever: A bacterial infection characterized by fever, red spots on the chest, abdomen and back, and severe intestinal irritation.

Ureter: The tube that transports urine from a kidney to the bladder.

Urethra: The tube that transports urine from the bladder to the exterior.

Uric acid: A slightly soluble, crystalline substance that is present in the urine. It is formed by the liver and removed from the blood by the kidneys.

Urinary system: An excretory system responsible for the removal of urine from the body. It comprises of the kidneys, ureters, bladder and urethra.

Uterus: A tough, muscular sac suspended by broad ligaments, situated between the bladder and the rectum in the female. If fertilization occurs, the uterus provides a source of attachment and nourishment for the fertilized ovum.

Vas deferens: A tube of the male reproductive system that transports sperm from the testis to the urethra, ready for ejaculation.

Vein: A vessel that carries blood back to the heart.

Venous: Pertaining to the veins.

Verruca: Small, horny, highly infectious tumour of the skin caused by the papova virus. Verrucae usually form on the sole of the foot and are quite painful as they grow into the skin rather than outwards. Also called plantar warts.

Vertebral column: Commonly called the spine. The adult vertebral column comprises of 26 individual bones (vertebrae).

Vishnu: One of the three most important Hindu Gods, known as the preserver of the universe.

Vishnu-padas: A painting showing the feet of the Hindu God Vishnu marked with symbols to represent the unity of the universe.

Waist line: The main guideline that runs across the middle of the foot. Drawing a line across the foot from the metatarsal notch shows its position. On the hand, the waist line runs across from the base of the thumb.

Zone therapy: A belief, rediscovered by Dr. William H. Fitzgerald, that the body is divided into 10 longitudinal zones of energy, extending from the feet and hands to the brain. In each of these zones it is believed that nothing occurs in isolation. Any abnormality, sensitivity or congestion in any part of a zone causes an imbalance throughout that whole zone. Likewise, any treatment performed on any area within a zone will have a healing effect on the whole zone.

Product List

Books published by Essential Training Solutions include:

Essential Anatomy & Physiology – The Elementary Guide
Written for those who require just the basics, this elementary guide provides a clear, simple account of all the main body systems.

Essential Anatomy & Physiology
Ideal for first year nurses and students studying for a Level 3 Diploma, this book comprehensively covers all the main body systems. The content has been approved by the Royal College of Nursing Accreditation Unit and the 475 questions provide valuable opportunities for self-testing.

Essential Aromatherapy
Produced as a part of an award-winning package, this book covers the theoretical aspects of Aromatherapy from its history to the chemistry, safety and practical uses of the oils. It contains details about 44 essential oils and 46 conditions, and includes more than 400 glossary terms and over 500 questions.

Essential Reflexology
This book is an invaluable asset to any conscientious reflexology student or practitioner. Core reflexology information, including details of 72 conditions, is supported by graphics, photographs and self-testing questions. It also includes our Elementary Guide to Anatomy & Physiology.

Interactive revision/reference products include:

Essential Anatomy & Physiology – The Elementary Guide CD ROM
Essential Anatomy & Physiology CD ROM
E-ssential Anatomy & Physiology e-learning
Essential Aromatherapy CD ROM
Essential Reflexology CD ROM

Courses:

Online VTCT Level 3 Diploma in Anatomy & Physiology

Support Software:

Client Management System

Web: www.essential-training.co.uk
Tel: +44(0)1604 879110

This page has intentionally been left blank.

Index

Achilles pinch and slide	80
Adrenal glands	307
Alcohol	99
Amenorrhoea	107
Amphetamines	71
Ankhmahor	19
Ankle circles	83
Ankle freeing	84
Antacids	71
Antibiotics	70
Anti-depressants	71
Anti-histamines	70
Anxiety	108
Areas of assistance	59
Arthritis – osteo	109
Arthritis – rheumatoid	110
Aspirin	70
Association of Reflexology	202
Asthma	98, 111
Athlete's foot	98
Autonomic nervous system	321
Babies, treating	93
Back pain	112
Bell's palsy	113
Beta-blockers	71
Bile	294
Bladder	258
Blood vessels	285
Blood	282
Blurred vision	114
Bowers, Dr. Edwin	23
Brain	318
British Complementary Medicine Association	202
Bronchitis	115
Byers, Dwight C.	25
Cancer	97, 116
Cardiovascular system reflex areas	41
Cardiovascular system	282
Case histories	203, 211
Catarrh	117
Cells	223
Central nervous system	318

Chemicals   223
Chilblains   118
China   21
Circulation   284
Client care   211
Codes of ethics   202
Colds   119
Compression of spinal nerves   120
Constipation   121
Contagious illness   96
Contra-indications   96
Counselling   219
Cramp   122
Creeping thumb   11, 72
Crescent moon   81
Cystitis   123

Depression   124
Diabetes   99, 125
Diaphragm line   9
Diaphragm relaxation   81
Diarrhoea   126
Digestive system reflex areas   46
Digestive system   290
Dobbs, B.Z.   87
Dorsal channels   81
Dorsal foot charts   399
Dorsal hand charts   407
Dorsal stroking   82
Double hand effleurage   80
Drugs   70, 99
Dysmenorrhoea   127

Ear   250
Eczema   128
Egypt   19
Elderly, treating   93
Emperor Hwang   21
Employment options   206
Endocrine system reflex areas   52
Endocrine system   304
Endometriosis   129
Energy hypothesis   87
Epilepsy   98
Exam tips   356
Eye   247

Facial neuralgia 130
Female infertility 131
Fever 98, 132
Fitzgerald, Dr. William H. 22
Fixed premises 209
Flu 119
Foot charts 395
Foot conditions 98
Foot moulding 85
Frozen shoulder 133

Gall bladder 295
Gangrene 98
Gillanders, Ann 25
Gliding off 86
Glue ear 134
Guidelines – foot 9
Guidelines – hand 191

Hand charts 395
Headache 135
Health and Safety Acts 202
Heart attack 136
Heart conditions 98
Heart 283
Heartburn 137
Hiatus hernia 138
Hormones 304
Hypertension 99, 139
Hyperthyroidism 140
Hypotension 141
Hypothalamus 304
Hypothyroidism 142

Immunity 269
India 20
Indigestion 143
Infectious illness 96
Ingham, Eunice 24
Insomnia 144
Insurance 202
Integumentary system 237
Internal bleeding 97
Irregular ovulation 145
Irritable bowel syndrome 146

Joints 231

Kidney stones 147
Kidney 258
Knuckling 84
Kusinara 21

Lactic acid hypothesis 87
Large intestine 297
Laryngitis 148
Lateral foot charts 403
Ligament line 10
Limited company 208
Liver 294
Lumbago 149
Lungs 243
Lymphatic inflammations 97
Lymphatic system reflex areas 55
Lymphatic system 269

Marquardt, Hanne 24
Mastitis 150
Medial foot charts 401
Medial petrissage 83
Menopause 151
Menorrhagia 152
Menstruation 98, 266
Metatarsal kneading 85
Metatarsal see-saw 82
Migraine 153
Mobile practice 209
Multiple sclerosis 154
Muscular fatigue 155
Muscular system 275
Myalgic encephalomyelitis 156

Nausea 157
Negative reactions 97
Nervous system reflex areas 38
Nervous system 316
Neurons 316
Nutrition 216

Oedema 158
Olfactory system 255
Organisms 225
Organs 225
Osteoporosis 99
Ovarian cysts 159